MARKETS WITHOUT LIMITS

May you sell your vote? May you sell your kidney? May gay men pay surrogates to bear them children? May spouses pay each other to watch the kids, do the dishes, or have sex? Should we allow the rich to genetically engineer gifted, beautiful children? Should we allow betting markets on terrorist attacks and natural disasters?

Most people shudder at the thought. To put some goods and services for sale offends human dignity. If everything is *commodified*, then nothing is sacred. The market corrodes our character. Or so most people say.

In *Markets without Limits*, Jason Brennan and Peter M. Jaworski give markets a fair hearing. The market does not introduce wrongness where there was none previously. Thus, the authors claim, the question of what rightfully may be bought and sold has a simple answer: if you may do it for free, you may do it for money. Contrary to the conservative consensus, they claim there are no inherent limits to *what* can be bought and sold, but only restrictions on *how* we buy and sell.

Jason Brennan is Associate Professor of Strategy, Economics, Ethics, and Public Policy at Georgetown University's McDonough School of Business, and, by courtesy, Associate Professor of Philosophy. He is the author of *Why Not Capitalism?* (Routledge, 2014), *Compulsory Voting: For and Against*, with Lisa Hill (2014), *Libertarianism: What Everyone Needs to Know* (2012), *The Ethics of Voting* (2011), and *A Brief History of Liberty*, with David Schmidtz (2010).

Peter M. Jaworski is Assistant Teaching Professor of Strategy, Economics, Ethics, and Public Policy at Georgetown University's McDonough School of Business. Prior to joining the faculty at Georgetown, Peter was Visiting Research Professor at Brown University's Political Theory Project. He is a senior fellow with the Canadian Constitution Foundation and serves on the Board of Directors of the Institute for Liberal Studies.

MARKETS WITHOUT LIMITS

Moral Virtues and Commercial Interests

Jason Brennan and Peter M. Jaworski

Routledge
Taylor & Francis Group

NEW YORK AND LONDON

First published 2016
by Routledge
711 Third Avenue, New York, NY 10017

and by Routledge
2 Park Square, Milton Park, Abingdon, Oxon, OX14 4RN

Routledge is an imprint of the Taylor & Francis Group, an informa business

© 2016 Taylor & Francis

Library of Congress Cataloging in Publication Data
Markets without limits : moral virtues and commercial interests / edited by Jason Brennan and Peter Jaworski.
pages cm
Includes bibliographical references and index.
1. Exchange--Moral and ethical aspects. 2. Economics--Moral and ethical aspects. 3. Value--Philosophy. 4. Markets--Social aspects. I. Brennan, Jason, 1979- II. Jaworski, Peter.
HB72.M24725 2015
174'.4--dc23
2015008148

ISBN: 978-0-415-73734-0 (hbk)
ISBN: 978-0-415-73735-7 (pbk)
ISBN: 978-1-315-81808-5 (ebk)

Typeset in Bembo
by Taylor & Francis Books

To the authors, supporters, and readers of the *Business Ethics Journal Review* (bejr.org)*

*Chris MacDonald and Alexei Marcoux, editors, *BEJR*, paid $275 for this dedication

CONTENTS

ACKNOWLEDGMENTS

We've benefitted enormously from many discussions, manuscript fora, conferences, author-meets-critics sessions, and the like.

Brennan greatly thanks the F. A. Hayek Program for Advanced Study in Philosophy, Politics, and Economics at the Mercatus Center at George Mason University for their support of his research.

Jaworski thanks the Political Theory Project at Brown University for a space to finish this project, and for lively debates about this paper.

We especially thank Pete Boettke, Claire Morgan, and Aurelian Craiutu for organizing and leading a workshop on an early draft of this book, and, once again, Pete Boettke and Claire Morgan for arranging an author-meets-critics session at the Southern Economic Association on a later, more polished draft of the manuscript. We thank James Otteson, Karen Vaughan, Andrew Young for their valuable feedback at that event.

For their helpful comments and feedback, we also thank Andrew Botterrel, Ted Burczak, Eric Campbell, Simone Chambers, Zac Gochenour, David Faraci, Andrew Farrant, Christopher Freiman, Bill Glod, Richard Greenstein, Joshua Hall, John Hasnas, Joseph Heath, Kendy Hess, Steve Horwitz, Hartmut Kleimt, Cathleen Johnson, Michael Kates, Kimberly Kraweic, Daniel Layman, Peter Loewen, Loren Lomasky, Ed Lopez, Adam Martin, Stephen Miller, Aaron Novick, Mark Pennington, Douglas Rasmussen, Mario Rizzo, David Schmidtz, Daniel Shapiro, David Sicilia, Daniel Silvermint, James Stacey Taylor, John Tomasi, James Ullmer, Steven Wall, and Matt Zwolinski. We thank audiences at Brown University, New York University, UCLA, the University of Pennsylvania, the University of Buffalo, the University of Toronto, McGill University, George Mason University, West Virginia University, St. Lawrence University, the College of New Jersey, the Southern Economics Association, the Association for Private Enterprise Education, two anonymous referees for the journal *Ethics*, and the editors for helpful comments and criticisms.

We also wish to thank the following people, each of whom greatly assisted us by putting their money where our mouths are.

Silvermint Tier Acknowledgments

Our highest thanks extend to the following good and noble people and organizations:

Jacob Levy
Businessethicsblog.com
Christopher Nelson: "Mom, Dad, Kelly, and Simon: Surprise!"
Michael Lopiansky
Jeremy McClellan: "Jeremy McClellan. Google his name and he'll tell you the"
Philip Magness: "May Sandel enjoy a fair & equal eternity in a circular TSA queue."
Sean Starcher: "Visit echopointsbooks.com."
Cris Hernandez
Art Carden: "Buy & Read my book with Deirdre McCloskey on the Bourgeois Era!"
Michael Thomas, who thinks the price is too low.
Benjamin Kirkup: "Prioritizing value creation over value capture."
Alex Krimkevich
Jared Silver, whom you should follow on Twitter @jaredsilver.
Thomas Sewell, Libertarian Writer – SharperSecurity.com
Sarah and Sofia Inkapool, "Declare Your Independence! GIZLOT!"
Hugh MacEroy: "Laurier MacEroy, for being the cutest Westie in the world."
Chad Swarthout
Brad Wall
Tom Palmer

Platinum Tier

Our second highest thanks go to the following supporters:

Tracy Wilkinson
Rebecca Lees
Carrie Figdor
Jo-Are Bjerke
Aristotle Magganas
Matthew Manning

Gold Tier

We extend our third highest thanks to the following supporters:

Michael Wiebe
Kyle J. Hartz
Peter McCaffrey
Daniel Bier
John Palmer
Pierre Lemieux
Pierre Lemieux
Pierre Lemieux
Pierre Lemieux
Pierre Lemieux
Peter McCaffrey
Ekin Can Genç
Andrew Pearson
Sven Gerst
Derrill Watson
Mark Roh
@FakeNassimTaleb
Ian Stumpf
Nick Partington
Matt Bufton
Matt Bufton
Matt Bufton
Matt Bufton
Matt Bufton
Sally Jurica
Shiraz Allidina
Samuel Bowman
Kyle Walker

PART I

Should everything be for sale?

" ... modern civilization has become largely possible by the disregard of the injunctions of those indignant moralists."

—F.A. Hayek

1

ARE THERE SOME THINGS MONEY SHOULD NOT BUY?

The Debate's Over, And Markets Won, But ...

Market institutions, for all their terrible shortcomings, are the best thing that ever happened to humanity.

Deirdre McCloskey says we can boil economic history down to a simple story: "Once upon a time we were all poor, then capitalism flourished, and now as a result we're rich."[1] Even, say, an American living at what the US government considers the poverty line today has a standard of living around three times higher than that of the *average* American in 1900 AD.[2] Or, as Paul Krugman wrote in 1996, " ... most families in 1950 had a material standard of living no better than that of today's poor or near-poor. ... it does not seem at all absurd to say that the material standard of living of the poverty-level family in 1996 is as good as or better than that of the median family in 1950."[3] On average, the global standard of living has increased by a factor of at least 20 in the past two hundred years. In some countries it has increased by far more.

We owe this all to markets and economic growth. The wealth we enjoy did not exist 50 years ago, let alone 1000 years ago. The US by itself in 2013 produced something like 50% more than the entire world's economic output in 1950, and close to 80 times the entire world's economic output in 1000 AD.[4] Wealth has been *made*, not just moved around. Even if all of the wealth that existed in the world as of 1000 AD had been distributed equally among everyone then alive, the average standard of living would be no better than that of Haiti or Malawi today.

Economists have known these kinds of facts for a long time. These claims about growth may be controversial among pundits and voters, and even among some professors in certain ideological and anti-scientific humanities departments, but not among experts. But the message of development economics is now going mainstream. Consider: U2 front man Bono, long known for his social activism, now "preaches capitalism":

> ... imagine for a second this last global recession but without the economic growth of China and India ... without the hundreds of millions of newly minted middle class folks who buy American and European goods ... Imagine that. Think about the last five years.
>
> Rock star preaches capitalism. Shocker. Wow. Sometimes I hear myself and I just can't believe it ...
>
> But commerce is real. That's what you're about here. It's real. Aid is just a stub cap. Commerce, entrepreneurial capitalism takes more people out of poverty than aid, of course, we know that.[5]

Of course, growth has not touched everyone equally. Critics of market society, following Marx, say that what matters most is what common people have the real ability to do, and this means giving them real resources to achieve their ends. But this kind of prosperity—where common people have real resources—is found in market societies and nowhere else.[6]

For informed humanitarians, the debate is no longer whether we should have market societies or not, but rather *which kind* of market society we should have.

But *Which* Market Society?

A market is a relationship where the mode of interaction is consensual exchange.[7] Broadly speaking, a market is the voluntary exchange of goods and services for valuable consideration.[8]

One might ask: what kind of market society should we have? That is a broad and imprecise question. We need to break it down into a set of narrower questions, such as:

1 How much should governments intervene in and regulate the market?
2 What sorts of property rights regimes and background legal institutions are best?
3 How much should governments provide social insurance or other welfare programs to protect citizens from misfortune on the market?

These are all worthy questions, but they are not our concern in this book. Here, we focus on a fourth question:

4 What sorts of things should be and should not be for sale?

This question concerns the *scope* of the market. Even if we accept that a market economy is best, there remains the question of just what should and should not be part of that market economy. Most people think that some things should be kept out of the market, that some things are not properly the kind of thing that should be bought and sold.

Noxious Markets?

Consider the following examples, some familiar, some not. Ask yourself; do you think it is morally wrong to sell the goods or services in each example?

- *Human Billboards*. In Tokyo, the PR firm Wit Inc. paid young women $121/day to wear sticker advertisements on their thighs as they go about their days. The women must be young, popular, thin, and pretty. They agree to wear short skirts or shorts. Wit's CEO explains, "It's an absolutely perfect place to put an advertisement, as this is what guys are eager to look at and girls are eager to expose."[9]
- *Watch My GF*. In the United States and elsewhere, one can purchase subscriptions to websites that collect nude or sexual pictures men have submitted of their ex-girlfriends. These pictures were meant to be private; the women intended only for their then-current boyfriends to see them. Sometimes men submit these videos to humiliate their exes. (It's called "revenge porn.")
- *Prostitution*. Of course, rather than looking at pictures, you can always buy sex. For example, Yessica on Washington, DC's www.backpage.com charges $200/hr for companionship, while Jessica on www.eros-dc.com charges $280/hr.
- *What's Your Price?* WhatsYourPrice.com is a dating website in which users pay other users to go on first dates with them. 22-year-old college student Vva33, who posted a picture of herself emerging from a pool in a little black bikini, tells men that she "won't meet for less than $300" as she gets "too many higher offers." Related websites promise to help match would-be "sugar daddies" with would-be "sugar babies."
- *Wigs*. Hair extensions and wigs are often made from real human hair. This hair frequently comes from poor women in the third world, many of whom sell "their treasured asset[s]" because they have few options.[10]
- *The Other Express Lane*. In airport queues, not everyone is equal. For a long time, first-class passengers have been able to use a separate line, cutting ahead of everyone else. But now some airlines sell access to these expedited security lines and for early boarding on the plane. For $18, you can skip ahead of everyone else.
- *Human Eggs and Pregnancy Surrogacy*. When I (Brennan) was in college, an infertile couple ran an ad in the college newspaper offering to buy an egg from a tall, blonde, blue-eyed woman for $25,000. Relatedly, one of my homosexual friends and his husband, recently married as of the time I am writing this, will soon look to purchase an egg and hire a surrogate to bear the couple a child after the egg is inseminated. They will likely pay nearly $100,000 total for these services.

- *The Greatest Movie Ever Sold*. Why does fictional billionaire Tony Stark (aka Iron Man) drive an Audi rather than, say, an Aston Martin or a Bugatti? Simple: Audi paid to have its products placed within the film. In fact, in any high budget summer film from Hollywood, if you can see the logo or brand of the product the characters use, chances are, you're viewing a paid product placement.
- *Payola*. Sometimes the music on the radio is itself the placed product. Record companies sometimes pay radio stations to broadcast music signals. In the United States, this is legal so long as the radio station discloses that the song is sponsored, but this rule is difficult to enforce, and many radio stations do not disclose that they received money.
- *Pay for Grades*. Following the work of economist Roland Fryer, many school systems are starting to experiment with paying underperforming students for good grades.

Noxious Potential Markets?

All of the examples above are markets that either currently exist or used to exist until recently. But also consider the following possible markets, which some people wish to see legalized:

- *Tiger Farming*. Tigers are nearly extinct. A large part of the problem is that hunters poach tigers for their fur. Laws against poaching and trade in tiger pelts fail to stop the problem—it's just too difficult to stop poachers and the black market tiger trade. This raises the question: in order to save tigers from extinction, should governments allow tiger farming? That is, should governments allow private farmers to raise and slaughter tigers for their fur, just as they allow ranchers to raise cattle for meat and leather or rabbits for their pelts? Defenders of tiger farming say that there is no moral distinction between pigs and tigers—if one may be farmed, so may the other—but allowing tiger farming would remove the economic incentives behind poaching and thus prevent extinction in the wild.
- *Betting on Terror*. In the early 2000s, following the work of many economists on the predictive power of information markets, the Pentagon considered creating a Policy Analysis Market (PAM). These information markets would have allowed people to bet on when certain events would occur, such as terrorist strikes or certain kinds of conflict in the Middle East. The markets are designed such that the market price of a bid indicates the probability that an event will occur (e.g., $.87/share on a bet that terrorists will attack Boston tomorrow = 87% chance that terrorists will attack Boston). Defenders of PAM believe the Pentagon, CIA, and other agencies would in turn have used this information to save lives.

Chances are, you oppose some of the markets above. You find at least some of these markets offensive, repugnant, degrading, or evil. If so, you are not alone.

Most people think there are some things that money should not buy, that should be insulated from the market forces of supply and demand.

We Are the Critics' Critics

Debra Satz refers to those markets that generate "extreme revulsion" as noxious markets.[11] She says there is "an intuitive disgust or abhorrence to certain kinds of market transactions … "[12] Margaret Jane Radin describes the objects of sale on these markets as "contested commodities,"[13] and insists that some things are "market-inalienable," meaning they are not the kinds of things we should have permission to sell.[14] Contested commodities include markets in organs and blood, sex, surrogacy, line-standing services,[15] and the like.

There seems to be a limitless market for books about the moral limits of markets. (Critics of the market all agree that it is permissible for them to sell books on the limits of the market, and some of them have made piles of money selling such books.) In recent years, Debra Satz, Ruth Grant, Michael Sandel, Robert Skidelsky, Margaret Jane Radin, Benjamin Barber, and George Ritzer, among others, have each argued that certain things should not be for sale, and the spread of the market corrupts our personal and civic character. We will refer to these thinkers and their intellectual allies as "anti-commodification theorists." They are opposed to what they call "commodification," where "commodification" is a pejorative word for putting something up for sale that was not previously the kind of thing people tended to buy and sell.

The common theme in their work is that the market is mutinous servant of the public good. The market may be good—or tolerable—for some purposes, but it spreads and takes over like pigweed.

Commodification, they say, is a built-in defect of the market mentality. People—from arch-capitalists like PayPal-founder Peter Thiel to anti-capitalists like filmmaker Michael Moore (net worth: $50 million[16])—are always looking to make a buck. If someone can figure out a way to make a profit by selling something that was not previously for sale, pretty soon it will be for sale. And so, the complaint goes, the market leaves nothing sacred. It gets its greedy, grubby fingers in everything.

We think rumors of the evils of markets have been greatly exaggerated. It is time to give markets a fair hearing.

Our goal in this book is deflationary. We want to show anti-commodification theorists that their complaints about the scope of the market are misplaced. There are, we agree, things that should not be bought and sold, but that's only because they are things people shouldn't *have* in the first place. Beyond that, we argue, there are legitimate moral worries about *how* we buy, trade, and sell, but no legitimate worries about *what* we buy, trade, and sell.

In this book, we will argue that anti-commodification theorists' objections to markets are mistaken—in almost every *interesting* case where they have argued markets are morally impermissible, on the contrary, we argue such markets are permissible. Where they see the market as having a fundamentally amoral ethos or as tending to corrupt us, we see it as moral and morally ameliorative. Where they think the solution is to contract the market, we think the solution is to expand it.

Why This Debate Matters

Right now, about 99,000 Americans are on the active waitlist for kidney transplants. *Most* will not get kidneys. Last year, over 3,000 of them died waiting for a kidney. In 2010, about 4,300 Canadians were on a waiting list for organs, 80% of them for kidneys. In 2012, 84 people died for want of a transplantable kidney. Most likely you, the reader, have an extra kidney, and could donate your extra kidney to a needy person with only relatively minor negative long-term consequences for your health.[17] However, like most people, you are not kind, loving, or altruistic enough to do so.

So, this raises the question, should governments allow individuals to sell their extra kidneys on the market? People are simply not willing to give away the organs others need. The government sets the legal price of organs at $0, far below the implicit market price. Thus, an economist might say, *of course* there is a shortage—whenever the legal price of a good is set below the equilibrium price, the quantity demanded will exceed the quantity supplied. Many philosophers and economists thus think that markets in organs will eliminate the shortage. You aren't kind enough to give away your extra kidney to a stranger, but you might do it for $100,000. Defenders of organ sales believe that organ sales will save hundreds of thousands of lives annually and will help make the poor rich.

Still, most people recoil at the thought of organ sales. Hollywood movies, such as *Repo Men* or *Never Let Me Go*, portray organ markets in horrifying ways. Most people feel down in their guts that organ sales are gross, repugnant, repulsive, and disgusting. They put a moral name to their revulsion: they complain that organ sales commodify the human body and fail to treat the body with proper respect. Or they argue that there's no way to sell organs without wrongfully exploiting the poor.

We'll discuss many markets over the course of this book. Sometimes, what's at stake is banal: should a Japanese businessman be allowed to satisfy his fetish for schoolgirl panties, or should an overworked surgeon be allowed to pay for someone to hold his place in line at the festival? But even when we're discussing these banal markets, we should recognize that a great deal is at stake in how we answer questions about the morality of the market. At the end of day, we'll be talking about whether couples can have children, about whether we should use the best methods available to predict terrorist attacks, or whether sick people live and die. This book is an entry into an academic debate, but it's not merely an academic debate. How we answer these questions matters.

Notes

1 McCloskey 1991, 1.
2 We use Angus Maddison's historical gdp/capita data, available here: http://www.ggdc. net/maddison/Maddison.htm. See also Maddison 2003.
3 Krugman 1996.
4 Schmidtz and Brennan 2010, 122; and URL http://www.ggdc.net/maddison/Maddison. htm
5 Bono, speech delivered at Georgetown University, November 12, 2012. Text available here: https://www.youtube.com/watch?v=PUZFgBqcYt8
6 See Schmidtz and Brennan, 2010.
7 Thanks to David Schmidtz for suggesting this definition.
8 We mean "voluntary" in the sense of uncoerced. We recognize that a market exchange can be "involuntary" when, for example, background circumstances exert pressure on someone to sell a childhood toy, or to enter into prostitution or a sweatshop contract.
9 http://qz.com/107236/the-latest-trend-in-japan-is-to-advertise-on-womens-thighs/
10 http://www.guardian.co.uk/lifeandstyle/2012/oct/28/hair-extension-global-trade-secrets
11 Satz 2012, 4.
12 http://www.econtalk.org/archives/2011/08/satz_on_markets.html
13 See Radin 2000.
14 See Radin 1997.
15 Sandel 2012a, 5, 22–28.
16 http://www.celebritynetworth.com/richest-celebrities/directors/michael-moore-net-worth/
17 E.g., see Ramcharan and Matas 2002.

2

IF YOU MAY DO IT FOR FREE, YOU MAY DO IT FOR MONEY

We're going to spend some time clarifying just what our thesis is and what the commodification debate is about. We need to do so in part because many of the people who participate in the debate get the debate confused. Simply by clarifying what's at stake, we'll take care of perhaps half of the cases we've seen the anti-commodification critics complain about.

Our Thesis

No one thinks that literally everything and anything should be for sale under any circumstances, no matter what. Everyone thinks there are at least some cases in which certain things should not be for sale.

Despite this admission, our title *Markets without Limits* is not misleading. There is an important sense in which we do advocate markets with unlimited scope. Our view of the scope of the market can be summarized as follows:

Markets without Limits:

If you may do it for free, then you may do it for money.

To put it in a more long-winded way, if you may have, use, possess, and dispose of something (that does not belong to someone else) for free, then—except in special circumstances—it is permissible for you to buy and sell it. Another way of expressing our thesis is that the market does not *transform* what were permissible acts into impermissible acts. It does not *introduce* wrongness where there was not any already. Yet another way of expressing this is that, in the debate on commodification, to produce a successful argument for a limit on markets, the fact that something is on the market must cause or contribute to the wrongness. It must feature in an explanation for why it is wrong.

To illustrate these ideas, consider the following two markets:

1   *Child Porn*. A market in which people sell pornographic images of young children.
2   *Nukes*. A market in which arms dealers sell nuclear weapons.

We agree that child porn and nuclear weapons should not be for sale. But the problem with these markets isn't the markets themselves—it's that the items for sale should not be possessed, period. It's wrong to possess child pornography even if you acquired it for free. The wrongness of markets in child pornography does not originate in the market, but in the existence of the traded item in the first place.

We think the same goes for nuclear weapons, though this claim is more controversial, and we will not defend it here. We think no country should have nuclear weapons. But suppose we are wrong—suppose relatively peaceful countries like England and France may permissibly have nuclear weapons, even if Myanmar and the average citizen may not. If so, then our view is that England and France may sell nuclear weapons to one another, but not to Myanmar or the average citizen.

So, we agree that buying and selling is wrong in cases 1 and 2, but this is because *possessing* the items in question is wrong, not because buying and selling introduce wrongness where there was none to begin with. That it's wrong to buy and sell these items is a trivial consequence of their being wrong to *have*.

Thus, we agree to the following principle:

The Principle of Wrongful Possession:

If it is inherently morally wrong for someone to possess (do, use) X, then (normally) it is morally wrong for that person to buy or sell X.[1]

As far as we can tell, everyone in this debate agrees to the Principle of Wrongful Possession. It follows trivially, on that principle, that if someone inherently shouldn't have something, then he or she should not sell it or buy it. Because child porn shouldn't exist, it also shouldn't be for sale.

Similarly, consider the case of dog fighting. For the sake of argument, let's agree that dog fighting wrongfully mistreats dogs. If so, then we agree that people shouldn't sell tickets to dog fights or bids on dog fights. But, again, the reason people shouldn't sell dog fight tickets is that dog fights shouldn't exist. It would be wrong to host dog fights *for free*. Selling tickets doesn't *introduce* wrongness where there wasn't any to begin with.

Or, to take another obvious example, it's wrong to pay someone to murder someone else, but that's just because it's wrong to murder people, period. Perhaps paying someone to kill another person might *amplify* the wrongness, under certain circumstances, of killing, but it's not that the market in killing introduces wrongness into what was otherwise a permissible act.

Or, to take another example, Michael Sandel complains about parents trying to sell naming rights to their children. He worries children might end up being named "Pepsi Peterson" or "Jamba Juice Jones."[2] But, in our view and in Sandel's, the problem here is that these names are humiliating. If so, then parents shouldn't give their kids these names, period, for free. If so, the market for naming kids Pepsi is wrong because naming kids Pepsi is wrong. The problem isn't the *market*. In contrast, Brennan named his children Aiden and Keaton. Since it was permissible for him to do so for free, it would be, in our view, permissible for him to do so for a fat check from Pepsi.

Or, as a final example, drawn from the list above, we agree that it's wrong for students to buy essays from AstonishingPapers.com and then submit those papers as if they were their own. But the problem here isn't the *buying*. It's that the students plagiarize. We've both seen plenty of students plagiarize essays they acquired for free. The market in academic dishonesty is wrong only because academic dishonesty is wrong. A fortiori, if the students purchased papers from AstonishingPapers.com without any intention to pass these papers in as their own, they would do nothing wrong at all. But if the students acquired those same papers for free and then passed them in as their own, they would act wrongly. Thus, imagine that we decided, as an experiment, to pay AstonishingPapers to write a five-page essay on some silly topic, such as "the importance of purple fruit." We have no intention of submitting this work as our own; we just want to see what they come up with. If we never try to pass off someone else's work as our own, then it is perfectly permissible to buy a paper from them.

When critics of the market, such as Sandel or Satz, write books about what should not be for sale, what they intend to do is to identify things that are normally permissible for adults to possess, own, have, occupy, provide, or use, but which are not permissible for those adults to trade, sell, and/or buy. They intend to discuss cases where markets really do transform otherwise permissible activities into wrongful actions. They intend to identify cases where the wrongness of buying and selling an object originates in the buying and selling, not in the object itself.

So, for instance, Sandel of course thinks it is permissible for you to stand in line at Disney World. He even thinks it is permissible for you to hold a spot in line for your kids, only to jump out at the last minute so they can ride the roller coaster in your place. But he doesn't want people to sell line-standing services. You can hold the line for free, but you can't sell your spot.

Elizabeth Anderson has no problem with you having casual sex or with you serving, for free, as a pregnancy surrogate for your infertile sister. But she doesn't want people to sell sex or surrogacy. For her, you can give it away, but you can't sell it—and others shouldn't buy it.

Sandel and Anderson would have no problem with you deciding to donate a kidney to a needy stranger for free. But they think that selling your kidney would show disrespect for the human body, as you would be treating your body like a mere commodity.

Filmmaker Morgan Spurlock has no problem with *Iron Man* series writers deciding to have Tony Stark drive an Audi supercar, so long as the *Iron Man* series producers do this for free, because they happen to like Audis or because they think Tony Stark would drive a car like that. But Spurlock thinks it is problematic for the producers to turn their movie into a paid advertisement.

We disagree in every case. We will argue that if you can do it for free, you can sell it.

Incidental Vs. Inherent Wrongness

There are many cases where—thanks to special circumstances—it can be wrong for particular people to buy and sell certain things that would otherwise be permissible to buy and sell. We want to explain here why this does not conflict with our thesis. In fact, it's just an extension of it.

Consider two new cases

3 *Civic Duty, for Profit.* It's November 8, 2016, election day in the United States. Mary doesn't plan to vote. Her friend Natalie—a long-time activist—says, "What if I pay you $100 to vote a straight Democrat ticket?" Mary agrees and votes accordingly.

4 *But You Promised!* Kevin and Jane are in the process of moving. Kevin wants to have a yard sale to reduce the amount of stuff they have to pack. Jane is sentimental and wants to keep as much stuff as possible. After some discussion, Kevin promises Jane that he will not sell any of his vintage cameras, even though he does not want to keep them all. However, during the yard sale, he sells one for $50 behind her back. Jane never notices, but he knows she would be enraged if she learned he'd sold the camera.

Most people believe that selling is wrong in both cases. They think it is wrong for Mary to sell her vote (and for Natalie to buy it) and wrong for Kevin to sell the vintage camera.

But most people also think the cases are importantly different. Most people would say that selling a vote is *inherently* wrong. Votes are simply not the kind of thing that should be for sale. (We disagree, but right now we're just reporting what others tend to think.)

In contrast, most people think there is nothing inherently wrong about selling a vintage camera. Instead, what makes selling wrong in this particular case is that Kevin promised not to do so. So, it's just incidental, accidental, or contingent that selling a camera was wrong here. In short, the difference here, most people would say, is that votes are just *not the kind of thing that should be for sale*, while cameras are the kind of thing that may be sold, except in special circumstances.

Consider another example:

> 5   *Batterer*. Orin appears at Dick's Sporting Goods and asks for a baseball
> bat. He loudly explains that he plans to use the bat to beat his cheating
> girlfriend to death.

This case is more like case 4 than case 3. It's wrong to sell Orin the bat, but that's
just because we know Orin plans to kill someone with it. Bats are not the kind of
thing it's wrong to sell; it's just wrong to sell one to someone you know will use
it to harm an innocent person.

Consider another example:

> 6   *Hot iPad*. Suppose you are walking down the street, when a shady-
> looking guy offers to sell you a used iPad for half price. You ask if it's
> stolen, and he says, "So what if it is? Do you want it or not?"

Again, in this case, most people would judge that it's wrong to buy the iPad and
wrong for the thief to sell it. However, it's not because iPads are inherently the
kind of thing that should not be for sale, but because the iPad *isn't his to sell*.

Consider a final case:

> 7   *Hurt Kid*. Nate's child is badly hurt. But, rather than take him to the
> hospital, Nate spends the next hour trying to sell his car.

There's nothing wrong with selling cars. The problem with Nate isn't that he's
trying to sell something that should not be for sale, but that he should be doing
something else at that moment other than trying to sell his car.

But You Promised, Batterer, Hot iPad, and *Hurt Kid* are each cases where it
would be wrong to sell something, but not because the thing being sold is
inherently the kind of thing that should not be for sale. Rather, in each case, there
is some other moral duty—a duty to respect promises, a duty not to cause harm, a
duty to respect property, or a duty of care—that incidentally attaches to that
particular transaction or that situation. We accept that these kinds of case are
genuinely cases where it is wrong to buy and sell certain things. So, we agree that
it's wrong to sell the items in question in cases 4 through 7. So, in that sense, we
accept limits to markets.

But, call these *incidental limits*. In each of the cases, the good in question is
normally something that it's permissible to sell.

In case 4, Kevin promised to keep the cameras, so he should keep them. That's
not very interesting. Almost any otherwise permissible act can be rendered
impermissible if one promises not to do it. It's permissible for us to listen to thrash
metal today, but if we promised our loved ones that we'd abstain from listening
to thrash metal today, it would then become wrong to listen to it. That doesn't

show there are limits to what kinds of music it can be permissible to listen to—it just shows that promises can introduce obligations where there were none. It's permissible for you to sing in the shower, but not if you promise not to. It's permissible for you to eat spaghetti, but not if you promise not to. It's permissible for you to use a red toothbrush, but not if you promise not to. Etc.

In case 5, it would be wrong to give Orin a bat for free, because Orin will use it to hurt someone. In case 6, it would be wrong to give away or take the iPad for free, because the iPad is stolen. In case 7, it would be wrong to spend that time trying to give away one's car, because doing so means one will neglect one's child. But these are clearly special cases. It's not that the things in question are inherently wrong to buy and sell, but just that these special circumstances where buying and selling *anything* would be wrong.

Almost any otherwise permissible act can be rendered impermissible by such circumstances. So, again, it's normally permissible for me to listen to thrash metal, but not if doing so comes at the expense of feeding my hungry child. Here, the issue isn't that listening to thrash metal is inherently wrong, but rather that, in my special circumstances, I should be doing something else.

In contrast, when people say that votes or organs should not be for sale, they mean that votes or organs just are the kind of thing that people should not buy or sell. Even if we specify that no one will be harmed by Mary selling her vote to Natalie, most people would still judge that it is wrong to buy and sell individual votes. (We disagree.)

Three Kinds of Limits

To summarize, we have so far discussed three kinds of limits to markets:

A *Limits Due to the Principle of Wrongful Possession*: There are some things that people inherently should not have—indeed, that should not even exist—and, as a consequence, people should not buy or sell.

B *Incidental Limits to the Market*: There are cases where particular people should not sell particular things—things that normally would be permissible to sell—because of special circumstances, such as that they promised not to sell those items, or the items will be dangerous in these special circumstances, or because they have pre-existing duties that require them to do something else other than engage in buying or selling.

C *Inherent Limits to the Market*: There are some things that people are normally allowed to own or possess in some way, but which should not be for sale.

A and B are in some sense limits on the market, but only in boring, trivial ways. A and B are not what anti-commodification theorists have in mind when they say we ought to limit the scope of the market. C is where the action is.

We accept A and B, but reject C. We think there are no *inherent* limits to the market. If you can have it, you can buy it; if you can give it away to someone, you can sell it to her.

To illustrate, we think that if it is morally permissible for you to vote a particular way, then it is also morally permissible for you to be paid to vote that way or to pay someone to vote that way.[3] We think that if it is permissible for you to have sex with someone for free, then it is permissible to buy and sell sex with that person. We think that if it is permissible for you to stand in line at the amusement park, then it will by default be permissible for you to accept money to stand in line for someone else. We think that if it is permissible for you to choose to act as someone's slave for the rest of your life for free, then it would also be permissible for you to take money to do so.

Notice that many of these claims take a conditional form: if it is permissible to do X for free, then you may do X for money. In many of these cases, we don't know whether it is permissible to do X for free. So, for instance, we aren't sure whether it is morally permissible for you to choose, voluntarily, to become someone else's slave for the rest of your life. We can come up with good arguments for and against this. We don't know how to balance these arguments. That said, we think that whatever wrongness exists in voluntary *paid* slavery emerges from voluntary slavery, not from the payment. If it turns out to be wrong for you to voluntarily accept $1 million to be someone's slave, then what makes it wrong is that you shouldn't choose to be someone's slave period, not that you received $1 million to do so. The market does not figure into the explanation of what makes this transaction wrong.

We agree that, say, a married man should not buy sex from a prostitute without his spouse's permission. But this is because he should not have sex with someone else, period, without his spouse's permission. The problem here isn't *prostitution*, but *cheating* on his spouse.

Or, to extend this example, we agree that a person should not buy sex from pimps who deal with involuntarily enslaved, trafficked women. But here the problem is one of wrongful possession—the trafficker shouldn't *own* the women to begin with. The market doesn't introduce wrongness where there wasn't any. It would be wrong to have sex with the trafficked women against their will even if the pimp offered them to you for free, and even if he never tried to make any money from the women.

We think you may buy or sell line-standing services, unless there are incidental reasons or special circumstances that explain why not. One such special circumstance would be if the park forbade such services. In that case, you would have promised not to sell line-standing services as a condition of buying your admission ticket. But this is incidental—it's no different from promising not to sell your cameras in case 4. Another special circumstance would be if, during the time you are standing in line, you promised to attend your friend's birthday party. Here, you shouldn't sell line-standing services at that time, not because it's inherently wrong to sell line-standing services, but because (incidentally) you promised to be at a birthday party instead.

We think it is permissible for you to sell a kidney. Indeed, we hope you do. (It's illegal in most places to do so, but we hope you break this law if you can get away with it.) Many people are convinced that kidney selling is inherently degrading and inherently expresses disrespect for the human body, but, we will argue, they are mistaken.

Similarly, we think buying a subscription to WatchMyGF.com is immoral, but not because it is inherently immoral to buy and sell pornographic images of adults. *Playboy*, *Penthouse*, and *QXMen* are permissible businesses, while Watch-MyGF.com is not. The problem with WatchMyGF.com is that the images are stolen. Our opposition to WatchMyGF.com is the same as our opposition to the sale of stolen watches. Buying and selling stolen watches is wrong because it's wrong to exchange stolen items for free, not because it's wrong to buy and sell watches. In the case of WatchMyGF.com, buying and selling the stolen images doesn't transform what was otherwise a permissible action into a wrong action. It would be wrong of you to view the images on WatchMyGF.com for free.

We think it is wrong to sell crystal meth to fifth graders, but it's not because the market corrupts what was otherwise a permissible act. You shouldn't give crystal meth to fifth graders for free. In contrast, if there are cases where you could permissibly possess crystal meth and give it to someone else, then in those cases, we would view it as permissible to buy and sell crystal meth.

And so on. Our view is that—except in weird circumstances, like when one promises not to buy and sell—if it is permissible to have, possess, and give away something, then it's permissible to buy and sell it. Sure, there are incidental limits to what we can buy and sell, but there are exactly the same incidental limits to all actions that would otherwise be permissible.

Bad to Worse, If Not Okay to Bad

There are certain activities people shouldn't do and things they shouldn't have, period, and markets in those activities might make them worse. Incentives incentivize. Child pornography is bad even when not traded on a market, and it's likely that a market in it makes it worse, by increasing the number of children who are harmed.

While we don't think a market transforms permissible activities into wrongful activities, we agree that markets in wrongful goods and services can sometimes make things even worse. Murder is bad, and a market in murder might compound the problem. We don't want to industrialize the production of murder.

On the other hand, in principle, there could be cases where markets in bad things might make things better. Imagine that some new drug is developed, a drug that, suppose, everyone ought to avoid. People only give the drug to each other as gifts. The drug is poorly made, and, as a result, causes additional health problems from impurities. It's at least possible in this case that a fully legal, regulated market in that drug would make things better, not worse. Suppliers might produce higher quality, higher purity drugs in order to avoid lawsuits. And use might go down, not up, after the drug is legalized, just as drug use and its associated dangers dropped in Portugal and Colorado after they legalized certain drugs.

Our point here is that even if there are goods and services that ought not be possessed in the first place, it's an open, empirical question whether commodifying those goods and services might improve upon the status quo. To find out, we'd need to see how such markets would operate in practice. Examining just when this is so goes beyond the scope of our book. Still, we want to note that the question, "Is it a good idea to commodify things that no one ought to have?" doesn't wear its answer on its sleeve.

Notes

1 The word "inherently" is doing work in this principle. After all, consider a case where Bob promises to sell his cameras, but then does not. Here, Bob should not possess his cameras any longer, but it is permissible, indeed, obligatory, for him to sell them. Without the "inherently" qualifier, this principle would be false.

2 Sandel 2012a, 188.

3 Brennan first argued for this position in Brennan 2011, 135–60.

3

WHAT THE COMMODIFICATION DEBATE IS AND IS *NOT* ABOUT

Seven Kinds of Objections to Commodification

In this book, we will consider and refute a wide range of arguments against "commodification," i.e., against allowing certain things to be for sale. Here, we provide a taxonomy of the kinds of objections people raise. We will explain each of these kinds of objections, and the arguments behind them, in greater detail in subsequent chapters.

> A *Rights Violations:* Markets in some goods or services might violate people's rights. So, for instance, there should not be markets in stolen watches, child porn, or slaves, because these violate people's rights.
> B *Harm to Others:* Markets in some good or service might lead to greater violence or might cause harm to innocent bystanders. So, for instance, perhaps people should not be able to sell pit bulls, because pit bulls are extremely dangerous, and pit bull owners impose too much risk upon their neighbors.

We accept that A and B can impose limits on the market, but only because A and B determine what kinds of things people can have in the first place. A and B explain not why commodifying pit bulls or child porn are wrong, but instead explain why people should not have pit bulls or child porn at all. A and B limit not the scope of the market in particular, but instead the scope of what can be possessed or done, period. As we've said before, if you can have it for free, you can buy it; if you can give it to someone for free, you can sell it to her. Anti-commodification theorists intend to find limits to the market in which the market itself is the thing that introduces wrongness where there wasn't any to begin with.

> C *Exploitation*: Markets in some good or service might encourage the strong to exploit (to take unjust advantage of) the vulnerable. Some anti-commodification theorists oppose markets in women's sexual services or in organs for these reasons—they worry that such markets will allow the rich to take advantage of the poor. Some Marxists oppose *all* wage labor, because they think paying people to work is inherently exploitative.

Our view is that there is a prima facie duty to avoid exploitation. (As a result, we think certain contracts are unconscionable and should not be enforced.) However, this duty will only incidentally make certain market transactions immoral. There are no *kinds* of goods and services that are inherently exploitative. Instead, there are just particular cases where a particular transaction involves immoral exploitation. Anti-commodification theorists who rely upon exploitation objections want to say that certain kinds of things—such as women's sexual labor—should not be for sale, period. For them, it will be important to prove that all such sales inherently involve wrongful exploitation. Otherwise, at best, they will not have shown that it's wrong to buy that *kind* of thing, but just that it is being sold the wrong way, and is in principle something that could be for sale.[1]

> D *Misallocation*: Markets in certain goods and services might cause those goods to be allocated unjustly. So, for instance, Michael Sandel thinks line-standing services and paying to avoid queues are immoral because they are inegalitarian—rich people can pay to avoid standing in line, but the poor often cannot. Or, consider that Ivy League schools and their analogs sometimes admit lower quality students—students who would normally be denied admission, because the students have rich or celebrity parents. Legacy children—children of alumni—have lower admissions standards, because the schools expect the parents will donate more money to the schools. One might describe this pejoratively as the parents "buying" their children admission to prestigious colleges.
>
> E *Paternalism*: Markets in some good or service might cause people to make self-destructive choices. So, for instance, the Center for Science in the Public Interest lobbies the government to prohibit the sale of many different food items that people want to consume, on grounds that people will make unhealthy choices if such foods are available. Or, one might think it is immoral to buy and sell crystal meth, because using crystal meth is harmful to oneself.

As with exploitation arguments, we will show that whenever these kinds of arguments appear to succeed, they succeed only incidentally, or they just show that certain things should not be possessed at all. Anti-commodification theorists will not be able to show, however, that there are certain kinds of things that it is acceptable to have or do for free but which must not be placed on the market.

F *Corruption*: Participating in certain markets might tend to cause us to develop defective preferences or character traits. So, for instance, some people think we should avoid buying Disney Princess dolls for our daughters, because this will reinforce certain defective gender norms. Others think we should avoid participating in information markets, because these markets might cause us to develop immoral preferences. Still others think that participating in the market, period, generally tends to make us more selfish and callous.

Note that most philosophers who make corruption objections to markets mean to make a general complaint about the market. They do not simply mean to say that it's wrong for individuals who are corrupted by particular markets to participate in those markets. Rather, they usually mean to say that because the markets in question usually corrupt most people, no one should participate in them. Thus, suppose buying and selling sex has a negative effect on everyone's character, except for two unusually imperturbable individuals. Most, if not all, anti-commodification theorists would say that those two individuals should also refrain from buying and selling sex, even from each other.

The claim that markets corrupt us is serious indeed. If and when such complaints are true, the markets thereby implicated are lamentable if not downright damnable. We will take these claims very seriously, to a point of wanting to be very sure that the damnations are not mere witch-hunts. We will ask, what kind of evidence would it take to make good on the claim that possessing or trading in certain commodities genuinely is corrupting?[2] And what does that evidence actually show?

In response to corruption objections, we will show again that when there is a problem, it is not the market per se that is causing the problem. But, more strongly, we will argue that corruption objections are usually false or that those advancing such objections lack sufficient empirical evidence to justify their claims. On the contrary, we will argue, the best available empirical evidence suggests that the market is ennobling rather than corrupting.

G *Semiotic*: Participating in markets can express or communicate certain negative attitudes, or is incompatible with holding certain positive attitudes. A semiotic objection to commodification holds that, independently of objections A–F, to allow a market in some good or service X is a form of communication that expresses the wrong attitude toward X or expresses an attitude that is incompatible with the intrinsic dignity of X, or would show disrespect or irreverence for some practice, custom, belief, or relationship with which X is associated. So, for instance, some hold that organ sales communicate the idea that the human body is a mere commodity—a piece of meat—and thus fail to show proper reverence for the body. Others say that markets in surrogacy services express the idea that women are mere incubation machines.

Against semiotic objections, we will argue that the meaning of markets is largely a social convention, and that such conventions can be judged by their consequences. Thus, whenever allowing a market in X would produce good consequences, but our culture's semiotics imply that markets in X are bad, rather than this giving us reason to forbid markets in X, it instead requires us to change our semiotics. So, for instance, American culture views organ sales as vile and disgusting degradation of the human body. In turn, we will argue that this is because American culture disregards the sanctity of life—if Americans treated life with more respect, they would not imbue organ sales with such negative meaning. Anyone who raises a semiotic objection to organ sales is, in our view, glorifying vice.

Our Strategy

So far, we have just been focused on explaining what the debate is and what our position is in that debate. We have not yet articulated the best arguments the anti-commodification theorists have. Nor have we yet argued for our thesis and explained why we think the critics are mistaken. This will form the bulk of the book, and we'll get to that shortly.

Our strategy in this book is, for the most part, to articulate, explain, and then debunk the various arguments anti-commodification theorists have produced to try to show that commodification is wrong. We know of no general permissibility proof for all possible trades and markets that, in our mind, succeeds on the terms provided by the anti-commodification theorists. But, if we can repeatedly show that the critics' complaints are unfounded, this builds a case for our thesis. It's always possible that the critics will produce a good criticism down the road, but we're pushing the burden of proof back onto them.

Part of our strategy will be to accept most of the moral commitments of the anti-commodification theorists and still debunk their conclusions. We want to play and win in their ballpark. We're not going to base our arguments on controversial political or moral theories. Rather, we'll base our arguments as much as possible on 1) commonsense moral principles that most people accept and 2) the best available social science. While our conclusion is not itself commonsensical, we're going to use the good parts of commonsense to fix the broken parts.

A different book might attempt to argue that we need to play in a different ballpark. So, for example, some market enthusiasts want us to first agree that a controversial moral view is correct, and then go on to demonstrate that markets "without limits" follows from that view. Many libertarians, for example, argue that we have certain negative rights, and that these rights are such that voluntary capitalist acts between consenting adults should all be considered morally permissible. If this is our guiding slogan, it follows that we ought to permit prostitution, the sale of kidneys and blood, sale of line-standing services, and so on, the only limit being coerced trades and transfers. And since coercion violates the definition of what a market is in the first place, it is correct to say that this limit is a conceptual, rather than a moral, limit on markets. Many other contemporary libertarians attempt to first argue that the truth about ethics reduces to self-ownership, natural rights, non-aggression, consent, and/or contract. The guiding slogan for these libertarians is "anything consensual" or, as a bumper sticker for the US Libertarian Party once read, "we are pro-choice on everything." So long as the adults consent to an exchange, without coercion or fraud, that consent is sufficient to make the exchange morally permissible. Worries about exploitation from weak agency, misallocation like inequality, and other worries that anti-commodification theorists raise, simply don't register as genuine moral worries. Rights violations are the only category of real moral force. Everything else fails to take seriously the singular importance of agreement to terms between two or more adults.

But we didn't write that book. We wrote this book. We didn't write that book for two reasons. First, anti-commodification theorists do not accept libertarian political morality, and neither do the majority of professional philosophers and others whose profession obliges them to think long and hard about foundational issues in ethics. We want to have a conversation with them not about foundational issues in ethics, but about the moral limits of markets. We want to meet them on their moral diamond, rather than stomp our feet and threaten to take our ball and go home unless they come to a different ballpark.

More importantly, we did not write that book because neither of us agree with libertarian political morality. We have classical liberal sympathies, but we are not cartoon libertarians. We are in this ballpark, on this moral diamond, because this just happens to be our ballpark as well. We share similar, often identical, basic moral convictions as the anti-commodification theorists we strive to have a conversation with in this book.

So, instead, we aim to show that the anti-commodification theorists' complaints are mistaken, ill-grounded, confused, missing the point, or that they lack sufficient philosophical or empirical evidence for their positions. We defend our position—that if you may X for free, you may buy it; if you may give X away to someone for free, you may sell it to her—by debunking theirs.

Business Ethics Vs. What Can Be For Sale

We want to make sure people, including the anti-commodification theorists themselves, do not confuse the question of this book—what kinds of things may be for sale—with another closely related issue.

Sometimes people say we should not buy certain things because of how companies run their businesses. For instance, many people advocated boycotting Chik-fil-A when they learned that Chik-fil-A's owners donated money to fight same-sex marriage rights. Others advocate boycotting Apple because one of its subcontractors—FoxConn—has bad working conditions for its employees. Others might advocate boycotting payday loans stores for predatory lending practices, or boycotting certain car dealerships for being dishonest or too aggressive in their sales techniques.[3]

For the sake of argument, suppose that in these cases, we should boycott the businesses in question. In that sense, there would be a limit to markets. However, this is not what the anti-commodification theorists have in mind when discussing what should and should not be for sale. The problem with these businesses, according to their critics, is not that their products—chicken nuggets, iPhones, payday loans, or used cars—are inherently the kind of thing that should not be for sale. Rather, the problem, according to the critics, is just that these particular businesses are not being run according to ethical business practices.

Now, it might even turn out that all the businesses of a particular sort have such bad business practices that they all should be boycotted. So, for instance, imagine it turned out that, for some bizarre reason, *all* extant chicken nugget sellers were homophobes who donate half their profits to fight against civil rights. In that case, perhaps, one might have grounds not to buy the products in question, but that's just *incidental* to the products. It would not show that the nuggets are the kinds of things that should not be for sale, but rather that they are not being sold the right way, or that they are being sold by unscrupulous people whom one should avoid.

We both teach business ethics classes. We don't tell our students that businesses may just do as they please. Instead, businesses are bound by a wide range of negative duties—to avoid coercion, harm, exploitation, dishonesty, and so on—and can also acquire a wide range of positive duties. We agree that in some cases, when businesses egregiously violate the basic principles of business ethics, one should stop buying from or selling to those businesses.

But the debate over commodification is not about business ethics. (Anti-commodification critics frequently get this issue confused.) It is about whether certain things should not be for sale, period. It's important not to get these distinct issues confused. If buying Chik-fil-A nuggets is wrong, it's not because it's wrong to buy nuggets, but because Chik-fil-A is unscrupulous. If they sold carpets instead of nuggets, the issue would be the same. So, in this case, it's not the product being sold, but the seller that's the problem. In contrast, when anti-commodification theorists say it's wrong to buy line-standing services, the problem for them is not *who* sells the services, or *how* the services are sold, but the product itself.

Consider the following three claims:

1 It is immoral to lie.
2 It is immoral to cheat.
3 It is immoral to steal.

From 1–3, we can deduce 4–6:

4 It is immoral to lie while wearing a hat.
5 It is immoral to cheat while wearing a hat.
6 It is immoral to steal while wearing a hat.

4–6 follow logically from 1–3—if 1–3 are true, then so are 4–6. But suppose someone wrote a book called *The Moral Limits of Hats*, which tried to argue against universal hat-wearing by arguing for 4–6. We'd realize that the problem isn't with wearing hats, but with lying, cheating, and stealing. Wearing a hat is incidental. Similarly, in the debate here, we're considering what the moral limits of markets are. As we keep stressing, it's imperative, in discussing the limits of markets, that the *market* be the problem, rather than be incidental, like wearing a hat in 4–6.

Regulated Vs. Free Markets

We once watched one of our colleagues debate an anti-commodification theorist over whether certain goods or services should be for sale. The anti-commodification theorist said that free markets in certain goods and services would be bad in various ways. Our colleague took the bait, and spent his time trying to show that free markets in those goods and services would not be so bad.

We bring up this example in order to clarify the debate. The question of whether it is morally permissible to have a market in some good or service is not the same as the question of whether it's permissible to have a *free, completely unregulated* market in that good or service. Our thesis is that there are no inherent limits to what can be bought and sold. But that's compatible with thinking that some things, or even *all* things, should only be bought and sold in highly regulated markets. The question of whether or not markets should be free and unregulated is a red herring in the anti-commodification debate.

To illustrate, notice that the following two positions are coherent:

A *Anti-Market Libertarian*: G. A. Rothbard, the genetically engineered child of Marxist G. A. Cohen and libertarian Murray Rothbard, thinks markets are bad, and that we should never buy or sell anything. He opposes all commodification, even of mundane items, such as books and pencils. However, G. A. Rothbard also believes that people have absolute negative rights against being interfered with when they buy and sell goods. Just as our rights of free speech allow us to say things that are wrong to say, he thinks we have rights to buy and sell even though doing so is always immoral. Thus, G. A. Rothbard thinks justice prohibits any coercive regulation of the market, but also thinks nothing should be for sale.

B *Pro-Commodification Regulation Czar*: Murray Cohen, a different genetically engineered child, believes that literally everything that can be possessed may be bought and sold, but also advocates having extensive government regulation of every transaction.

We don't know of anyone who takes such positions, but they are positions in the logical space.

Thus, once again, we remind the anti-commodification critics that the commodification question is not about libertarianism or free markets. It's a separate question. It turns out empirically that free market enthusiasts are less worried about commodification, but they remain separate questions.

Law Vs. Ethics

Law and morality are not the same thing, though they sometimes overlap. Thus, when people say that certain things should not be for sale, it's important to distinguish between legal and moral impermissibility.

1   *Legal Impermissibility:* The law ought to prohibit the buying and/or selling of X.
2   *Moral Impermissibility:* It is morally wrong (regardless of whether it is illegal) to buy and/or sell X.

Sometimes anti-commodification theorists mean just to say that it is wrong to sell certain goods and services. Other times they mean to say it should be illegal to sell these goods and services.

Sometimes anti-commodification theorists believe that the law should let people sell things, but it is immoral to do so. For instance, some anti-commodification theorists think that it is immoral to sell cocaine, but they think that drug prohibition does more harm than good, and so they think governments should let people sell cocaine.

Generally, unless we indicate otherwise, the discussion in this book concerns whether buying and selling a certain thing is morally permissible, not whether the law should allow it. When we get into discussions about what the law should allow, we will explicitly indicate that we are doing so.

The Right to Sell Vs. The Rightness of Selling

Our view is that anything you may do for free, you may do for money. A corollary of that is that if it is permissible for you to own something, then it is permissible for you to sell it.

Here, we want to make sure people avoid thinking that our argument will be predictable and boring. Let's consider what ownership amounts to.

To own something is to have a *property right* in it. But, as most philosophers of property rights have noted, a property right is not just one right, but a *bundle* of separate rights. As David Schmidtz explains:

> Today, the term 'property rights' generally is understood to refer to a bundle of rights that could include rights to sell, lend, bequeath, use as collateral, or even destroy. (John Lewis generally is regarded as the first person to use the 'bundle of sticks' metaphor, in 1888.) The fact remains,

though, that at the heart of any property right is a right to say no: a right to exclude non-owners. In other words, a right to exclude is not just one stick in a bundle. Rather, property is a tree. Other sticks are branches; the right to exclude is the trunk.[4]

A property right is really a collection of separate rights, which generally include the right to sell, to buy, to lease or rent, to destroy, to modify, and to use. The central right of property is the right of exclusion. So, for instance, my right to my house means I have the right to exclude you from using my house—except in special circumstances, you need my permission to occupy my land. If property rights are a bundle, we might think of the right to exclude as the trunk from which the other rights grow as branches.

We want to be clear that we are *not* arguing that it follows, as a matter of logic (from the meaning of the concept of "property right") that if something is permissibly someone's property, that she may then sell it. Certain libertarian thinkers might be tempted to make this argument, but we reject it, for three reasons.

First, if we did try to ground our thesis on property rights, it would not really settle the debate. It would just shift the debate to a related debate. If we did insist that to have the right to own something meant a right to sell it, then at best, the question for debate would just become what people have the right to own. Nothing would change.

Second, we think this argument rests on a conceptual mistake in its analysis of property rights. After all, we have the rightful power to determine what happens to different things in different ways—and the bundle of rights that attaches to this rightful power varies. The strength of our rights also varies. I can have property in a cat and a car, but my power over the cat—which may be better understood as "guardianship" rather than ownership—doesn't allow me to do as much with it as my ownership of the car does. The way I have a property in a cat is different from how I own a car, which is different from how I own a guitar, which is different from how I own a plot of land, etc. So, for instance, my ownership right to my guitar includes the right to destroy it at will for any capricious reason, but my right to my cat does not include such a right. My right to my house includes the right to sell it, but, because of a restricted covenant, it does not include the right to paint it neon orange with neon pink polka-dots.

Now consider the right to sell. Certain property rights come with restricted covenants—you can buy some things, but lack the corresponding right to sell them, or have only limited rights to sell. So, for instance, I (Jason) have a property right to a pool club membership, but I may sell my membership only to someone who buys my house, and only at a price set by the pool club. My ownership over the membership is not the same as my ownership over my guitars, which I have the right to sell at will on any mutually agreeable terms. Another example: you probably own a license to use many forms of software, but you agreed, as part of the purchase, that this ownership did not include the right to resell the software when you are finished with it.

Third, we think this argument makes a further conceptual mistake in that it conflates two separate questions:

A What do you have the right to do with your property?
B What is right for you to do with your property?

A and B are distinct. In general, if you have the right to do something, this does not presuppose that it is morally right for you to do it. Rights are not about what's morally permissible for the right-holder to do. Instead, they are more about what's morally permissible for other people to do to the rights-holder. So, for instance, suppose my wife lovingly gives me a new guitar for my birthday. The guitar is mine, and I have the right to destroy it—no one should stop me from doing so. But, if I were to destroy it, I'd act badly, as I would hurt my wife's feelings. Or, as another example, I have the right to join a Neo-Nazi political rally and express hatred of Jews, but it would be immoral to do so. No one should stop me from being a Nazi, but I also shouldn't be a Nazi.

Thus, an anti-commodification theorist could simply agree that people have the *right* to sell certain things (line-standing services, sex, organs, etc.) but then claim that it remains immoral and wrong to buy and sell those things, even though it is within people's rights. The anti-commodification theorists would then conclude that certain markets should be legal, even if they are deeply immoral. Our goal here is to challenge the moral condemnation of these markets. We want to argue that markets in contested commodities like organs and sex are not merely within people's rights, but are morally permissible.

Notes

1 Satz 2012, 153, agrees—she thinks that markets in women's sexual services are only contingently wrong, in light of extant "status inequality between men and women." If this inequality were removed, as it may well be in a few hundred years, then markets in sexual services would be permissible. In that sense, Satz and we fundamentally agree. However, we disagree with Satz on the particulars. We think it is often permissible to buy sex *now*, despite extant status inequality.
2 We owe these sentences to David Schmidtz.
3 For a philosophical discussion of this issue, see Hussain 2012.
4 Schmidtz 2013.

4

IT'S THE HOW, NOT THE WHAT

Over the next few chapters of this book, we will address the best arguments against commodification, one by one. We examine a variety of such objections to markets and a range of cases where markets in goods and services supposedly introduce wrongness where there wasn't any. In each case, we find the objections unsound. Sometimes these objections rest upon mistaken empirical premises. Sometimes they rest upon bad moral premises. At the end, we conclude that none of the best arguments against markets in everything succeed.

Here, we offer a general challenge to anti-commodification theorists. We hypothesize that their problem is not really with *what* is being sold, but *how* it's being sold. This isn't to say the problem doesn't matter, but that the anti-commodification theorists have misdiagnosed the problem.

We argue that even if selling certain goods and services a certain way might be bad, there is always a different time, place, and manner for selling those goods and services that would remove those objections. So, for instance, if someone complains that selling kidneys would lead to the exploitation of the poor, we can in principle eliminate that problem through regulation.

Our thesis in this book is that if you can give something to someone, then you can normally sell it to that person. If you can take something from someone, then you can normally buy it from that person. There are no inherent limits to markets. There are only incidental limits. If we steal the BMW, we can't sell it to you, not because BMWs are the kinds of things that can't be sold, but because it's not ours to sell. If you're only two years old, we can't sell a tricycle to you, not because tricycles shouldn't be bought and sold, but because you aren't old enough to consent to the purchase. And if we promise not to sell our watches, then we can't sell them, not because watches are not the kind of things that must never be bought or sold, but just because we happened to have promised not to do so. And so on.

Time, Place, and Manner

The United States Constitution includes, as the First Amendment, a guarantee to freedom of speech. The United States Supreme Court has seen fit to distinguish three different kinds of speech, each receiving a different level of protection. "Obscenity" gets very little protection, "Commercial speech," receives intermediate scrutiny, while political and expressive speech gets the highest level of protection. When it comes to political and expressive speech, the Supreme Court describes the limits and regulations that are permissible as not limits on the content of speech. Apart from cases where a restriction on speech serves a compelling state interest that cannot be served in any other way, the limits that they have found consistent with first amendment guarantees are described as content-neutral. It's not *what* you say, but *when, where,* and *how* you say it.

Consider some famous First Amendment cases:

1   *Burning the flag:* Gregory Lee Johnson set an American flag on fire in Dallas, Texas, in 1984. He did it during the 1984 Republican National Convention, which was being held in Dallas. And he did it in order to protest then-president Ronald Reagan's administration, as well as corporations. The authorities in Texas quickly arrested him, and charged him according to a statute that prohibited the desecration of a "venerated object." A State Court permitted the charge to go through but the Texas Court of Criminal Appeals reversed the decision. On appeal, the US Supreme Court sided with the latter, and Johnson was set free to burn more flags if he wanted to.[1]
2   *Rock Against Racism:* New York City's *Central Park* has an amphitheater. It also has a place called "Sheep Meadow" that the city has designated as a quiet place for reading, walking, and relaxing. Rock Against Racism is a group that had, since 1979, used Central Park's amphitheater for anti-racist speeches and concerts. On many occasions, people at Sheep Meadow, and at some apartment buildings on the edge of Central Park West complained about the volume from the anti-racist concerts. In 1984, the concert was still too loud, leading to two citations, and, eventually, the police cut off the power to the concert altogether. The next year, the city decided that the best way to regulate the volume was to require everyone to use city-provided sound equipment that was to be operated by an independent sound technician, rather than permitting each event host to provide their own equipment and technician. Rock Against Racism took the city to court, insisting that these requirements violated their first amendment rights. But the Supreme Court ruled for the city, arguing that the city had a substantial interest in limiting sound volume, that the particular regulations were sufficiently narrowly-tailored to this goal, and that these regulations were content-neutral.
3   *Public political meetings:* In the 1960s, Baton Rouge, Louisiana had segregated lunch counters. The segregation led to pickets and protests. At one point,

23 students from a black college were arrested. After the arrest, B. Elton Cox, a minister, organized a protest at the courthouse which drew 2000 protesters across the street from the courthouse. On the other side of the street, between 100 and 300 whites gathered. Cox gave a speech urging the protesters to sit at the segregated lunch counter, which resulted in grumbling amongst the counter-protesters, and then the sheriff to try and disperse Cox's crowd. When they didn't, the sheriff ordered Cox's arrest and he was charged with breach of peace, picketing near a courthouse, and obstruction of a public passageway. The Supreme Court overturned all of these convictions, but did insist that their reason for so-doing had a lot to do with the fact that the protest was peaceful until the police showed up, and because the protesters did not actually obstruct a public passageway. If there had been a breach of peace, or if the protesters had gathered at a time when the thoroughfare had been particularly busy with commuters and thereby obstructed the public, the outcome would have been different.

In each of these cases, the Supreme Court insisted that the First Amendment prohibits legislating against the content of the speech. In this sense, when it comes to political and expressive speech, Americans legally have "speech without limits." There are no speech-specific, or content-specific restrictions on speech. Whatever you want to say, you can say. At the same time, the Court imposed or upheld *incidental* limits having to do with the time, place, and manner of speech.[2] In effect, the Courts have said that it's the how, not the what.

When it came to Johnson, the Court said that even though his activity caused deep offense, he had the right to burn a flag as a form of expression. This case turned, in part, on the manner of the activity. Had Johnson burned the flag in a way that might provoke a reasonable person to violence, then the Texas authorities would have been right to arrest him.

The Rock Against Racism case was also about the manner of the speech, not its content. Of course people are free to host a concert in opposition to racism. But if you're going to host a concert in a place like Central Park, you have to do it in a manner that is in keeping with the State's sound-amplification requirements.[3] And of course people are free to urge their friends and neighbors and even strangers to vote for a particular candidate. But you can't go into a suburban neighborhood in the middle of the night and promote your candidate with a noisy megaphone. Similarly, you can have a political meeting in a public place like a sidewalk adjacent to a courthouse, but you can't "insist upon a street meeting in the middle of Times Square at the rush hour as a form of freedom of speech".[4]

There are no legal inherent limits on political and expressive speech in the US, only incidental limits having to do with the time, place, and manner of that speech. So, too, might there be analogous time, place, and manner restrictions on markets that are similarly incidental, having nothing to do with the moral permissibility of a market in this or that good or service.

Demonstrating this means that at least some anti-commodification theorists are over-generalizing. They are confusing incidental with inherent limits. Demonstrating this would also mean that we would thereby deflate the anti-commodification thesis into a question about business ethics.

Some Cases

Consider the following cases:

Case 1: Life (insurance) and death

Suppose your friend has recently passed away. He was a close friend, but he never bothered to buy life insurance, despite the fact that you sell life insurance. He has left his wife with a very significant price tag for the funeral. So significant, that his wife and children will now be destitute. He could afford insurance, he just didn't bother getting it. You attend the funeral, and you bring your business cards. Meeting all sorts of people, you tell them about your friend's circumstances, hand them your business card and say, "Here. Buy some life insurance. Don't let what happened to James happen to you."

Case 1 presents a case of bad timing. Very few of us now think that there is anything morally problematic about selling life insurance. Indeed, it is a mark of responsible people that they purchase life insurance at some point. What we object to in case 1 is not the buying and selling of life insurance, but the *timing*. There is an appropriate time for a market in life insurance, and selling it at a funeral is just really bad timing.

Case 2: Location, location, location

Real estate agents are fond of the expression, "Location, location, location." What they mean is that the value of a piece of property is very often determined by where it's located. Something similar might be said about certain markets.

The story of Jesus knocking over the tables and wares of the Pharisees in the Temple is a good illustration of the point. Jesus did not, on his way to the Temple, knock over the tables and wares of outdoor shopkeepers in the town; he restricted his upsetting of tables to Temple grounds. In effect, Jesus was saying to the merchants, "Location, location, location"—sometimes, there's a wrong place for market behavior. And while neither of us are theologians or Biblical scholars, we don't see the point of this story as supporting a supposed conflict between the "sacred" Temple and the "profane" market. We suspect that if the Pharisees were practicing Yoga or playing Bocce ball at the Temple, Jesus would have been similarly upset and would have similarly upset the Yoga mats or Bocce balls. The Temple was for contemplation and prayer, not for anything else. As for commercial activity, Jesus probably had no problem with Pharisees and others selling things, he just had a beef with the ones who chose to do it on Temple grounds.

Similarly, a shopkeeper can't go out in the middle of a road to display her wares. It is not an objection to markets when we agree that homeowners are not required to accept door-to-door vacuum salesman into their homes or to host Tupperware sales parties if they don't want to. It's not because there's something wrong with the buying and selling of Tupperware or vacuums, it's just that *where* you choose to do it is sometimes bad. For speech purposes, US courts distinguish between traditional public forums, limited public forums, and nonpublic forums as part of their place-relevant test. When it comes to speech, there are different kinds of places, and the kinds of places impose sometimes fewer and sometimes greater restrictions. They are still content-neutral; they merely discriminate on the basis of location.

This is part of our much broader point: often, the problem is not *that* something is sold, but *how* it's done that matters. Sometimes the timing is bad, and other times the location is not the right one. Anti-commodification theorists see this fact. They recognize that time and place restrictions on commercial activity are not restrictions on commercial activity as such. What they fail to recognize, we will argue, is that there is not one way that something is sold on the market, but very many very different ways of buying and selling the very same thing—markets come in different modes. Adjusting the mode of the market is a way of adjusting the manner in which a market operates. Sometimes, the problem may very well be that a particular kind of market, with its particular features, is inappropriate for some good or service. The manner of selling it is objectionable (or is more repugnant, even if that repugnance turns out to be not morally relevant). In short, it's the *how*, not the *what*.

The analogy to the first amendment test might be misunderstood, so let's get it right. The analogy is not that political and expressive speech acts are like market exchanges. Instead, market exchanges are better seen as speech acts performed in some specific language, like English or French. The broader category of speech acts as such would be similar to the broader category of exchanges as such. So an argument about the moral limits of markets is similar to an argument about the moral limits of English speech acts, not speech acts as such. This is important for the following reason. We have already ruled out objections to markets that are really objections to exchanges as such. We can't have slaves for sale or murder for hire, but that's not because the market somehow makes what would otherwise be morally right into something immoral. These things are inherently wrong, and their wrongness has nothing to do with their being exchanged as gifts, as part of communal sharing, or on the market. It's the "slaves" part not the "for sale" part that is objectionable, the "murder" part not the "for hire" that is repugnant to our conscience.

If we were to write a book about the moral limits of English speech acts, we could similarly rule out the expression of content that it is inherently wrongful to express in any language, as saying nothing of significance about the English language as such. We could then go on to discuss how time, place, and manner restrictions on non-inherently wrongful English speech acts make all the difference to the wrongfulness of the act. Altering these variables can turn non-inherently wrongful speech acts from wrongful to non-wrongful (and sometimes rightful) speech acts. It would be wrong of us to scream "fire" in a crowded theater when there is no fire. But now imagine that there is a fire, then it would be right for us to do so. It would be wrong of us to sincerely express racist sentiment, but it could be non-wrongful if we are saying so sarcastically or ironically or satirically, in a context where listeners understand the satirical or sarcastic upshot. The fake documentary about the Confederate States of America, for example, expresses racist sentiment but does so in a way to poke fun at that sentiment, to satirize people with such views. If it were expressed sincerely, it would be wrongful, but as a piece of satire, it is not.

This is what we intend to now do for markets. We intend to demonstrate that our attitudes and judgments about markets often depend not on inherent or essential features of all markets, but on the specific features of particular markets. When we alter the time, place, and manner of a market, we do not thereby change the nature of the exchange from a market to a non-market exchange. Selling t-shirts at 5 p.m. is a market activity just as surely as doing so at 10 p.m. So is selling iPods in an Apple store, or at a university. Selling a horse at auction or through Craigslist are both examples of different kinds of market exchange. We are saying that anti-commodification theorists need to be careful to distinguish objections to this or that market from objections to markets as such.

Our claim here is that the time, place, and manner of markets can change our attitudes towards the objects of sale and the people we engage in market exchanges with, can alter the allocative outcomes, can remove concerns about exploitation, and so can remove or eliminate the wrong-making features of a particular market exchange.

Designing the Manner

We don't merely have markets in different kinds of things, we have different *kinds* of markets for the very same thing. Some markets have a fixed price, like at your local Walmart. Other markets have prices that you are expected to haggle over, like at a garage sale. Sometimes you are required to enter into a pool of buyers at a clearinghouse. Some require you to make a secret bid, with the highest or second-highest bidder getting the goods. Sometimes you have to buy the bids separately before you can place a bid. Sometimes you have to join a club before you can buy anything, like at Costco. Some markets prohibit money, like at bartering websites. Other markets prohibit mass manufacture, and require items to be hand-made, like on Etsy. Still other markets are constructed such that you are expected to become at least somewhat familiar with a product before you can buy it, like test-drives at car lots. Sometimes, we restrict the sale of some good to those with licenses, or to those in certain professions, like with health care.

With respect to some goods, our objection may not be to the buying or the selling of the thing itself, but, rather, to the *way* that something is bought or sold. When Debra Satz and others worry about the endogenous effects of certain kinds of markets on the character, virtues, and cognitive abilities of the participants, they should recognize that different kinds of markets for the very same good or service will have different endogenous effects. This is a problem with market design[5] or what we'll call "market architecture", rather than a problem with markets as such.

A simple and common example is this. Suppose you want to distribute pie between your two children. One way to design a pie-splitting game is to make one child cut the pie, while the other child gets to choose the slice. This has the benefit of reducing complaints, as well as making it more likely that the eventual distribution will be regarded as fair by both parties. Here, we can regard the sense of unfairness and the bitterness of complaints from the parties as negative outcomes of pie distribution. Designing the distribution in this way minimizes (or eliminates) those negative outcomes. Now imagine for a moment a critic of pie splitting before anyone had invented this clever way of splitting the pie. The critic might complain that we should not split pies, because pie splitting made people feel bitter and angry and sometimes led to fights. The critic might confuse the negative outcomes of one way of splitting a pie with splitting pies as such. "There are some things that ought not be split," he might say, "especially pies." But the criticism would fail, precisely because there are other ways of doing the very same thing, of splitting pies without the attendant negative effects.

We will show that many of the objections to money and markets raised by anti-commodification theorists can be conceived of as complaints about particular markets, rather than about markets as such. If so, we will ask, are there ways of altering market architecture that reduce or eliminate these complaints? Our answer to that question is "yes." For the very different kinds or modes of markets, there is a sociology of that particular market. People have constructed different meanings that correspond with different *kinds* of markets. In Part II, we argue that purely semiotic objections to markets fail. However, suppose we are mistaken. Here, in this chapter, we argue that even if it's wrong to sell certain goods through certain kinds of markets, it remains permissible to sell those goods through *other* kinds of markets.

Holding those social conventions about meaning constant, we will conclude that anti-commodification theorists ignore the heterogeneity of market modes, and too often confuse objections to one way of exchanging something with an inherent conflict between markets as such and the inherent features of some object, good, or service.

Elizabeth Anderson's Surrogacy Market

Elizabeth Anderson says,

> Commercial surrogacy substitutes market norms for some of the norms of parental love. Most importantly, it requires us to understand parental rights no longer as trusts but as things more like property rights – that is, rights of use and disposal over the things owned. For in this practice the natural mother deliberately conceives a child with the intention of giving it up for material advantage. Her renunciation of parental responsibilities is not done for the child's sake, nor for the sake of fulfilling an interest she shares with the child, but typically for her own sake (and possibly, if "altruism" is a motive, for the intended parents' sakes). She and the couple who pay her to give up her parental rights over her child thus treat her rights as a kind of property right. They thereby treat the child itself as a kind of commodity, which may be properly bought and sold.[6]

Anderson's objections to surrogacy arrangements are varied. She objects to the attitude that surrogates take towards the child. She objects to the attitude she discovers towards women's reproductive labor that she believes is inherent to surrogacy arrangements.[7] She objects to the contractual features that require a woman to give up her baby despite the fact that women may change their minds. They change their minds, when they do, partly because of a gross lack of information—surrogates do not now know how much they will bond with the child once it comes time to fulfill the contract. She objects to the fact that no one represents the interests of the child, just as "no industry assigns agents to look after the 'interests' of its commodities."[8] Finally, she objects to the role that brokers play in contemporary surrogacy arrangements, which can be corrupting. The broker, says Anderson, is motivated and incentivized to try and get the surrogate to release the product of her labors, even if she becomes attached, or changes her mind.

In order for Anderson to get the conclusion that she wants—that we ought to have a full prohibition on surrogacy arrangements—it must be the case that there is no way of forming or creating a surrogacy market that is consistent with taking the right attitude toward women's reproductive labor or towards the child. Perhaps a case like this can be made, but this case has not been made. Instead, and at best, what Anderson has demonstrated is that women's reproductive labor (and the children that are the product of that labor) are wrongfully and disrespectfully commodified in a market *like the one we currently have*, with brokers, and so on.

In order for the argument that markets, as such, are inappropriate for surrogacy to be successful, she would need to demonstrate either that the form that the market currently takes with respect to surrogacy is a necessary and not merely contingent form given the kind of thing that surrogacy is, or that there does not exist a possible form that a market could take that would not wrongfully commodify women's reproductive labor and the children that are the product of that labor.

Consider: the broker is a contingent, and not a necessary element to the surrogacy market. Brokers probably make the market more "efficient," and permit us to economize on information and transaction costs (brokers are, after all, experts of a sort). Nevertheless, they are hardly constitutive of markets. We could have surrogacy arrangements without brokers, and these arrangements would still rightly be called "markets." So the broker objection can be overcome by designing brokers out of a surrogacy market. Alternatively, we might distinguish between "mean" and "nice" brokers. Mean brokers are brokers that prioritize making money rather than ensuring that each party is treated as an end, and gives genuine and uncoerced consent to the transaction. So we shouldn't have commercial surrogacy arrangements with mean brokers, but it would be the meanness, and not the broker-ness, that would be objectionable.

The nature of the contract is also contingent. Anderson worries that the terms of contemporary surrogacy arrangements require that a woman give up the child even if she becomes attached, or changes her mind. We note, as a side issue, that courts have not required specific performance, preferring, instead, to grant parental rights to the surrogate as well as the biological or genetic father of the child when surrogates have changed their mind. We can put this worry about surrogacy aside merely by redesigning the terms of the contract in order to include a "change of mind" clause: if, for any reason, the surrogate changes her mind, the contract is null and void. It would still be a market. So, again, Anderson's objection to surrogacy markets seems to be about the how, not the what.

The fact that no one represents the interests of the child is not a necessary feature of the market. We could institute a rule that requires an agent to function on behalf of the child's interests in all surrogacy arrangements. We do precisely this during disputes over inheritance if the inheritor is a child who happens to be too young to defend her own interests, and we could do the same for surrogacy arrangements.

The more significant objections, the ones that come closest to being genuine in-principle objections to markets in surrogacy, are the objections to the attitudes people either take, or are seen as taking, towards the child and women's reproductive labor. As Anderson sees it, she appears to think that it is an inherent feature of any and all markets that the participants view the child and women's reproductive labor in the wrong way. They conceive of the child as a profit-possibility, rather than as a creature with a dignity; and conceive of women's reproductive labor not as a special form of labor, but merely as an abstract input in an economic process that delivers a product.

At first, we want to register our skepticism about this sort of claim. We want to note the similar worries that people used to have towards children's insurance. Once upon a time, people objected to such insurance schemes as "putting a price on children's lives," as "commodifying children."[9] Maybe, for a time, this is the attitude that people took towards their own children when taking out insurance, and maybe the insurance companies had this attitude as well. But times have changed. We now rightly regard these attitudes as being inessential, indeed bizarre and unusual, to children's insurance. People who take out such insurance are no longer regarded with mistrust, we no longer believe that getting children's insurance *means* that you regard the child as a commodity, as a profit-possibility, or that you are pricing human life. Is it possible that the attitudes Anderson takes to be constitutive of surrogacy arrangements is merely an artifact of the novelty of these arrangements, rather than intrinsic parts of these kinds of exchanges? We're skeptical, but on Anderson's behalf, let's put this skepticism aside.

We can register a different kind of skepticism as well. We don't see the connection between our attitudes and property rights. Many of us have property rights in objects that we do not regard as mere commodities. I (Peter) have a watch that I received as a gift from my grandfather who has now passed away. My attitude is deeply sentimental toward it. In no way do I regard that watch as a mere commodity, despite the fact that I recognize and am aware of my property rights in the watch. So I am able to hold two thoughts in my mind—"this watch is my property" or "I have property rights in this watch" and "this watch is not a mere commodity to me"—that simply are not incoherent or in any way in conflict. But, again on Anderson's behalf, let's put this skepticism aside as well.

Our more significant response accepts Anderson's worries. Let us suppose, for the sake of argument, that the current surrogacy market really does generate or produce a disrespectful attitude towards the child and towards women's reproductive labor. And we of course agree with Anderson that these attitudes are the wrong attitudes, that it would be immoral to regard a child or the capacity for childbirth as primarily or exclusively a mere commodity. Let us suppose that this continues to be the case even if we prohibit brokers and include a "change of mind" clause in the contract. Let us also agree to hold the socially constructed meanings of markets constant as well. But suppose you are not persuaded, or suppose that surrogacy is not the kind of thing that generates sufficiently positive consequences to give us grounds to object to the contingent cultural practice of attaching the social meaning to surrogacy that Anderson sees in surrogacy. Are there other variables that could be adjusted in order to overcome the repugnance of such a market based on the commodification attitude that, as we are supposing, is generated by this market?

The Manner of Exchange

Guitar amplifiers have a bunch of knobs on the front, knobs that control the volume, the equalization, the gain (also called "overdrive" or "distortion"), and other factors. Some amplifiers are "touchy" or "hard to dial in"; that is, they sound good only with very specific settings. For instance, the Mesa Boogie Mark series of amplifiers—a famous type of amplifier you have heard on thousands of rock, metal, and jazz songs—only sounds right with very specific settings. (Specifically, one needs to keep the bass knob almost off, the midrange knob fairly low, the treble and gain knobs high, and must make a V-shape with the included five-band equalizer.) Another example: legendary guitarist Steve Vai's signature Carvin Legacy amplifier needs to have the "presence" knob at 7; any higher and the amp sounds shrill, any lower and it sounds flubby. Other amplifiers are "easy to dial in". For instance, the legendary Marshall Super Lead—another amp you've heard thousands of times in thousands of recordings—sounds good at basically any setting.

Markets are a bit like guitar amplifiers. Just as guitar amps have various knobs (gain, volume, bass, midrange, treble, presence, resonance, top cut, boost, mid cut, etc.), so markets might have a range of variables that can be put to different settings. Just as some guitar amps sound good only on very specific settings, some markets might be good only on very specific settings. Or, just as other guitar amps sound good no matter what the settings, so other markets might be good no matter what the settings.

So, if a market is kind of like an amplifier, what are the different knobs and what do they do? What we are calling the manner of a market exchange consists of the following variables, which we can call the seven dimensions of market manner:

1   Participants (buyer, seller, middleman, broker, etc.)
2   Means of exchange (money, barter, local currency, bitcoins, gift cards, etc.)
3   Price (high, low, moderate, etc.)
4   Proportion / Distribution (how much each party gets)
5   Mode of exchange (auction, lottery, bazaar, co-op, etc.)
6   Mode of payment (salary, scholarship, tip, charitable contribution, etc.)
7   Motive of exchange (for-profit, public benefit, cost-recovery, non-profit, charitable, etc.)

If each of the seven dimensions had only three options (although there are many more), that would give us 3^7 possible permutations, or 2,187 different kinds of market manner. If we were to add time and place, we would have many, many more. To overcome the anti-commodification objection to commercial surrogacy, we need to find only one out of at least 2,187 different kinds of manners of markets that overcomes the objections to make our point. When it comes to a surrogacy market, we can change the manner in very many different ways. The participants can be (and are) restricted. The price could be different, and the proportion of the money can be distributed between the seller of the service, the broker, any agencies involved, and so on, differently. The payment need not be money that the seller personally receives, she could be paid in a charitable contribution made on her behalf, or the money could go into a scholarship fund for the baby, or for a baby she might have in the future. We could also insist on price floors or ceilings, or a uniform, standardized price consistent across all surrogates.

Apart from the participants, the mode of payment, the price, and the proportion or distribution, we could also change the mode of exchange. Surrogacy arrangements could make use of lotteries, with surrogates receiving a fixed payment from a pool of hopeful parents who enter a lottery with equal odds of ending up with a child. The babies could, perhaps, be auctioned, although we suspect many of our readers will find that especially distasteful. That distastefulness, however, may be a function of not understanding the sociology of auctions, which we will describe in greater detail below. (That is, baby auctions might actually be an especially tasteful market.)

Each of these changes to the variables can change the symbolic meanings associated with the various exchanges. These changes remain consistent with the exchange felicitously being described as a market. It would still count as a surrogacy market, it would just be different. Can we find a market architecture that would result in people having the right attitude towards the child as a predictable feature of some or another market manner? In what follows, we will first address ourselves to a worry that might have occurred to you already. Namely, is our understanding of what makes something a "market" too broad? Aren't markets necessarily for-profit, and isn't the use of money, rather than barter or scholarships, as an instrument of exchange an essential feature of modern-day markets? Once we address this worry, we will then try to demonstrate that altering the manner is a real possibility before we turn to the empirical literature. If we find that changes in market architecture have overcome similar problems with other kinds of markets, we should expect that changes in market architecture can overcome problems not only with commercial surrogacy, but in a wide range of other kinds of markets as well.

This is our general challenge to anti-commodification critics. It won't be enough for them to show us that some markets are bad—morally impermissible—on some or even many "settings". They need to show us that markets in certain commodities are bad on all the possible settings. Otherwise, if we can find even one "setting" for a particular market, then our thesis stands. So, to take a silly example, suppose it turns out to be permissible to buy and sell kidneys only for exactly $56,000 in bitcoins, only while the buyers and sellers are singing "When I'm 64," and only on the fourth Friday of May. Even then, that means that kidneys are properly the kind of thing that can be bought and sold. The anti-commodification critics would be wrong.

One might be tempted to think that if a certain commodity can be permissibly bought and sold only on say, one very specific "setting" of these nine variables, then that market is *close* to being evil. One might think that good commodities are the ones that can be bought and sold with almost any combination of these variables. One might think that as the acceptable "settings" of a particular commodity become more constrained, then that market is for that reason *less* good.

But this doesn't hold for markets in various goods and services anymore than it holds for amplifiers. Consider again: the Mesa Boogie Mark IIC+, III, and IV sound right only on a few very specific settings, but they aren't for that reason *bad* amplifiers. On the contrary, they are *excellent* amplifiers, which is why you've heard them thousands of times on thousands of recordings. You just need to know how to dial them in. Similarly, it might be that a market in kidneys is permissible only on very specific "settings," but that market might still be a wonderful market, one that does far more good for the world than most other markets.

That said, we don't want to make it too easy for us to claim victory. After all, suppose a certain market could, in principle, be permissible, but only under highly fantastic conditions, conditions that are highly unlikely ever to obtain.[10] If so, our thesis would remain intact, but would be significantly less interesting. Fortunately, though, as far as we can tell, it seems we avoid this problem in the book. We don't just find, e.g., that selling kidneys could be permissible only if one first flips heads 666 times in a row. Rather, most of the repugnant markets could be "fixed" rather easily.

Outline

In the first few chapters, we clarified just what the commodification debate is about. We've learned through experience—through presenting pieces of this book at over 20 different venues—that clarifying just what the debate is does a lot of work. Many of the people we've met who are inclined to complain about commodification realize, after some prodding, that they are actually concerned with *possessing*, not with *buying and selling*.

In this chapter, we issued a general challenge to anti-commodification theorists: for them to show that some goods (that it is permissible to possess, and to give away or take for free) may not be bought and sold, they need to "fiddle with the knobs" of the market and make sure that those goods cannot be bought or sold on any "setting". It might be that some goods—such as kidneys—can only permissibly be bought and sold under very specific conditions. But, if so, they can still be bought and sold, and our thesis stands.

In Parts II, III, and IV of this book, we will examine and attack a number of arguments that try to meet our challenge. In Part II, we look closely at semiotic objections to certain markets. Part III focuses on corruption objections. Part IV focuses on exploitation, harm, and misallocation objections. In each case, we argue these specific objections are unsound.

By Part V, we've debunked the major arguments against commodification. However, we expect that many readers will still have a gut-level feeling that something is just plain wrong with buying and selling certain goods. Part V takes a close look at this gut-level feeling. We argue that at least some opposition to commodification is based on feelings of disgust, and we argue that such feelings are not reliable indicators of right and wrong.

Notes

1 *Texas v. Johnson*, 491 U.S. 397 (1989).
2 There is controversy about whether or not this is, strictly speaking, true. The courts have ranked speech in order of importance, with commercial speech, obscenity, and fighting words receiving a lower standard of protection as compared with speech the courts have deemed to be more important, like political speech. But for our purposes here, we will simply accept them at their word. Not much hangs on whether or not, in fact, US courts consistently live up to their own proclaimed standards.
3 *Ward v. Rock Against Racism*, 491 U.S. 781 (1989).
4 *Cox v. Louisiana*, 379 U.S. 536, 85 S. Ct. 453, 13 L. Ed. 2d 471 [1965].
5 Market design is a particular kind of mechanism design within game theory. In market design, economists attempt to alter relevant features within a market (or a "game") in order to generate or avoid some outcome. Most often, economists are interested in increasing the efficiency properties of a market. So, for example, some attempt to minimize transaction costs or reduce negative externalities.
6 Anderson 1990, 76.
7 " ... the sale of an infant has an expressive significance which this argument fails to recognize. By engaging in the transfer of children by sale, all of the parties to the surrogate contract express a set of attitudes toward children which undermine the norms of parental love. They all agree in treating the ties between a natural mother and her children as properly loosened by a monetary incentive." Anderson 1990, 77.
8 Anderson 1990, 76.
9 Zelizer 1994.
10 Thanks to an anonymous referee for this point.

PART II
Do markets signal disrespect?

5

SEMIOTIC OBJECTIONS

Money Means Something

Buying and selling is not just about getting goods or making money. It can also be an expressive act, a kind of performance, or a way to signal attitudes and beliefs to one another.

Consider, as the popular critic of markets Naomi Klein observes, that name brands used to just be a way for customers to identify and differentiate among products. Coca-Cola and Pepsi taste somewhat different, and the branding allows you to pick your preferred choice wherever you go. However, branding expanded beyond that, such that we now identify different brands with different lifestyles, attitudes, and ideologies. Buying certain products is buying into an image or a lifestyle.

So, for instance, one reason people buy Apple computers over less expensive but equally well performing PCs is that they want to signal to others and themselves that they are a certain kind of person. Or, perhaps, in virtue of buying the Apple, they *become* (to some extent) that kind of person. We imbue certain goods and services, or certain brands that provide these goods and services, with meaning. Like it or not, it says something about you that you have an Apple rather than a PC.

Or, for example, consider the market in luxury sport sedans. The BMW 335i and Mercedes C400 do not have identical performance—there are real differences between the two cars. But most buyers do not simply choose between them on the basis of their physical differences or differences in price.

Rather, BMW and Mercedes—both equally high status—have consciously and carefully cultivated different images of what BMW and Mercedes drivers are like. Many people who buy a BMW are thus signaling (or trying to signal) that they are exciting driving enthusiasts, who demand precision and performance. Buying a Mercedes tends to signal that a person is refined, sophisticated, and elegant.

We imbue the willingness and unwillingness to buy certain things with meaning. For instance, consider common attitudes in the United States towards prostitution. Some people believe it is not immoral to buy sex, but even most of these people *look down* upon men who do so—buying sex is seen as low status, because a high status man should be able to get sex for free. People also draw limits to what they will buy and sell in order to express certain attitudes or to evince certain philosophies. Or, for instance, some people take pride—acquire a sense of dignity—in performing certain tasks—such as installing new drywall in the basement—rather than hiring others to do it for them. These people see their unwillingness to pay others to do the work as expressing certain virtues. Or, consider "freegans": people who choose not to buy food, but who instead search dumpsters for discarded but edible food. They describe themselves in self-congratulatory ways as "embrac[ing] community, generosity, social concern, freedom, cooperation, and sharing in opposition to a society based on materialism, moral apathy, competition, conformity, and greed."[1] Being a freegan is not just about trying to get stuff for free rather than buying it, but about expressing an identity and political ideology.

As we saw in Chapter 1, there is a large range of moral objections to "commodification," to having markets in everything, including:

A Exploitation: Markets in some good or service—such as organ sales—might encourage the strong to exploit (to take unjust advantage of) the vulnerable.

B Misallocation: Markets in certain goods and services—such as Ivy League admissions—might cause those goods to be allocated unjustly.

C Rights Violations: Markets in some good—such as slaves—might violate people's rights.

D Paternalism: Markets in some good or service—such as crystal meth or cigarettes—might cause people to make self-destructive choices.

E Harm to Others: Markets in some good or service—such as pit bulls or handguns—might lead to greater violence.

F Corruption: Participating in certain markets—such as buying luxury goods for oneself or Disney Princesses for one's daughters—will tend to cause us to develop defective preferences or character traits.

We will get to each of these objections over the course of the book. In this chapter, we are concerned with objections based on the idea that buying and selling certain things can be a form of *wrongful expression*.

Certain forms or instances of expression are wrong. One shouldn't go around flipping other drivers the bird at random. One shouldn't write Neo-Nazi music expressing the hatred of Jews. One should not just say to one's kind, loving mother, "Hey Mom, I hope you die and rot in hell." And so on. Even when it is within our rights to express such attitudes, it is still wrong to do so. (To say we have the right of free expression is just to say that others shouldn't stop us from expressing certain attitudes. This says nothing about whether it is right or wrong for us to express these attitudes.)

Consider how, say, a committed Christian might feel if you told her that you once used the Bible as toilet paper, because you were out of toilet paper and it was the only thing available. Even if you did not intend to express contempt for Christianity, she would likely feel deeply offended. Even many non-Christians would find this behavior offensive.

Many people think that markets in certain goods and services are offensive in just this way. They think we ought morally, and perhaps even legally, to limit what can be for sale, because extending the market into certain domains is offensive or contemptuous of things that deserve reverence and respect. Many philosophers, political theorists, and laypeople are convinced that there is an additional class of objections to markets in everything, beyond the objections outlined in A–F. These philosophers advance what we will call semiotic objections to markets in certain goods and services. Michael Sandel says, "markets don't only allocate goods; they also express ... certain attitudes toward the goods being exchanged."[2] Semiotic objections are based on this kind of idea. They take the following form:

G Semiotics: Independently of objections A–F, to allow a market in some good or service X is a form of communication that expresses the wrong attitude toward X or expresses an attitude that is incompatible with the intrinsic dignity of X, or would show disrespect or irreverence for some practice, custom, belief, or relationship with which X is associated.

Semiotic objections rely upon the idea that markets in certain goods communicate, signal, express, or symbolize the wrong attitude. Markets are a kind of language, or a kind of social meaning system. Market activities like bringing goods and services to market, buying those goods and services through financial instruments like money, the instruments themselves, and so on, all come bundled with meaning. According to the semiotic objection, the act of commodifying certain objects is essentially disrespectful and degrading of those objects (or of something associated with those objects) because of a meaning that attaches to market activities.

Semiotic Objections Are Not Supposed to Be Redundant

Semiotic objections—as we identify them—are independent of worries about exploitation, misallocation, rights violations, self-destructive behavior, harm to others, or character corruption. Thus, to understand what we are calling a semiotic objection to commodifying some good, imagine that buying and selling that good would not lead to any exploitation, would not undermine distributive justice or result in morally bad distributions, would not cause inefficiencies, would not violate anyone's rights, would not cause self-destructive behavior, would not lead to others being harmed, and would not corrupt us. Semiotic objections hold that markets in that good would still be wrong because such markets would express or communicate something disrespectful, or would violate the meaning of some relationship.

For example, many people are convinced sex services or pornography should not be for sale because such sales are inherently degrading.[3] Many would say the same about organ sales. But suppose Bill Gates decided to sell his kidney to Warren Buffett for $1,000,000. Here there is no exploitation. Yet many would regard this transaction as communicating disrespectful attitudes about the human body. Satz discusses a case where students at a university were paid to keep their rooms clean in order to impress prospective students and their parents. She is not worried about exploitation or deceptive advertising. Rather, she finds the transaction at odds with the kind of relationship a university should have with its students.[4] Anderson worries that markets in pregnancy surrogacy are inherently disrespectful of women and children. Some of her concerns involve purported rights violations. Yet, rights violations aside, she is worried that paying women for surrogacy communicates that women are "incubation machines," and that such services violate the intimacy of the pregnancy relationship.[5]

Some apparently semiotic objections to markets are parasitic on non-semiotic objections. Buying people as slaves communicates disrespect because slavery violates their rights. The standard and main objection to sweatshop labor is that it is exploitative. If so, then buying sweatshop labor communicates disrespect because it is exploitative. Markets in child pornography involve harming and exploiting children. The harm and exploitation involved in child pornography explains why child pornography communicates disrespect. We do not include these in our assessment of semiotic objections, because we mean to include only objections that are independent of concerns about harm, imprudence, rights violations, exploitation, misallocation, and corruption.

Note that semiotic objections are not unique to the debate about what should not be for sale. Many democratic theorists defend democracy in part on semiotic grounds, on the idea that democracy and only democracy *expresses* our fundamental moral equality.[6]

Consider some examples of semiotic objections. Sandel objects to adoption auctions: "Even if buyers did not mistreat the children they purchased, a market in children would express and promote the wrong way of valuing them. Children are not properly regarded as consumer goods but as beings worthy of love and care."[7] Later he objects to gifts of money or gift certificates, claiming that "traditional gift-giving" expresses "attentiveness" while these gifts do not.[8] He also objects to information markets in terrorism or death, saying, "If death bets are objectionable, it must be ... in the dehumanizing attitudes such wagers express."[9]

Elizabeth Anderson claims that in order to produce the social conditions under which people can be autonomous, "Constraints may be needed to secure the robust sphere differentiation required to create a significant range of options through which people can express a wide range of valuations."[10] She says "people value different goods in different ways," and to preserve their freedom we must create different "spheres that embody these different modes of valuation," boundaries "not just between the state and the market, but between these institutions and other domains of self-expression."[11] Anderson's semiotic objections are less explicit than Sandel's. However, as the previous quotations reveal, one of her main arguments against certain markets is that to preserve Kantian autonomy, we must separate different goods into different spheres so that we can express different modes of valuation.

Similarly, Michael Walzer says that distributions of goods are unjust when these distributions violate the social meaning of those goods.[12] Different goods—such as office, honor, and love—are governed by different norms, and represent autonomous spheres that must be kept apart. Walzer complains that money can "intrude" into other spheres. He says, the "words *prostitution* and *bribery*, like *simony*, describe the sale and purchase of goods that, given certain understandings of their meaning, ought never to be sold or purchased."[13] So, for Walzer, as with Anderson, certain things cannot be for sale because that violates the *meaning* of those goods.

David Archard, following similar arguments by Richard Titmuss and Peter Singer, claims that selling blood is "imperialistic" because it involves a "contamination of meaning."[14] He says that if we allow blood sales, "the meaning of non-market exchanges would have been contaminated by the existence of the market exchanges. The monetary value which the latter attributes to any good exchanged would have 'leaked into' the former and changed its meaning."[15]

As far as we can tell, semiotic objections are the *most common* class of objections against commodifying certain goods and services. Nearly every anti-commodification theorist at some point relies upon or advances a semiotic objection, though every theorist also advances non-semiotic objections. However, despite this, there has been no systematic investigation or criticism of semiotic objections as such.

Three Semiotic Objections

Our thesis, in a nutshell, is that semiotic objections to commodification are unsound. (We remain agnostic as to whether semiotic arguments in other debates are sound.) In Part II, over the next three chapters, we examine and rebut a number of plausible-sounding semiotic arguments:[16]

1 The Mere Commodity Objection: Claims that buying and selling certain goods or services shows that one regards them as having merely instrumental value.
2 The Wrong Signal Objection: Claims that buying and selling certain goods and services communicates, independently of one's attitudes, disrespect for the objects in question.
3 The Wrong Currency Objection: Claims that inserting markets and money into certain kinds of relationships communicates estrangement and distance, and is objectionably impersonal.

One of our main responses will be to explain how the meaning of markets is, in general, a highly contingent, fluid, socially-constructed fact. There is little essential meaning to market exchanges. What market exchanges mean depends upon a culture's interpretative practices. These interpretative practices are themselves subject to moral evaluation. In our view, cultures sometimes impute meaning to markets in harmful, socially destructive ways. Rather than giving us reason to avoid those markets, it gives us reason to revise the meaning we assign to these markets, or, if we can't, to conscientiously rebel against or ignore the meaning our society attaches to these markets.

Notes

1 Quoted from http://freegan.info. The Freegans are so anti-consumerist they wouldn't even buy the more expensive .com domain.
2 Sandel 2012a, 9.
3 Anderson, 1995, 45.
4 http://news.stanford.edu/news/2010/june/class-day-lecture-061210.html
5 Anderson 1990, 71. For a similar view, see Pateman 1998, 207.
6 E.g., Christiano 2008, 98–99, 287; Gilbert 2012; Rawls 1971, 234; Rawls 1993, 318–19; Rawls 2001, 131; Freeman 2007, 76.
7 Sandel 2012a, 10.
8 Sandel 2012a, 106.
9 Sandel 2012a, 146.
10 Anderson 1995, 142–43.
11 Anderson 1995, 141.
12 Walzer 1984, 7–10.
13 Walzer 1984, 9.
14 Archard 2002, 87–103.
15 Archard 2002, 95.
16 A note on our method: Anti-commodification theorists, such as Michael Walzer, Anderson, Sandel, Satz, and Radin together give hundreds of cases where they think commodifying certain goods would be immoral. Many of these cases involve concerns about exploitation, misallocation, harm to others, self-destructive choices, corruption of character, or rights violations. Other times, these theorists advance semiotic objections as well. To definitively nail down our thesis in response to their arguments, we would have to examine each of their cases, and then try to show A) that a market in the relevant good or service does not communicate what they suggest it communicates, or B) that if it is impermissible, what makes it impermissible is not some "semiotic" concern, but instead that commodifying it harms others, violates their rights, causes self-destruction, causes misallocations, causes corruption, is unfair, or involves exploitation. In this book, we simply do not have the space to do that. So, instead, what we will do is examine a number of general semiotic arguments to commodification and a number of key examples. We generate a line of argument that casts suspicion on the cases we do not cover.

6

THE MERE COMMODITY OBJECTION

The Argument

We begin by rebutting one of the weaker semiotic objections. We do so in part because it will help us understand what goes wrong with some stronger semiotic objections.

Consider the connotation of the word "commodity." Suppose someone complains, "The Picasso painting is treated like a mere commodity!" Here the complaint is that in the process of buying and selling the painting, people are failing to appreciate and respect the painting's non-instrumental value. In common English, we often use the word "commodity" to refer to things that are bought and sold and seen as having merely instrumental value. When anti-commodification theorists complain about things being turned into commodities, they often mean that we are treating something as if it were merely a tool of satisfaction, when in fact the object (or something associated with it) deserves reverence or respect.

Thus, one semiotic objection holds that when we offer certain goods or services for sale, we thereby necessarily fail to regard whatever non-instrumental value those objects have. One way a market in some good or service X might be immoral is if the people in that market view X as a mere commodity, when X is not a mere commodity. We can express the argument as follows:

The Mere Commodity Objection

1 Some things are not mere commodities. They have a non-instrumental value that cannot be captured in their market price.
2 To offer certain goods and services for sale necessarily shows that one regards those things as mere commodities.
3 If 1 and 2, then it is wrong to offer certain goods and services for sale.
4 Therefore, it is wrong to offer certain goods and services for sale.

This argument tries to establish a necessary connection between A) buying and selling something and B) having disrespectful attitudes toward that thing.

Commodities Vs. Mere Commodities

One problem with the argument is that it subtly trades on two competing definitions of "commodity." So, for instance, Elizabeth Anderson says,

> A practice treats something as a commodity if its production, distribution, or enjoyment is governed by one or more norms distinctive to the market. Market norms structure relations among the people who produce, distribute, and enjoy the thing in question. For example, in market transactions the will and desire of the parties determines the allocation between them of their freely alienable rights. Each party is expected to look after her own interests, neither party is expected to look after the interests of the other, or of third parties, except to the minimal extent required by law.[1]

Perhaps Anderson means this to be a definition of a commodity. A commodity just is, by definition, a thing governed by norms distinctive of the market, and the market norms are fundamental amoral, as they are about seeking maximum satisfaction. But if so, then she loads the word "commodity" with all sorts of potentially negative connotations. To think of something as a commodity in the sense above just is to regard it as having purely instrumental value, and in buying and selling that good, people are expected only to observe some minimal set of negative moral obligations.[2]

But this cannot form the basis to an objection to universal commodification. If we decide to define "commodity" this way, it becomes trivial that thinking of something as a commodity is incompatible with thinking of that thing (or some practice associated with it) as deserving respect or reverence. However, it is not trivial that the buying and selling of an object is the same thing as viewing it as a commodity so defined. Instead, it is always an open question whether a person who buys or sells an object actually views the object as a commodity in the above sense.

Anderson and Walzer[3] appear to think that there is a necessary connection between buying and selling something on a market, and regarding that object as a commodity in the loaded with negative connotations sense discussed above. But we can distinguish between something being A) a commodity and being B) a *mere* commodity. Let us say that a commodity is simply anything with a price tag, anything that could be exchanged on a market. Calling something a commodity in this sense does not carry with it any judgment about its moral status or about how people might mistreat it. However, to call something a mere commodity does carry moral overtones. A mere commodity is something with a price tag, exchanged on a market, that is properly viewed as merely having instrumental value, as something that may properly be used solely as a tool to satisfy the (non-moral) desires and preferences of the exchanging parties.

By distinguishing between a commodity and a mere commodity, we see why the Mere Commodity Objection is flawed. If something is bought and sold, it follows trivially—as a matter of definition—that it is regarded as a commodity. However, it is an interesting, substantive thesis to say that a person buying and selling something regards the object as a *mere commodity*. From the fact that someone treats something as a commodity, we cannot automatically infer that she views it as a mere commodity. We know something is a commodity in the neutral sense if that thing is for sale. But to know that people regard something as a mere commodity, we would need to conduct additional psychological research into their attitudes and beliefs.

When you buy something, you might treat it as a mere instrument of pleasure to be disposed of at will. This is true of, say, apples, condoms, and sandwiches. But we do not think of all commodities this way. In fact objects routinely are bought and sold without the buyers or sellers considering those objects to be mere commodities.

Commodities, But Not Mere Commodities

Consider pets. At least some non-human animals, like dogs, dolphins, and chimpanzees, matter intrinsically and non-instrumentally. They ought not to be treated or regarded as mere commodities. Yet, of course, pets are routinely bought and sold. While many people (regardless of how they acquired their pets) do mistreat their pets or fail to recognize their inherent value, many people cherish their purchased pets, and many pet breeders have a deep love for the animals they breed.[4]

Similarly, on the art market, Alfred Barnes accumulated one of the most prized collections of masterpieces in the world. Barnes would agree with Elizabeth Anderson when she writes that "[t]he person who truly appreciates art does not conceive of art merely as a thing which she can use as she pleases, but as something which commands appreciation. It would be contemptible to willfully destroy the aesthetic qualities of a work of art simply to satisfy some of one's nonethical preferences, and it is a mark of a cultivated and hence admirable person that she has preferences for appreciating art."[5] Barnes and hundreds of others live up to bearing the mark of a cultivated and admirable person, and participate in buying and selling masterpieces. Barnes appreciates art far more than most—that is why he bought all that art.

Many Catholic bookstores sell candles, rosaries, prayer cards, and other devotionals. It is routine in many Catholic traditions to buy such devotionals. But the Catholics who consume them do not regard these commodities as being no different from similarly priced regular candles. A private company—the Cavanagh Bread Company—produces and sells nearly all the altar bread consumed during Eucharist in the United States.[6] The Cavanaghs are devout Catholics and treat their product—which they sell for profit—with appropriate sanctity. (For example, they do not allow the finished wafers to be touched by human hands.)

With examples like these—and there are many others—we can conclude that the fact that people buy and sell things does not automatically show us that those people have the wrong attitudes towards those things. As a matter of fact, people can and do regularly buy and sell things while at the same time maintaining an attitude of respect or reverence for the commodities or for practices and customs associated with the commodities. We will return to this point many times over the course of the book.

Now, an anti-commodification theorist might respond to our argument by instead trying to argue that when people buy and sell certain objects, this tends over time to *cause* them to view the objects as mere commodities. This new argument admits that people can buy and sell, e.g., works of art without regarding those works of arts as mere decorations. However, it holds that over time, as more and more people buy and sell more of these objects, the market will wear away at our respectful attitudes.

But this new argument is a corruption objection, not a semiotic objection. Note that this new argument is not completely philosophical—it would need to be substantiated with empirical psychological or sociological research. The person advancing this argument would bear the burden of proof, and would need to conduct or find sufficient empirical evidence to support her premises. However, since our focus in this chapter is just on semiotic objections to markets, we leave it open here whether this new argument succeeds. We will respond to this objection in Part III. But we regard this move as supporting our hypothesis that semiotic objections are at best parasitic on other objections. At this point, what seemed like a semiotic objection has turned into a corruption objection, and so this semiotic objection fails.

Thus far, we have shown that people who buy goods and services need not necessarily regard the objects they buy and sell as mere commodities. However, this does not settle the matter. We have deflated one of the weaker semiotic objections to commodifying certain goods and services, but we must now turn to stronger objections.

The Meaning of Markets

Similar remarks apply to the word "market." For the purposes of this book, we define a "market" broadly. (Note that, as far as we can tell, others who participate in this debate also use a broad definition.) Broadly speaking, a market is the voluntary exchange of goods and services for valuable consideration. Since the commodification debate primarily concerns whether it is permissible to exchange certain goods or services for money, we will by default consider all voluntary exchanges of goods and services for money part of the market.

Now, some may wish to attach additional criteria for something to be called a "market," such as that market exchanges must involve purely selfish motivations, or that market actors must regard the exchanged object as lacking intrinsic value. As we just saw, this seems false—as a matter of fact, people do buy and sell things without having such attitudes. But another reason to avoid loading the term "market" with such negative criteria is that it makes the anti-commodification theorist's argument facile. After all, if market exchanges are by definition selfish and indifferent to the real value of things, then it follows almost trivially that marketizing certain goods and services will fail to express proper respect for them. But that leaves open the possibility that there are *schmarkets*, in which people buy and sell goods and services, but lack all the bad attitudes some may wish to say are essential to markets. If we accept that markets by definition have these amoral attitudes, then the anti-commodification theorist can easily show us that markets in certain goods and services are disrespectful, but she would not have shown us that schmarkets in those goods and services are disrespectful. In addition, the anti-commodification theorist wants to tell us something about actual market behavior. By loading the definition like this, it becomes an empirical question whether any given sale in the real world is in the markets or the schmarkets. For all we know, it could turn out that all actual markets are schmarkets. Thus, nothing is gained from loading the definition of "market" with negative connotations. We should just use a broad definition, and treat the question of what motivates people in markets as an empirical one.

Upon further reflection, the Mere Commodity Objection is not really an objection to markets or commodification per se; it's at most an objection to the attitudes buyers and sellers might have or lack while buying or selling. So long as buyers and sellers have the right attitudes, then the objection doesn't hold. It's a complaint not about *what* is being sold, but *how* it is being sold. It's a complaint not about the objects of sale, but about the people selling them.

A Note on the Meaning of Prices

Complaints about commodification are closely associated with complaints about the ways in which economists model human rationality. Many critiques of com-modification, including Anderson's *Value in Ethics and Economics*, Walzer's *Spheres of Justice*, and Radin's *Contest Commodities,* include lengthy attacks against cost-benefit analysis or about whether all values can be expressed on a common, numerical scale. Anti-commodification theorists argue:[7]

- There are not merely many different valuable things, but many different *kinds* of values and *ways* of valuing things.
- Accordingly, these goods cannot be placed on a common *cardinal* scale of value, especially a monetary scale. The value of something is not simply its price.
- But economists write as though all of our values can be expressed on a common cardinal monetary scale and the value of something just is its price. Thus, economists *distort* the kinds of value things actually have.

- As a result, many of economists' explanations of the world and their policy prescriptions come from a distorted or mistaken conception of value.

So, for instance, an economist might advise a politician that when faced with deciding between saving the rainforest or allowing more industrial production, we should just determine how much money the rainforest is worth, compare that to the expected monetary value of increased industry, and then pick the choice that's worth more in monetary terms. The sensible economist would no doubt admit that such measurements are hard to make, but would insist that in principle there are such measurements to be made. But many philosophers, including all the major anti-commodification theorists, dispute this very point. The value of the rainforest just cannot be expressed on a monetary scale, even if some of the items it produces can.

Or, consider a personal example. On the day Brennan met his future wife Lauren, he also met another girl (whom Lauren and he now refer to as "Shiny Pants") who made it very clear she was interested in dating him. An economist might say that while Brennan strictly preferred at that time dating Lauren to dating Shiny Pants, he might still have preferred A) dating Shiny Pants *and* receiving $10,000 to B) dating Lauren. If so, then it seems plausible that by examining preferences like these, we could put a monetary price on how much Brennan initially valued Lauren over Shiny Pants. And that's not just because Brennan is a strange person, the kind of person who teaches political economy classes and who would write a book defending commodification. Lauren similarly had options, and while she chose Brennan over the other guy, she might well have tried dating the other guy for $10,000 instead of dating Brennan. If so, then it seems plausible that by examining preferences like these, we could put a monetary price on how much Lauren initially valued Brennan over that other guy. Or, at least, that's how economists are inclined to talk, and anti-commodification theorists worry that economists thus misunderstand how people value things.

We're worried that the anti-commodification theorists misunderstand what economists are up to. It may well be that economists commit many philosophical sins. However, even if one accepts that 1) there are a plurality of different kinds of values, and 2) the way we value these different things is different, it's still possible that the value of these goods can be expressed on a single, *cardinal* scale. This follows from a number of plausible assumptions about rationality. The proof of this is rather technical. But we'll summarize the main moves here.

Suppose Randy is fully rational. Here, don't read "rational" as saying that Randy is homo economicus, some kind of cartoon self-interested maximizing sociopath. Assume Randy has a proper regard for all things moral and sublime. But suppose Randy is, unlike the rest of us, fully rational and fully informed. It seems like the following statements about Randy would be true, because each of these describes what appears to be an axiom about how rationality works:

1 At any given moment, Randy can always determine whether one option is better than the other or if they're equally good (or bad).

2 If Randy strictly prefers A to B, then he does not strictly prefer B to A. But if he is indifferent between A and B, then he is indifferent between B and A.

3 If Randy prefers (at any given moment) A to B and B to C, then he prefers A to C.

4 Randy prefers each of his preferences at least as much as he prefers it.[8]

From these axioms, we can generate an "ordinary utility function" for Randy. That is, we can rank all possible states of the world from better to worse (including ties) for Randy. To say that Randy has a utility function is *not* to say that Randy thinks all values reduce to one *common denominator* called "utility." For Randy, there may indeed be a plurality of different kinds of values and modes of valuing. "Utility" in the economist's sense isn't the *fundamental value all things have*. Rather, it's just a way economists *represent* Randy's preference rankings. The economist isn't asserting here that all values are subjective, either. Instead, the economist remains agnostic. He is just trying to represent how fully rational Randy's mind works.

So far, these axioms just get us an *ordinal scale*. Some things (such as the achievement of a perfectly just society) are better than others (such as getting a new high score on Flappy Birds). But, anti-commodification theorists complain, economists don't just say that a rational (and moral) person might rank options, by preferring one thing to another. Instead, anti-commodification theorists complain that economists think we can, in addition to ranking values, put them all on some *cardinal, numerical scale*. This seems to suggest every value is simply fungible with every other, and thus seems to reject the starting assumption that there is a plurality of different kinds of value.

Here, in the interest of avoiding making this book overly technical, we have to briefly explain *why* economists think that without getting into a proof of it. As far as we can tell, the anti-commodification theorists are not familiar with the work of John von Neumann and Oskar Morgenstern, two economists who revolutionized utility theory in economics. Von Neumann and Morgenstern showed that if you add a few more plausible axioms to the list above, in particular, axioms about how rational people respond to *lotteries* and deal with *risk* (for example, that rational people prefer better prizes to worse prizes and better odds to worse odds), then we'll be able to translate any ordinal utility function into a cardinal utility function. That is, given A) Randy's ranking of all possible states of the world and B) Randy's rational way of choosing among lotteries, we generate C) a new utility function, in which all values can be expressed on a cardinal, numerical scale.[9] (And if Randy values money, we'll be able to express this scale in monetary terms.) It turns out that *every* possible set of trade-offs a rational agent might have, regardless of whether that agent is selfish or altruistic, amoral, immoral, or moral, a monist or a pluralist, can be expressed on a continuous, numerical utility scale. Again, that's not to say that the only thing that the agent really values is *utility*, but just to say that we can correctly represent the agent's values on this one scale.

In summary, it's not true that economists crudely assume that there is only one kind of value—*utility, as expressed by prices*. Rather, economists conclude on the basis of a number of plausible axioms about rational preferences that all such preferences can be represented on a single continuous numerical scale. This is true regardless of whether the agent is a value monist or pluralist. Anti-commodification theorists thus can't just complain that some things have a more than instrumental value, or that not everything is fungible with money, or that there is a plurality of values. Economists can and do accept all that.

Instead, if anti-commodification theorists want to attack economists, they must make more radical claims (and, indeed, many of them have). It won't be enough to assert that some things are incommensurate, in that they have a different *kind* of value. (After all, I value $10,000 in purely instrumental terms, while I value the last Father's Day card my kids gave me intrinsically, as a sentimental object. But, frankly, I value $10,000 more than I value the card, in part because I can use that $10,000 to make even more memories with my kids.) Rather, they need to show (not merely assert) some values are *radically incommensurate*, such that we cannot compare them in any way, or have any preferences between them.

So, for instance, Anderson says that Bach was brilliant and Darwin was brilliant. They have a different kind of brilliance—Bach had musical brilliance and Darwin had scientific brilliance. Anderson claims we cannot meaningfully compare their brilliance. We cannot say Bach was more brilliant than Darwin, that Darwin was more brilliant than Bach, or that they were equally brilliant. Note that she is not simply saying that we don't understand them enough to compare them, or that this comparison is a hard case. Rather, she's saying that in principle no such comparison, ranking, or equation is even possible. Even God, if there is one, couldn't claim that one was more brilliant than the other or that they were equally brilliant. If so, then Anderson might say that it is impossible to say in principle which person's brilliance is more valuable.[10]

Anderson might be right, but we have to admit we don't find her argument even slightly convincing. Her main rationale for it is that Darwin and Bach had a different kind of brilliance, and so we cannot compare them. But that doesn't seem right. Consider: Darwin was a brilliant scientist. Brennan is a mediocre musical composer. (He has less significantly less musical brilliance than Bach did.) It seems obvious to us that Darwin is more brilliant as a scientist than Brennan is a composer. (Though Brennan is somewhat flattered if Anderson is committed to denying this.)

Anderson says,

> Neither [Bach nor Darwin] was superior in brilliance to the other, nor were they roughly equal in brilliance. If this were so, then a small but significant improvement in the brilliance of one would suffice to tilt the

judgment in his favor. But it is silly to claim that, say, had Darwin achieved some brilliant insights into genetic theory as well as evolution, he would thereby have exceeded Bach in brilliance.[11]

That doesn't seems silly to us. Instead, it seems obvious to us that adding brilliance to one eventually tilts the judgment in favor of one over the other. Had Darwin, say, achieved everything Einstein did plus what Darwin in fact did, he would be more brilliant, tout court, than Bach. The reason we're not sure of Anderson's example, of whether adding a small but significant improvement to Darwin would tilt the balance in his favor, is that we're not sure whether Darwin or Bach was more brilliant overall, or just how close in brilliance they were. As far as we can tell, Anderson does not really have an argument to help us distinguish A) whether Darwin and Bach cannot in principle be compared from B) whether they can be compared, but we just don't have enough information to quite make the comparison. Anderson has strong intuitions in favor of A, while we have strong intuitions in favor of B.

Rather than press this point further, we'll leave this as an impasse. Our arguments in this book do not depend upon what we've said here. Our main goal is just to inform the anti-commodification theorists that they seem to be loading economists with a bunch of intellectual baggage that economists need not accept.

Notes

1 Anderson 2000a, 19–20.
2 Similar remarks apply to Walzer 1984, 95–127.
3 Walzer 1984, 95–115.
4 We should point out that this is empirically testable. We could look at, for example, rates of abuse of pets as a proxy for the wrong attitude, and the means of acquiring those pets. If anti-commodification theorists are right, we can hypothesize a connection between buying pets and a higher propensity to abuse them compared with people who acquired their pets by gift or through adoption. Provided we control for other factors (like antecedent attitudes towards dogs, cats, or other pets), this would be one way to test the anti-commodification thesis.
5 Anderson 1990, 72–73.
6 Katie Zezima, "Bread of Life, Baked in Rhode Island," *New York Times* Dec. 24, 2008, URL http://www.nytimes.com/2008/12/25/business/smallbusiness/25sbiz.html?page wanted=all&_r=0
7 Anderson 1995, 44–64, 190–216; Radin 2000, 2–3, 88–94, passim; A. Brennan 1992; Kelman 1981; Sandel 2012a, 47–51; Walzer 1984.
8 Gaus 2008, 36–37.
9 Gaus 2008, 40–49; von Neumann and Morgenstern 1944.
10 Anderson 1995, 56.
11 Anderson 1995, 56.

7

THE WRONG SIGNAL AND WRONG CURRENCY OBJECTIONS

The Arguments

The last chapter showed it is possible for people to believe both A) that an object may permissibly be bought and sold on the market, and yet B) that the object in question has significant or profound non-instrumental value. However, the anti-commodification theorist can just respond that there is a difference between C) regarding something as a mere commodity versus D) treating it like a mere commodity. A person who offers things for sale or who purchases things on the market might believe that these things have non-instrumental value and must be treated with reverence or respect. However, anti-commodification theorists could still argue that at least *sometimes*, when we buy and sell certain things, we treat the objects the wrong way, as if they were mere commodities, even if we do not personally regard them as mere commodities. Our actions toward things might be out of alignment with our attitudes toward them. Our actions might express disrespect even if we do not have disrespectful attitudes.

Thus, one common and intuitively plausible semiotic argument focuses on what markets communicate, not what market agents *intend* to communicate. Consider:

The Wrong Signal Objection

1 Buying and selling certain objects tends to express certain morally deplorable attitudes, or tends to fail to communicate proper respect for something that deserves respect.
2 This expression occurs independently of any attitudes that the person commodifying the object may happen to have.
3 If so, then commodifying certain objects is wrong.
4 Therefore, commodifying certain objects is wrong.

Premise 2 of this objection gets something right. What we express through our words and actions is not simply a function of our intentions, and is often entirely independent of our intentions. For instance, the thumbs up sign expresses approval in our culture. Yet in other cultures, the thumbs up expresses something more like what we mean when we extend our middle finger. If we were to visit certain foreign countries, we might give someone else the thumbs up with the intention of expressing approval, but we would in fact express contempt. We should thus refrain from making that gesture in places where it will express contempt.

A closely related objection holds that there are some cases where introducing money into a relationship offends or clashes with or spoils that relationship. The worry is that introducing cash payments into a relationship is incompatible with the meaning of that relationship. Suppose we offered our romantic partners $100 to clean the house, watch the children, cook dinner, or have sex. They would be offended. Making such an offer would express disrespectful attitudes and would be incompatible with the kind of relationships we have.

One might try to generalize these kinds of concerns to try to show that some things should just not be for sale:

The Wrong Currency Objection

1   Offering money for services communicates estrangement.
2   There are some relationships—romantic partners, between fellow citizens, friendships, and so on—where it would be morally wrong to communicate estrangement.
3   If so, then offering money, or commodifying, certain services within certain kinds of relationships is wrong.
4   Therefore, commodifying certain services within certain kinds of relationships is wrong.

So, for instance, Anderson often relies upon the Kantian idea that some things have a dignity, not a price, and takes this quite literally as an objection to putting certain things up for sale.[1] She then complains that selling sex services corrupts the meaning of the sexual relationship, because the sexual partners in prostitution do not exchange the same kind of good.[2]

Note that the Wrong Currency Objection does not say that it is wrong to buy and sell certain goods and services *simpliciter*; it just says that it is wrong to exchange money for certain goods and services *within* certain relationships. If the Wrong Currency Objection holds it might be wrong to offer one's spouse money for cooking, cleaning, or childcare. But this is not because it is wrong to commodify labor in cooking, cleaning, or childcare. We do nothing wrong by paying for a meal at a restaurant, or in getting maid services, or by hiring a babysitter for the night. So, the Wrong Currency Objection does not appear to say that some things just should not be for sale, but rather that certain relationships should not involve monetary exchanges.

Philosophers concerned with over-commodification tell us that prices and markets are a kind of ritualistic language, a kind of social meaning system. These theorists worry that putting certain things on the market communicates disrespect or other bad attitudes, or is inherently incompatible with respect and good attitudes.

An Outline of Our Basic Response

Our basic response to both arguments will be to argue that when there are no non-semiotic objections to commodification, then the consequences of commodification set the main standard by which we should judge our culture's semiotics. That is, we will argue if there are no independent, non-semiotic objections to markets in certain goods or services, then the meaning of market exchanges in those goods and services is probably just a contingent, relative social construct. There is probably no essential meaning to market exchanges.

If certain markets express disrespect or selfish motives, in light of a culture's socially-constructed semiotics, but if those markets do or would lead to good outcomes (or if prohibiting those markets leads to bad outcomes), then (pro tanto) people in that culture should *revise* their social practices governing what counts as expressing disrespect or selfishness. Failure to do so—that is, taking our cultural practices for granted when they impose great costs—is itself morally misguided. We will further argue that if it's not possible or too difficult to revise the culture's social practices, individuals may conscientiously choose to reject their culture's social practices and instead participate in those contested markets. They will express disrespect or selfishness, but they will be justified, not merely excused, in doing so.

In short: our view is that when there is a clash between semiotics and consequences, consequences win. But we are not just saying that consequentialist arguments on behalf of markets trump or outweigh semiotic arguments against them. Rather, we will defend the stronger, more interesting claim that if there are no other deontic concerns about markets aside from semiotics, if there are no worries about wrongful exploitation, harm to others, rights violations and so on, then consequentialist considerations allow us to *judge* the semiotics of market transactions.

The Meaning of Money and Exchange Is a Contingent Social Construct

In this section, we present a range of sociological and anthropological evidence that there is no essential meaning to money or market exchange. Instead, the meaning of money is a contingent social construct. In the absence of non-semiotic objections to markets, the social meaning of money, of markets, and commodification, is relative, not objective. Note that we are not saying that *morality* is relative or a social construct, but, rather that the meaning we attach to market exchanges is.

Sandel, Anderson, or Carol Pateman claim in contrast that some markets necessarily signal disrespect—that it is not a mere contingent social convention that such commodification signals disrespect—even when these markets do not involve exploitation, harm, and so on, and even when market agents do not have any bad attitudes.[3] They might be right; we will consider their essentialist semiotic arguments in more depth later. But for now, we want to examine some sociological and anthropological evidence that the meaning of markets is contingent and socially constructed.

There are facts about what symbols, words, and actions signal respect. But—when there are no worries about exploitation, harm, rights, and so on—these facts appear to vary from culture to culture. Consider that King Darius of Persia asked the Greeks if they would be willing to eat the dead bodies of their fathers. The Greeks balked. Of course, the right thing to do was to burn the dead bodies on a funeral pyre. To eat the dead would disrespect them, treating them like mere food. Darius then asked the Callatians if they would be willing to burn their fathers on a funeral pyre. The Callatians balked. The thing to do was to eat one's father, so that part of the father was always with the son. Burning the dead would treat them like mere trash.

The Greeks and Callatians agreed about what their obligations were. They agreed that everyone has a moral obligation to signal respect for their dead fathers. Each group had developed a system of linguistic and cultural norms within which they could fulfill this obligation. They had developed rituals that signified respect for their fathers. The issue here is just that the Greeks and Callatians were, in effect, speaking different (ritualistic) languages. The Greeks and Callatians may have been mutually horrified. However, it is not obvious that there is any universal fact about what it takes to express respect or disrespect for the dead. Asking whether the Greek or Callatian practices are the correct way to express respect is, at first glance, a bit like asking whether English or French is the correct language. While it is not a mere social construct that we should express respect for one another, it appears at first glance that the symbols and rituals we take to express respect *are* mere social constructs.

Sandel complains that giving money instead of a non-monetary gift communicates a lack of concern. Yet there is evidence that this is merely a construct of current Western culture. For the Merina people of Madagascar, monetary gifts carry no such stigma of being impersonal or thoughtless.[4] For the Merina, giving what Sandel calls "thoughtful" non-monetary gifts expresses no greater concern or thoughtfulness than giving cash of equal value. Just as in some cultures giving a person the middle finger will not be interpreted as expressing disrespect, in the Merina culture, a "thoughtful" gift will not be interpreted as being more thoughtful than a cash gift.

In Western cultures, we are now more likely to view gifts of money or gift certificates as impersonal or thoughtless, but even this is just a recent cultural development. For Americans, monetary gifts used to have a different meaning.

Sociologist Viviana Zelizer says that in the 1870s–1930s United States, monetary gifts were seen as *especially* thoughtful:

> Families, intimate friends, and businesses likewise reshaped money into its supposedly most alien form: a sentimental gift, expressing care and affection. It mattered who gave gift money and who received it, when it was given, how it was offered and how spent. Defying all notions of money as neutral, impersonal, and fungible, gift money circulated as a meaningful, deeply subjective, nonfungible currency, closely regulated by social conventions. At Christmas, weddings, christenings, or other ritual and secular events, cash turned into a dignified, welcome gift almost unrecognizable as market money and clearly distinguished from other domestic currencies.[5]

Thus, from a sociological standpoint, the distinction between "thoughtful" and "unthoughtful" gifts appears to just be a contingent, culturally-relative, social construct. Indeed, Zelizer's extensive work on the meaning of money and exchange, work spread out over multiple books, seems to show us that the supposed "profanity" of commodification or cash is not a deep fact about market economies as such, or about money as such, but a peculiarity of our own culture at this particular time. In her work, Zelizer uncovers many other instances where different cultures at different times do not impute the meaning to money or to markets that Sandel thinks we should impute.[6]

Sociologists Maurice Bloch and Jonathan Parry concur:

> The problem seems to be that for us money signifies a sphere of "economic" relationships which are inherently impersonal, transitory, amoral and calculating. There is therefore something profoundly awkward about offering it as a gift expressive of relationships which are supposed to be personal, enduring, moral and altruistic. But clearly this awkwardness derives from the fact that here money's "natural" environment – the "economy" – is held to constitute an autonomous domain to which general moral precepts do not apply (cf. Dumont 1977). Where it is not seen as a separate and amoral domain, where the economy is "embedded" in society and subject to its moral laws, monetary relations are rather unlikely to be represented as the antithesis of bonds of kinship and friendship, and there is consequently nothing inappropriate about making gifts of money to cement such bonds.[7]

Bloch and Parry write this to summarize the findings of anthropologists and sociologists of money and markets. Like Zelizer, they conclude money and markets do not have the same meaning everywhere that they have here. Instead, the reason commodification seems so repugnant to us Westerners is because we Westerners tend to regard the sphere of exchange and money as a "separate and amoral domain." Bloch, Parry, and Zelizer say that we then mistakenly assume that this is just a "natural" or essential fact about money. We could think of money a different way, just as the Callations could think of burning the dead a different way.

Similarly, it's tempting to hold that when a man gives a woman money for having sex with him, this must mean, as a matter of logical necessity, that he is treating her like a prostitute, with whatever disrespect this characteristically imputes. But where philosophers see logically essential meaning, sociologists and anthropologists see contingent, socially-constructed meanings. There are cultures in which monetary exchanges in intimate relationships are normal. Among the Merina people, men are expected to give cash after sex. Failure to do so is seen as disrespectful. The Merina do distinguish between marital relationships and prostitution, and they do not believe cash exchanges for sex treat wives like prostitutes. Cash simply does not mean for them what it means for us. For them, the thing that separates wives from prostitutes is *not* the exchange of money for sex, but whether the relationship is formal or informal, loving or impersonal, serious or casual.[8] For Zelizer, the Merina men are in a sense buying sex, but they do so in order to express respect for their wives.[9]

One might be tempted to object that this practice is just an expression of patriarchy. On the contrary, sociologist Kirsten Stoebenau, in summarizing the work of Gillian Feeley-Harnick, explains that in Madagascar, sexual relationships were "open and easy: a young man will propose to have sex with a young woman who, if interested, allows the man into her home/living quarters. Traditionally, the man will place a small amount of money under the pillow to show respect to her for giving the power of her body (as representation of fertility) to him."[10] To fail to give such a gift would express profound disrespect to the woman. Stoebenau argues that patriarchal attitudes towards female sexuality in Madagascar were in fact introduced by French missionaries. The practice of exchanging money for sex pre-dates these attitudes toward sex.

One might also object that the Merina's practice of men paying their wives for sex doesn't count as a market, because the men are not 1) indifferent to their wives' subjectivity, 2) the men intend to express respect, 3) the men do not regard the value of sexual relations with their wives to be fungible with money, and so on. But, as we said earlier, anti-commodification theorists should be careful to avoid this kind of objection. If they decide to define "markets" as spheres of impersonal exchange in which participants care only about themselves and in which the participants regard the things exchanged as only having instrumental value, it follows trivially that markets in certain goods and services will express disrespect or fail to express respect. But then it remains an open question whether it is permissible to buy and sell those same goods and services, because it becomes an open, empirical question whether this instance of buying and selling is done on *schmarkets* rather than markets. Schmarkets, recall, function just like markets, except that people don't have whatever deplorable or amoral attitudes some anti-commodification theorists want to say are essential to markets.

Now consider what practices signal and symbolize closeness and estrangement. What signals estrangement or closeness can vary greatly from people to people, from culture to culture, or can vary greatly over time within a particular culture. So, for instance, in some parts of India, friends and family do not say "please" and "thank you" for something that is an expected part of the relationship. If you were Indian, you would cause offense if you started saying "please" and "thank you" to your loved ones for normal behavior. In certain parts of India, by expressing gratitude, you signal that you do not really consider your mother a friend or family member, that you regard her like you would some stranger. The same is generally true of introducing financial payments into our Western relationships. We offend because we signal estrangement from our family or friends.

We can at least imagine a healthy marriage in which the partners decide to pay each other for a wide range of services, even though they love each other deeply and have as firm a commitment as any other married couple. Imagine both spouses are economists, in particular the kinds of economists who favor information markets. Suppose they have a strong understanding of the role of money and prices in revealing confidence, sincerity, and the strength of preferences. They agree to commodify many aspects of their relationship because it is an efficient, more effective method for them to communicate their needs with one another. They decide to commodify their exchanges in part because they accept the large body of economic literature showing that forcing people to put prices on things penalizes them for insincerity. This literature shows that talk is cheap, but putting one's money where one's mouth is is not cheap. So, for instance, in a money-less relationship, partners may exaggerate the extent to which the other partners' behaviors bother them. But if, in a monetized marriage, a partner realizes she is not willing to put up even $5 to stop the behavior, then she might thereby realize that the behavior does not bother her nearly as much as she was letting on. (Note that this holds even if one thinks one is entitled to be rid of the behavior for free.[11]) Thus, our economist couple might rationally choose to commodify parts of their relationship in order to ensure they remain honest with one another and themselves.[12] So, in principle, a thoroughly commodified marriage between two economists could be as healthy as a typical marriage. There is nothing wrong with this kind of marriage; it's just a contingent fact about the rest of us that we prefer a different style of marriage.

In fact, NBC News recently ran a story about a couple, computer scientists Bethany Soule and Daniel Reeves, who commodified their relationship in just this way for just this reason.[13] (Soule and Reeves are alumni of the University of Michigan's Strategic Reasoning Group.[14]) The couple use the tools of computer science, behavioral economics, and game theory to improve their marriage. As they put it, they have replaced resentful "But I did the dishes last time" with "But I did the dishes last time and I got paid $40 for it, so that was kind of awesome!"[15] If this works for them—and it does so far—we do not find anything morally objectionable about it. Soule and Reeves live by a different code of meaning from Sandel or Anderson, and we do not see why Soule and Reeves have a duty to adopt Sandel's or Anderson's code of meaning.

Sandel asks you to imagine that on your wedding day, your best man's speech brings you to tears. But he then asks you to imagine you discover your best man didn't write that beautiful speech. Instead, suppose your best man paid a professional speechwriter to write it for him. Sandel says you would probably think the bought speech has less value than one the best man wrote himself. To prove this, Sandel offers a test—would you feel uncomfortable telling the person you're giving the item to that it was purchased, rather than something you made yourself? If so, Sandel says, there's "reason to suspect it's a corrupt version of the real thing."[16] He says that wedding toasts are "an expression of friendship," and so should be written oneself.[17]

Let's think a bit more about this case by asking some questions. Why is it okay to buy a Hallmark card on Valentine's Day, but not to buy a toast? Why is it okay to take your spouse out to dinner on her birthday, rather than cooking it yourself, but then it seems somewhat more appropriate to bake her a birthday cake yourself than to buy one? Why is it fine to buy your children presents on the holidays, rather than having to carve these presents out of wood by hand? Why is it permissible to buy your spouse flowers rather than have to grow them yourself?

In each case, it looks like a contingent phenomenon of our culture that we find one acceptable but not the other. Things could have turned out the opposite. There's no deeper truth here.

Consider a case like that of the wedding toast: imagine that it's your father's funeral. Hundreds of people gather to mourn his passing. Now, suppose your recently widowed mother learns that many of those mourners are not friends, family, or acquaintances, but strangers whom you paid to be there. How might she react? Well, if she's Romanian, or Chinese, or lived in England during the time of Charles Dickens' *Oliver Twist*, she might thank you for being a dutiful son or daughter. In some cultures, it's normal and expected that one will hire professional mourners for a funeral.[18] In these cultures, hiring people to mourn simply does not have the same meaning it has here and now. In the US, hiring professional mourners would seem offensive, given people's sensibilities, but we Americans don't have to think that way.

Imagine there is a Twin Earth with a Twin America. Twin America's culture is much like real America's. However, in Twin America, it's the norm for best men to buy their speeches. In Twin America, imagine, best men usually spend lavish amounts of money to buy the fanciest, most eloquent speech from the most famous speechwriters they can. In Twin America, suppose, to *write one's own speech* would be seen as cheap and uncaring. Also, suppose that it's expected in that culture that the father or mother of the bride must bake the wedding cake, rather than buying it from a bakery, as is the norm in the real America. Suppose, also, that in Twin America there's a Twin Harvard with a political theorist Twin Michael Sandel. Twin Michael Sandel recently wrote a book describing how awful it is that some parents on Twin Earth are choosing to pay professionals to bake the wedding cake, rather than baking it themselves. However, he doesn't blink an eye at the best men buying speeches, which he sees as normal and appropriate.

What's really going on here is that there are general cultural expectations that there are some things one should do oneself and some things one may buy. We imbue the first set of things with certain meaning. But all of this is highly contingent, as the professional mourners or the Twin Sandel case shows. In fact, it can and does vary from culture to culture and from person to person whether making something oneself is seen as meaningful, neutral, or cheap and uncouth.

Westerners now see monetary transactions as impersonal, instrumental, and selfish.[19] Sandel's, Walzer's, Anderson's, and others' semiotic complaints reflect this Western view. But, Parry and Bloch say, it appears we can almost always find real life examples where people of different cultures buy and sell something Westerners find repugnant to buy and sell, but for the people in those cultures, buying and selling has very different meaning than it has for us Westerners.[20] We Westerners could attach different meanings to markets than we do.

So, we have a dilemma here. On one hand, we have philosophical arguments from prominent theorists telling us that we can determine, a priori, that certain markets essentially signal disrespect. On the other hand, we have sociological and anthropological work that seems to show that extant markets in those very goods often have an entirely different meaning from what we Westerners attribute to them. We can side with the philosophers, in which case we must conclude that the people in these other cultures are just plain wrong. Merina men in fact disrespect their wives; they just fail to see it. When the Chinese give gifts of money in red envelopes on New Year's Day, they are impersonal and distant; they just fail to see it. Or we can side with the sociologists, and then conclude that people in these other cultures are doing nothing wrong when they buy and sell certain goods and services. Anti-commodification theorists who rely upon semiotic arguments have not discovered an essential meaning to money; they are instead reifying contemporary Western mores. But this comes with the implication that we Westerners *could* think differently about the meaning of money and exchange, and thus opens up the possibility that we *should* think differently.

We find the sociologists' story more persuasive. For now, we ask readers, for the sake of argument, to join us in siding with the sociologists and anthropologists, in order to see what philosophical implications that might have for the commodification debate. (Later, we will more directly respond to the philosophical arguments that markets have essential meaning.)

The Cost of Meaning: Why We Should Not Take Semiotics for Granted

Cultures imbue certain actions, words, and objects with symbolic meaning. In light of those codes, some behaviors will signify morally bad meanings. But this is not cost-free. We do not have to take those codes for granted. Instead, we need to ask whether we have reason to maintain, modify, or drop the codes altogether, or whether we have reason to conscientiously object to, rebel against, or ignore those codes. That will depend in great part upon the consequences and opportunity costs of using such codes. In general, if the consequences of using one set of signals turn out, on net, to be bad or costly, then we should stop using that set of signals. That is, we should subject our semiotics to a kind of cost-benefit analysis, and drop semiotics that fail this analysis.

Certain forms of symbolism are socially destructive—they cause great harm. Others could have high opportunity costs—they could prevent us from doing things that would be beneficial. Either case gives us strong pro tanto grounds to revise the current practice or at least to stop complying with it. So, for instance, if a culture regards contraception as expressing contempt for life, then it will tend to perpetuate poverty and low status for women. If a culture regards anesthesia as expressing contempt for a divine will, then people will suffer needlessly. And if a culture regards life insurance as expressing the desire to profit from death, then it thereby tends to leave orphans and dependents at the mercy of charity.

To illustrate, consider that the meaning of words is a social construct. The word "cat" really does refer to cats and not to dogs. However, it is a contingent social construct that the word "cat" signifies what it does. It could have signified nothing or something else, and in the future, it may well change to mean something else. In light of that, imagine it turned out—thanks to bizarre laws of physics—that every time we emit the sounds "I respect you as an end in yourself!" or "Some things have a dignity, not a price!" to others, an infant died. We had better then stop talking that way. If it also turned out that every time we emit the sounds "I despise you and hope you suffer forever in Hell" a person was magically cured of cancer, we would have every reason to start talking that way.

If we discovered these facts, we would have compelling moral grounds to modify our semiotics. We should, if we could, change the meaning of the English language, modifying it such that "I despise you and hope you suffer in Hell" did not have negative meaning. We might even make it an informal greeting. If we *refused* to change our practices—saying instead that it is just plain wrong to talk in certain ways—we would act disrespectfully. We would show a lack of concern for life, what really matters more.

To take a real-life example, consider that some cultures developed the idea that the best way to respect the dead was to eat their bodies. In those cultures, it really was a (socially-constructed) fact, regardless of one's intentions, that failing to eat the dead expressed disrespect, while eating rotting flesh expressed respect. But now consider that the Fore tribe of Papua New Guinea suffered from prion infections as a result of eating the rotten brains of their dead relatives prior to that practice being banned in the 1950s.[21] The interpretative practice of equating the eating of rotting flesh with showing respect is a destructive, bad practice. The people in that culture have strong moral grounds to change what expresses respect.

In some cultures women are expected to undergo genital mutilation. Now, these cultures offer many (mistaken) consequentialist reasons for female genital mutilation: they think it improves hygiene, prevents birth defects, eases childbirth, or prevents marital infidelity. But they also usually have semiotic reasons. In some cultures, mutilation marks fidelity and respect for the group, or fidelity and respect for the religion. Some versions of this practice (such as cliterectomies or infibilitation) are especially harmful. The cultures in question have strong moral grounds to revise the semiotics they impute to genital mutilation.

Now apply this kind of reasoning to questions about commodification and what markets mean. As an example of symbolism with a high opportunity cost, consider the issue of organ selling. Many people claim that organ selling would cause exploitation or the misallocation of organs, but we ask you to put those aside for the moment and focus only on the semiotic objection. Thus, to test whether such semiotic objections have any independent force, imagine instead that organ selling works the way that proponents believe it would.

To review, the argument for organ sales begins by noting there is a huge shortage in organs. People are simply not willing to give away the organs others need. The government sets the legal price of organs at $0, far below the implicit market equilibrium price. Thus, an economist might say, *of course* there is a shortage—whenever the legal price of a good is set below the equilibrium price, the quantity demanded will exceed the quantity supplied. Many philosophers and economists thus think that markets in organs will eliminate the shortage. For the sake of argument, suppose they are right. Suppose markets in organs make sick people healthier, make poor people richer, and prevent hundreds of thousands of deaths per year.[22] Suppose also that we are able to design or regulate such markets in such a way that no wrongful exploitation or misallocation takes place.

Perhaps, in light of pre-existing Western interpretive practices, markets in organs would still count as "commodifying life," as Sandel would say. But rather than this giving us reason to refrain from selling organs or to judge organ markets as immoral, we conclude it instead gives us reason to judge our interpretative practices as morally dysfunctional. If markets in organs did have such good consequences, this would be compelling grounds for us to revise our interpretative practices. Rather than saying that organ selling shows disrespect for the body, we should say that our culture's semiotics impute disrespect in a harmful way. If organ sales really do save lives, and if there are no other serious, non-semiotic objections to organ sales, then people should *get over* their aversion to these markets, just as they got over their semiotics-based aversion to life insurance and anesthesia.

Consider another example. In the early 2000s, following the work of many economists on the predictive power of information markets, the Pentagon considered creating a Policy Analysis Market (PAM). These information markets would have allowed people to bet on when certain events would occur, such as terrorist strikes or wars. Many economists believe that information markets are especially good at making predictions, because 1) they draw information from diffuse and diverse sources, and 2) they reward people for being right and punish them for being wrong.[23]

PAM never got off the ground—public outrage killed it. As Sandel says, the idea of "buying a stake in someone else's death" carries a certain "moral ugliness."[24] Senator Ron Wyden said PAM is "ridiculous" and "grotesque," while senator Byron Dorgan called it "offensive."[25] These critics did not deny PAM would work; they thought it was immoral for semiotic reasons.[26]

It may be that in our culture, given the meanings we have constructed, to bet on a terrorist attack is translated as callously buying a stake in someone else's death, just as in the past (given our culture's former semiotics) to buy life insurance for one's family really was interpreted as a disgusting act that commodified death. However, if PAM worked as intended, it would have saved many lives. If so, then having a culture that sees PAM as vile and offensive is itself vile and offensive—one of the misguided features of our culture is that we are willing to let people die because we imbued certain acts with negative symbolic meaning.[27] Our concern here is not whether PAM would really work better than the alternatives. Instead, our view is that *if* PAM worked as advertised, then we should not forbid it on semiotic grounds. Instead, we should modify the semiotics surrounding PAM (again, provided there are no independent non-semiotic objections to PAM).

Our semiotics can have more small-scale opportunity costs. Even if a market in certain goods does not save lives, when we see that people choose to participate in that market this usually means it has good consequences for the participants. It suggests that they regard themselves as benefiting from the exchange, and that to eliminate this opportunity for exchange would thereby eliminate their most-preferred option. We should thus be cautious in imbuing too many things with negative symbolic meaning to avoid unduly constraining options.

We do not claim that it is easy to revise our semiotics. And it is a complicated question just what responsibility individuals have in revising their culture's semiotics. But we do not think these complications amount to an objection to our thesis. Consider, in parallel: feminists argue that Western semiotics infuse gendered meanings onto a wide range of objects, practices, words, colors, careers, behaviors, and so on. They argue that these semiotics are harmful to both women and men, and thus claim we should modify our semiotics. We doubt anyone holds that because it is difficult to modify such semiotics, the feminist critique is therefore wrong. Similarly, we doubt that anyone holds that because determining the responsibilities of individuals is difficult, the feminist critique is wrong. One might argue that there are *moral* costs to changing our semiotics, and these considerations can count against changing them. We can accept this point, but note that similar remarks also apply to feminist arguments for changing the semiotics of gender. So, without exploring these issues at great length, we just note that whatever response feminists have to these purported objections, we should have as well.

Suppose instead that it is impossible to change the semiotics of one's culture. Suppose that a culture has a code of meaning about what it takes to signal respect or good motives, but this code of meaning is harmful, destructive, or has an unduly high opportunity cost. Suppose also that this code of meaning cannot be revised—while it's contingent that the culture has this code of meaning, the culture is so rigid that they will never change.

Must one then adhere to that code, refraining from actions that express disrespect or bad motives? We don't see why. Instead, it seems more plausible that one may conscientiously reject or ignore the code. To see why, consider some examples outside of the market:

1   It's a contingent fact that some cultures regard female genital mutilation as expressing respect. But suppose those cultures turned out to be impervious to change—try as we might, we cannot induce them to see things differently. Does a member of that culture thus have an obligation to mutilate her child's genitals? It seems not. Rather, it's more plausible that once a person recognizes that the social meaning of genital mutilation is contingent, and that the practice is deeply harmful, the person can unilaterally decide to reject the practice, thereby violating the semiotics of her culture. Others will regard this as disrespectful, but from a moral point of view, that's just too bad for them. Disregard for that culture's semiotics is not merely excused, but justified.

2   It's a contingent fact that the Fore regard endocannibalism as expressing respect for their dead. But this practice transmits kuru, a fatal prion-based disease. Now, suppose the Fore are rigid and will never change their semiotics. Ask: should an individual Fore who recognizes the dangers of the practice eat his dead relatives? Here, it seems more plausible that he may conscientiously refuse to participate in the practice, even though that will offend others. His disregard of the semiotics is not merely excused, but justified.

3   It's a contingent fact that some cultures used to regard anesthesia as expressing religious disrespect. Suppose you were part of a rigid culture that would never abandon this aversion to anesthesia. Now suppose your child is ill and needs surgery. Are you obligated to refrain from anesthetizing your child in order to avoid signaling disrespect in your culture? Here, again, it seems more plausible that you may conscientiously choose to anesthetize your child. You will end up expressing disrespect, but you would be justified in doing so.

Note that we said you *may* conscientiously choose to reject the code of meaning. This should be distinguished from conscientious objection: we don't make the stronger claim that you must engage in some sort of public protest, or that you should bear punishment for your actions in the hopes that your martyrdom will induce others to change.

Note also that we are not just saying in cases 1–3 above that consequences trump symbolic concerns. We are not saying that there is a pro tanto duty to comply with one's culture's codes of meaning, but this is outweighed by a duty to avoid harm. Rather, we're saying that in these cases the duty to comply *disappears* or is *silenced*, not merely defeated or outweighed.

Now, let's apply this kind of reasoning to markets. Suppose our culture just so happens to regard organ sales as disrespectful, though it doesn't have to. It could think of organ sales as no different from selling labor. Suppose our culture is rigid; there is no possibility of getting people to change their minds. Should we thus refrain from participating in organ markets, in order to avoid signaling disrespect? Our view is that one may instead conscientiously refuse to participate in the semiotics of one's culture. If most Americans reject organ sales on semiotic grounds, but organ sales would save lives, then some Americans may conscientiously refuse to abide by American semiotics. They are not merely excused, but justified.

Notes

1 Anderson 1995, 8.
2 Anderson 1995, 153. Anderson's argument reminds us of the argument against homosexuality in Finnis 1997. Satz 2012, 142–43, thinks this is an implausible objection.
3 Satz 2012, 117–19 describes Pateman and Anderson as advocating an *"essentialist thesis,"* that is, that "reproductive labor is by its nature something that should not be bought or sold."
4 Carruthers and Ariovich 2010, 68.
5 Zelizer 1997, 202–3.
6 Zelizer 2013; Zelizer 1994, Zelizer 2007.
7 Bloch and Parry 1989, 9.
8 Carruthers and Ariovich 2010, 68.
9 Zelizer 1995, 84.
10 Stoebenau 2010, 111.
11 Consider: I think my neighbor should quiet his barking dogs for free, but he refuses to do so. Now, suppose a genie offers to cast a spell ridding me of the noise for $10, but—even in a cool moment—I refuse to pay. This is evidence I do not care as much about the barking as I let on.
12 E.g., Hanson 2013, 151–78.
13 http://www.nbcnews.com/business/consumer/couple-pays-each-other-put-kids-bed-n13021
14 http://web.eecs.umich.edu/srg/?p=1508
15 http://www.nbcnews.com/business/consumer/couple-pays-each-other-put-kids-bed-n13021
16 Sandel 2012a, 98.
17 Sandel 2012a, 98.
18 Thanks to Vlad Tarko for this example.
19 Mitchell and Mickel 1999, 569.
20 Bloch and Parry 1989, 19–33.
21 Jamieson 2009.
22 E.g. Brennan 2012a, 91–92; Taylor 2005.
23 For an overview, see Luckner et al. 2012.
24 Sandel 2012a, 151.
25 BBC News, "Pentagon Axes Online Terror Bets," July 29, 2003, http://news.bbc.co.uk/2/hi/americas/3106559.stm.

26 They also worried these markets would corrupt us, but that's a different objection.
27 Sandel 2012a, 154, says that if we were convinced that PAM would save lives, then perhaps we should allow it. However, he contends, this would still cause us to have "morally debased sensibilities" and would be "morally corrupting." As we mentioned before, this is not a semiotic objection as framed, but a corruption objection.

8

OBJECTIONS: SEMIOTIC ESSENTIALISM AND MINDING OUR MANNERS

We have presented empirical evidence that in the absence of wrongful exploitation, harm, corruption, and so on, the meaning of markets is contingent and socially-constructed. Westerners right now happen to see markets and money as profane, amoral, impersonal, and so on, but Westerners do not *have* to think that way. If the meaning of markets is contingent, then, we argued, this cannot be a reason to forbid on-net valuable markets. Instead, if certain markets are valuable, we should revise the meaning we attach to these markets. Just as our culture modified the meaning of life insurance markets, so it could *and should* modify the meaning of, for example, organ markets (provided, of course, these markets work as proponents claim they would). In addition, people who recognize that we have dysfunctional semiotics may conscientiously disregard their culture's semiotics.

However, we will now briefly consider two major objections:

1 *The Essentialist Objection*: Bloch, Parry, Zelizer, and other anthropologists and sociologists are just wrong to claim that the meaning of money and markets is contingent. Some markets are essentially disrespectful, even if these markets do not involve exploitation, harm, rights violations, etc.
2 *The Argument from Civic Respect*: Even if the meaning of markets is contingent, it remains the case that some markets are contingently seen by one's culture as disrespectful, and this provides at least *prima facie* grounds for refraining from engaging in these markets.

The Essentialist Objection: The Case of Prostitution

Let's start with the Essentialist Objection. We have claimed that when a market does not involve exploitation, harm, rights violations, corruption, and so on, then the semiotics of that market are purely conventional, contingent, and socially constructed. There seems to be overwhelming sociological and anthropological evidence in favor of this kind of meaning relativism. However, an anti-commodification theorist might object that some markets necessarily have a particular meaning, regardless of what people in different cultures think.

We don't have space here, even in this long book, to examine every possible essentialist argument. Instead, we'll look in depth at essentialist arguments about the semiotics of prostitution, since this issue has the most developed and impressive literature.

Margaret Jane Radin says that prostitution detaches intimacy from sex, and that widespread use of prostitutes might cause us not to see sex as intimate at all.[1] But, as Satz responds, casual sex also detaches intimacy from sex, and widespread casual sex could cause a cultural change in which sex loses its intimate meaning.[2] If so, then the *market* plays no essential role in explaining the purported wrongness of prostitution or paid surrogacy—it would be wrong for the prostitutes to give sex away or for women to give their babies away, not just to charge for it. Radin's complaint is not properly a complaint about *commodification*. Consider, in parallel: we agree that it's wrong to buy and sell child pornography. But, we add, it would also be wrong to trade child porn for free, or even to have it, period. Buying and selling didn't *make* the transaction wrong; rather, it is wrong because one should not have it at all, regardless of whether money changes hands. So, Radin's complaint is not properly a semiotic objection to the commodification of sex.

Anderson complains that in prostitution, the buyer gives the prostitute cash, while the prostitute gives the buyer her body. The sexual partners in prostitution do not exchange the same *kind* of good. And so, Anderson seems to conclude, the buyer necessarily treats the prostitute as a mere object. But, as far as we can tell, Anderson does not have an argument about why, in the special case of sex, one must exchange the same kind of good. This is not immoral in other cases, such as when Anderson directly exchanges philosophy lectures for cash, or when she indirectly exchanges such lectures for food. And, as Satz notes, *all* labor involves one person purchasing to some degree the use and control of another person's body, such as what people wear, whom they will touch, how they will sleep, where they will be, what they will eat.[3] Yet, Satz responds, it does not appear that this is necessarily degrading or humiliating. So, Satz concludes, and we agree, we do not yet see from Anderson reason to think prostitution is essentially degrading in a way other forms of work are not.

Anderson has another argument. She claims that allowing the sale of sex reduces some people's freedom. In particular, it reduces some people's freedom to have sex have the meaning they want it to have.

According to Anderson, people value having the freedom of being able to induce sexual pleasure in those whom they love. But, Anderson claims, people not only want the freedom to induce sexual pleasure in those they love, they also want the freedom of having sex insulated from money. She says that a moral culture that accepts prostitution makes it hard to "establish insulated social spheres where [sex] can be exclusively and freely valued as a genuinely shared and personal good."[4] The idea here is that Jane might not just want to give sexual pleasure to Kevin. She also wants sexual pleasure to be insulated from the market, such that the sex they enjoy together is something they both recognize as a "genuinely shared and personal good." In a world where Kevin (or Jane) can buy sex, then the meaning of sex is different. So, Anderson concludes, allowing people to buy sex reduces the freedom of those who want sex to have a certain meaning.

Anderson is, in some sense, right. If people are free to treat sex as not having the meaning that Jane wants it to have, then Jane is not free to have sex have the meaning she wants it to have. So the freedom of some to treat sex as having one meaning conflicts with Jane's freedom to have sex have a different meaning.

But it's hard to see why this has any moral upshot. To show that buying and selling sex is wrong, it's not enough to point out, as Anderson does, that prostitution reduces Jane's freedom to have sex have the meaning she wants it to have. We need an additional premise, namely that Jane is *entitled* to have other people create a social environment in which sex has that special meaning.

Consider, as a parody: suppose we prefer that Swedish progressive death metal be seen as sacred. Suppose, in our view, Swedish progressive death metal should not be bought and sold on the market, but should only be developed through gift exchanges inside churches. If our culture allows Swedish progressive death metal to be bought and sold, it thereby reduces our freedom to have Swedish progressive death metal have the sacred meaning we want it to have. But, even if so, so what? Other people don't have any moral duty to ensure that Swedish progressive death metal have the meaning we want it to have. When they don't treat it as sacred, we lose our "freedom" to have it have the meaning we want, but we are not entitled to this freedom, and no one owes it to us to help us realize that freedom. We don't have any right to impose our view of the music on others, and they have no duty to comply with it.

Similarly, Anderson is correct that if people can buy and sell sex, this may reduce Jane's freedom to make sex with Kevin have exactly the kind of meaning she would like it to have. But that does not make it wrong to buy and sell sex. Rather, we need an independent argument here that shows us that other people are entitled to supply Jane with the social environment she desires, that is, that other people are obligated to impute the meaning onto sex that Jane wants sex to have. So, Anderson's argument doesn't *show* that selling sex is wrong because it reduces freedom. Rather, it presupposes that selling sex violates a particular meaning that some people are entitled to demand that others share. Jane wants sex to be seen as an exclusive gift. If others don't treat sex that way, this reduces her freedom to make sex be seen that way. But Jane isn't, as far as we can tell, entitled to have that kind of freedom, so there is nothing wrong with taking it away from her.

Philosophers often try to recast their arguments in terms of freedom, but this rarely does the work they want it to do. The problem is that "freedom" is a word which, in common English, has a large number of closely related but distinct meanings.[5] Thomas Hobbes wanted to define liberty and freedom as the absence of obstacles or impediments to achieving one's goals. On Hobbes's way of using the terms—a manner that is shared by many English speakers—anything that gets in the way of a person achieving his or her goals counts as a restriction on freedom. Others, such as certain Marxists, want to define freedom and liberty as the presence of the capacity to achieve one's ends. On this definition—the use of which is also widely shared by English speakers—anything that reduces one's ability to achieve one's ends also reduces one's freedom.

The thing is, on neither definition does "X reduces liberty" imply "X is wrong." Both definitions count any obstacle to getting what a person wants as a reduction in freedom. But these definitions leave open whether any particular degree of freedom is within that person's rights. So, for Hobbes, when a rapist forces a woman to have sex with her, he reduces her freedom. But when a woman sprays a would-be rapist with pepper spray and escapes, she also reduces the rapist's freedom. Hobbes would say that the difference between the two cases isn't about restrictions on freedom, but restrictions on *rightful* freedom. Preventing rape reduces rapists' freedom to rape, but rightly so, as rapists should not have such freedom. In contrast, preventing rape increases women's freedom of bodily security, etc. and rightly so, as they should have such freedom.

So, Anderson may be right that in one very important sense of freedom, it reduces some people's freedom for others to treat sex as a commodity. But it doesn't follow from this that treating sex as a commodity is wrong, because we don't yet have any reason to think that people are entitled to the freedom to live in a world where sex is never seen or treated as a commodity.

Second, Anderson and other critics of "women's sexual labor" often respond that sex is importantly different from other kinds of labor. Sex is supposed to be intimate and loving. But, as far as we can tell, this really just amounts to the assertion that at its best, sex is emotionally intimate and loving. As we saw earlier, it's possible for people to exchange money for sex and yet still having an emotionally intimate and loving sexual encounter—in some cultures, such exchanges are routine. Beyond that, though, it remains unclear why it would obligatory for every sexual encounter to be emotionally intimate and loving. Perhaps the very best kind of sex is emotionally intimate and loving. But, even if so, this does not imply that it is wrong to engage in emotionally non-intimate, casual sex.

The Haifa Daycare Case

There was a problem with too many parents picking up their children late from daycare in Haifa, Israel. Some economists proposed adding a monetary fine, penalizing the parents for late pickups. Ten daycare centers took part in the study. For the first four weeks, there was no financial penalty for late pickups. In the fifth week, they introduced a small fine—about $10 in today's money, adjusted for inflation. To their surprise, when the penalty was introduced, the number of late pickups increased—in fact, it more than doubled.[6] In effect, by introducing a small fine, the Israeli daycare transformed what was seen as a significant moral transgression into just another financial transaction—a price instead of a penalty.

Sandel and Satz view this as evidence of the badness of certain markets.[7] But we think they misdiagnose the problem. There is nothing morally wrong or inherently corrupting with charging people for picking up their kids late. Plenty of daycares do so without any deleterious results. Rather, the problem here is that these daycare centers seem to have had more than just an arms-length relationship with the parents. The addition of financial penalties for late pick-ups may have been interpreted by the parents as signaling that the daycare centers intended to switch to an arms-length relationship. The parents no longer viewed themselves as participating in a common venture with the daycare centers, where each owed something beyond payment to the other. We do not feel obligated to return movies on time to Redbox; we feel obligated only to pay the associated fees with "late" returns. The late fee is regarded as a price in a simple market transaction between strangers. The same is not true when we borrow a movie from a friend. If the friend introduced a fine for lateness, that may be interpreted in a way that estranges us from one another, and may thereby lead to more late returns. But this connection depends on a contingent interpretive practice—the practice of interpreting the sudden inclusion of financial fees or payments as signaling or meaning estrangement by being viewed as kinds of compensation. It is fine for daycares to have more impersonal relationships with parents. It is also fine for daycares to have more personal relationships with parents. What is morally problematic is communicating estrangement, when estrangement is inappropriate given the previously understood relationship.

Note that this goes both ways. It is also often bad to treat arms-length relationships as if they were not arms-length relationships. If we suddenly start offering our partners money to clean the house, they might both be angry, because introducing money would signal a violation of our previous understanding of the kind of relationships we have. Yet, it would also be bad if we suddenly asked the strangers we pay to mow our lawns to invite us to their children's birthday parties. It would be even worse if we told them we would pay them for mowing the lawn with a favor rather than with money.

Thus, pace Satz and Sandel, the issue here is *not* actually about commodification per se. Rather, it is about transgressing the boundaries of a relationship by communicating estrangement *or* friendship when that is not the nature of the relationship. Sometimes commodification is taken to mean estrangement and thereby transgresses the relationship, and, at the same time, sometimes non- or de-commodification is taken to signal friendship or a kind of closeness that transgresses the relationship. As we discussed previously, whether money communicates estrangement or closeness varies from culture to culture, or even among individuals within cultures.

In summary, anti-commodification theorists sometimes complain that commodification is incompatible with the kinds of relationships we want to have with one another, or that it deforms these relationships. In some sense, they are right, but this is not really a worry about commodification per se. The wrongness in these cases is not whether some things should be for sale or not, but whether it makes sense to introduce what are contingently seen as impersonal mechanisms into more personal relationships. Often it does not. Still, at least in principle, well-functioning, intimate relationships could be based heavily on market exchanges. We also noted that the problem goes both ways. Just as it can be improper to suddenly treat a personal relationship as if it were more arms-length and impersonal, it can be improper to suddenly treat arms-length, impersonal relationships as if they were more personal. And, again, the issue is not really about commodification. The principle at work here—treat personal and impersonal relationships by the appropriate norms—can be violated in all sorts of ways.

Sandel claims that when the Israeli daycares introduced financial penalties, they eliminated the moral sting of late pickups. He agrees that of course heavier penalties would have disincentivized parents more. However, since all disputants here agree that markets can communicate attitudes, we should also ask what message low prices communicate. The daycares introduced prices that were too low. Sandel correctly notes that low prices introduce too weak of a disincentive. But Sandel does not realize, as economists do, that prices not only create incentives, but communicate *information*. He thus fails to see that in addition, low prices communicate to parents that late pickups are not and never were a major transgression. Putting a tiny financial penalty on something is not the market crowding out non-market norms. Rather, the low price communicates that it is not and never was a big deal.

The Swiss Waste Facility Case

In discussing the siting of a Swiss waste facility, Anderson makes a similar argument as Sandel. The Swiss government sent out a survey asking residents how willing they would be to have the waste facility located near them. Many responded that they would be willing. Economists thought it would be interesting to see how much more willing the residents would be if a financial incentive was involved. Once again, a survey was sent out, with different financial incentives. The results were surprising: fewer, not more, residents were willing to have the facility constructed near them. Anderson offers the following explanation for why the residents were less rather than more willing:

> I suggest rather that the offer of compensation changed the perceived relationship of the Swiss government to the town residents and thus changed the practical identity they assumed in contemplating the waste facility. In asking the residents to accept the facility without compensation, the Swiss

state addressed the residents as citizens. It implicitly asked them to frame their practical dilemma as: "what principle for siting the facility should we accept, given that we (Swiss citizens, considered collectively) must process the waste somewhere?" This way of framing the question precludes a not-in-my-backyard response, because it recognizes that the facility must land in someone's backyard.

In offering compensation to the townspeople, the Swiss state represented their interest in a waste-free town as an entitlement, like a property right, and asked them their price for giving it up. It thereby implicitly asked each of them to frame their practical dilemma as: "how much is it worth to me (or we townspeople) to keep my town waste-free?" From that point of view it was harder to represent the siting of the waste facility in their town as desirable, because they no longer saw themselves as responsible for solving the collective problem they faced as national citizens, of finding some site for the facility.[8]

Anderson has offered us a plausible interpretation of the meaning of the offer of incentives in this case. But there are other equally plausible interpretations that do not support her argument.

Instead, it might be that the Swiss citizens only *seemed* altruistic because the survey was a mere survey. The original survey was not binding—nothing was at stake in the Swiss citizens saying, "Oh, sure, I'd take a waste facility in my backyard for free." Psychologists and other social scientists agree that people are biased to answer anonymous surveys in self-serving and self-promoting ways, or in ways that they would expect the surveyer to approve of. (This is called "social desirability bias."[9]) In non-binding surveys, people display much more altruistic attitudes than they do in real life. In the second survey, no real money was actually on the table. The Swiss were not offered actual money; they were just asked what they would do if they were offered money. In light of social desirability bias, we should be cautious in concluding, from this survey, that money corrupted the relationship or the people. Talk is cheap.

Another surprising problem with Anderson's interpretation of the Swiss waste case is that she misses, in this case, that offering money *communicates* something. (This is surprising because she is advancing a semiotic objection to commodification.) Consider: if Sally asks you to babysit her son for free, she signals one thing. If she asks you to babysit him for three hours and offers you $50 compensation, she signals something else. But if she asks you to babysit him for one hour and offers you $200 for that one hour, she might thereby signal that he's a real terror—and you might thereby be even less willing to babysit him.

Similarly, when a government offers to pay citizens to live near waste rather than have them accept the waste for free, this signals something to citizens. By offering compensation, the government signals (whether it intends to or not) that living near waste is bad and possibly harmful. By offering compensation, it signals that it believes that living near waste is *the kind of thing for which one should be compensated*. It will prompt citizens to believe that living near waste is a big deal, that it is worse than they may have thought, and so their willingness may go down. So, it should be stressed that the available evidence greatly underdetermines the meaning of the outcome, and Anderson is just reading the evidence in the way most conducive to her pre-existing conclusions, even though alternative readings that contradict her conclusions are equally or more plausible.

Minding Our Manners

Now let's consider the issue of civic respect. Earlier, we argued that many interpretive practices are highly contingent and culturally-specific. Even so, the anti-commodification theorist can respond: true, it is contingent that we drive on the right-hand side of the road around here, and it is true that the words "I disrespect you" contingently communicate disrespect in our language, but this doesn't change the fact that, once these practices get under way, we have reason to drive according to the social convention, and work within the meaning conventions of language around here. In short, the fact that, around here, buying a wedding speech, selling women's reproductive labor, and so on, is interpreted as disrespectful may be sufficient reason to denounce these practices. We should not give each other the middle finger around here, because around here the middle finger signals disrespect. And that's true despite the fact that it's contingent, culturally-specific, and not written into the moral fabric of the universe.

In response, we can just accept that people have at least a prima facie duty to obey the local norms of good manners *because* they have a duty to express respect for one another. There are cases where buying and selling certain goods is *impolite*—it communicates disrespect, given that culture's contingent semiotics. There could be cases where refraining from participating in these markets bears no significant cost or opportunity cost, and causes no significant harm. If so, then people should refrain from participating in those markets.

While we concede this, it is not a victory for semiotic arguments. We accept that manners matter. All things considered, we should have good manners, and play along with the manners of those around us. We should keep up the good manners when the good manners are good and useful, or at least not harmful. But, as we argued previously, we should reject these systems of manners when they are harmful or have high opportunity costs. We are not saying that manners have *no* hold on us, but are saying instead that we should replace or conscientiously reject codes of manners when these codes are dysfunctional, costly, and harmful. So, at this point, we're just haggling over the price of manners.

The semiotic objections we considered were intended to be powerful moral arguments for limiting the scope of the market. We have reduced what appeared to be significant moral arguments against commodification to issues of mere manners. Semiotic objections have force only in the way manners have force.

They hold only for minor markets of little consequence, only in cases where the cost of forbearance from the markets is not so high as to justify modifying our manners or conscientiously rejecting the code of manners. We take this, then, to be a vindication of Martha Nussbaum's claims when she wrote that "[a]n account of the actual social meaning of a practice is ... just a door that opens onto the large arena of moral and legal evaluation ... Social meaning does no work on its own: it offers an invitation to normative moral and political philosophy."[10]

Again, we note that the argument we've presented does not just imply that the bad consequences of forbidding certain markets sometimes *trump* a deonto-logical concern that such markets would express disrespect. We've made the much more interesting argument that in the absence of other deontological or non-communicative concerns, pure semiotic objections to markets fail, because consequentialist considerations allow us to put a price on and judge codes of semiotics. And just as we may often times shrug and say "manners schmanners," so we may with equal aplomb often times say "semiotics schemiotics."

The Feeling that It's Just Plain Wrong

Semiotic objections fail because there is no deep metaphysical fact about the meaning of money and markets. The meaning is entirely contingent, and, in principle, open to revision.

There is not one meaning to markets. Money and markets have very many different meanings, even in our own culture.[11] Sometimes, giving money means we are friends, or it can strengthen our bonds of friendship. Other times, the giving of money signals distance and estrangement. Zelizer suggests that this depends on whether the money is interpreted as a gift, compensation, or as an entitlement. But all of this is contingent and open to revision. Even if, in a specific context, money does mean estrangement, it must mean that only insofar as the "thumbs up" sign must mean "good job," rather than "up yours."

We have examined three distinct kinds of semiotic objections to markets—the Mere Commodity, Wrong Signal, and Wrong Currency Objections—and found each of them wanting. In each case, it turns out that these moral objections are based on contingent, culturally-relative interpretive schemas. Offering a good or service for sale does not necessarily mean that the participants to the exchange regard that good or service as of merely instrumental value. Introducing money (or favors) into personal (or impersonal) relationships may be the wrong currency for some relationships, but what counts as the right currency is merely a contingent fact with a high degree of variability. Finally, these interpretative practices—a culture's semiotics—can themselves be judged by the consequences they produce. In many cases, we are morally obligated to revise our semiotics in order to allow for greater commodification. We ought to revise our interpretive schemas whenever the costs of holding that schema are significant, without counter-weighted benefits. It is itself morally objectionable to maintain a meaning system that imbues a practice with morally objectionable meanings which would save or improve lives, reduce or alleviate suffering, and so on.

We make no claims about the ease or difficulty of altering our interpretive schemas. Perhaps it is practically very difficult, like altering or reforming whole languages. Perhaps the metaphysically contingent meaning of money and markets are nevertheless a deep sociological fact. But we should not be busy digging ourselves any deeper. Many people have a deep emotional aversion to certain trades. They find certain trades repugnant. But we have to ask whether disgust reactions are reliable guides to right and wrong. We also have to ask whether using these disgust reactions as the basis of a social code about the sacred and profane is worth the cost.

Notes

1 Radin 1997, 1884.
2 Satz 2012, 142.
3 Satz 2012, 143.
4 Anderson 2000a, 155.
5 See Schmidtz and Brennan 2010, 6–14.
6 Levitt and Dubner 2008, 15–16.
7 Sandel 2012a, 64–65; Satz 2012, 193–94.
8 Anderson 2000a, 197.
9 There is a massive literature on this. One classic piece is Paulhus 1991.
10 Nussbaum 1998, 695–96.
11 Zelizer 2013, 182, writes: "This, I claim, is how money works: in order to make sense of their complex and often chaotic social ties, people constantly innovate and differentiate currencies, bringing different meanings to their various exchanges. Thus, a multiplicity of socially meaningful currencies replaces the standard model of a single, neutral, depersonalizing legal tender." In Zelizer 1989, 343, she writes: "Yet, camouflaged by the physical anonymity of our dollar bills, modern money is also routinely differentiated, not just by varying quantities but also by its special diverse qualities. We assign different meanings and designate separate uses for particular kinds of monies. For instance, a housewife's pin money or her allowance is treated differently from a wage or a salary, and each surely differs from a child's allowance. Or a lottery winning is marked as a different kind of money from an ordinary paycheck. The money we obtain as compensation for an accident is not quite the same as the royalties from a book. Not all dollars are equal."

PART III
Do markets corrupt?

"Go into the London Stock Exchange—a more respectable place than many a court—and you will see representatives of all nations gathered there for the service of mankind. There the Jew, the Mohammedan, and the Christian deal with each other as if they were of the same religion, and give the name of infidel only to those who go bankrupt. There the Presbyterian trusts the Anabaptist, and the Anglican accepts the Quaker's promise. On leaving these peaceful and free assemblies, some go to the synagogue, others go to drink ... others go to their church to wait the inspiration of God, their hats on their heads, and all are content."

—Voltaire, Letters on England

9

THE CORRUPTION OBJECTION

"Business Ethics" Is an Oxymoron, Tee Hee

Every undergraduate at Georgetown—a Jesuit institution—takes a course in moral philosophy. But students in the McDonough School of Business (MSB) take an extra ethics course, "The Social Responsibilities of Business," in their senior year. When we ask our business students to guess why the university requires them to take this extra class, many of them answer, "Maybe they don't trust us."

Maybe they shouldn't. In fall of 2011, students in one section of Social Responsibilities of Business did a scientific survey of cheating and study drug use among their peers. They found that MSB undergraduates were almost twice as likely to admit to having engaged in some form of academic dishonesty or to have used study drugs as compared to undergraduates in the other three undergraduate colleges at Georgetown. Note, however, that MSB does *not* have a disproportionate number of violations reported to Georgetown's Honor Council. If MSB students cheat more, they get caught less.

Why do more MSB students cheat than students in the school of nursing and health studies, the college of arts and sciences, or the school of foreign service (which boasts President Bill Clinton as an alumnus)? Two years later, a different group of students argued that much of this is what psychologists call a *selection effect*. MSB students are predominantly male, while students at the other three colleges are predominantly female. Across the board, they argued, men tend to cheat much more than women. MSB also has more athletes, who are naturally competitive and tend to cheat more. Statistically, they argued, nearly half of the increased cheating at MSB can be explained by its having more men and athletes. Still, we'd like to know, even if they're right, what's causing the other half of the disparity?

Most people would be tempted to say it's *business*. A November 2012 Gallup poll asked subjects how they would rate the honesty and ethical standards of people in different professions. Only 21% of subjects would rate business executives very high or high. (These executives can take comfort in knowing that average Americans have an even lower opinion of lobbyists and Members of Congress.) In comparison, chiropractors—practitioners of a pseudoscience akin to palm reading—score better than bankers, business executives, stockbrokers, or advertising and marketing professionals.

According to popular perception, people attracted to business are more likely to have bad character, because their primary motivation is to make money. And, once in business, their environment consists of other such people. This creates a corrupting culture of greed, which leads to lying, cheating, and stealing on the margins. Perhaps when individuals work or study around others who lie and cheat, they come to be less bothered by lying and cheating.

Many people would be tempted to say that the corruption of business spreads to all who enter the market. The market is kind of a moral free-for-all zone.[1] In the market, we are all supposed to observe only minimal moral requirements to avoid theft, fraud, dishonesty, and coercion. Beyond that, we may do anything and make any trades we can with willing partners. Markets are thus about the naked pursuit of self-interest. Even capitalism's greatest defenders seem to agree. Adam Smith tells us, "It is not from the benevolence of the butcher, the brewer, or the baker, that we expect our dinner, but from their regard to their own interest. We address ourselves, not to their humanity but to their self-love ... "[2] That seems just a few steps away from the great Marxist philosopher G. A. Cohen's denunciation: "Every market ... is a system of predation."[3]

The historian Lord Acton said that power corrupts and absolute power corrupts absolutely. Most people think something like this is true of the market as well. The market attracts already corrupt people, and, once it gets them there, it further corrupts them. This may not be a decisive consideration against the market— maybe the benefits of markets in increased wealth, lifespans, and happiness exceed the costs to our souls—but nevertheless, it is a consideration against them. Markets put cash in our wallets but take a toll on our character. We buy a better life at the cost of our hearts.

Or so the common story goes. But is this story true?

Five Corruption Objections

Worries like these constitute what we will call *The Corruption Objection* to commodification. The Corruption Objection holds that participating in certain markets (or in any market, period) tends to cause us to develop defective preferences or character traits. This argument appeals to claims about how we respond to markets. It relies upon the view that the market is not simply a value-neutral mechanism for exchange, but is rather thick with a set of norms that influence and structure how and why we make exchanges, how we come to regard the objects of exchange, and we come to regard objects, people, and practices associated with the objects we exchange. Over time, the market makes us worse people.

Sometimes, when critics of the market advance a Corruption Objection, they just mean to say that the market or a specific market is bad for us. Sometimes they mean to say something stronger—that if introducing or participating in a market would be corrupting, this makes it *wrong* to do so. Note the difference between these two complaints. To say a market is corrupting is to say that you think the market has a bad side effect, a side effect you wish didn't exist. But to say that the corrupting effect of certain markets makes it *wrong* to participate in those markets is to say that others are morally obligated not to participate in those markets.

Here in Part III, we will first provide an outline of what it takes to make a successful Corruption Objection. We do so not to aid the other side of the debate, but because we want to make it clear just what's at stake in making these kinds of arguments work. Sometimes people who advance corruption objections need to do more work to get the arguments to go through. We will then consider and rebut five major versions of the Corruption Objection:

1 *The Selfishness Objection*: Claims that exposure to and involvement in markets tends to make people more selfish and less altruistic.
2 *The Crowding Out Objection*: Claims that providing cash rewards for certain activities tends to crowd out and reduce people's intrinsic motivation.
3 *The Immoral Preferences Objection*: Claims specifically that betting in information markets corrupts people by giving them a stake in bad outcomes.
4 *The Low Quality Objection*: Claims that certain goods and services should not be commodified—sold for profit—because doing so produces lower quality versions of those goods and services than if the goods were produced by a not-for-profit agency.
5 *The Civics Objection*: Claims that markets and commodification threaten civic engagement, because markets draw people away from active participation in politics.

We think all five versions of the Corruption Objection fail. Since these are the major variations of the Corruption Objection, we take this as strong evidence that the Corruption Objection is unsound.

Notes

1 Gauthier 1987, 83–112 argues that an ideal market—one without market failure—would allow participants freedom from morality.
2 Smith 1981, 26–27.
3 Cohen 2009, 82.

10

HOW TO MAKE A SOUND CORRUPTION OBJECTION

Evidence

In Chapter 6, we refuted arguments claiming that to sell something on a market just is to treat it as a mere commodity. We showed that on the contrary it is possible to buy and sell something and still regard it as having a higher status than a candy bar or a roll of toilet paper. However, in response, some might claim that in the long run, it is not psychologically possible to disaggregate or compartmentalize. If we allow certain things to be for sale, we will eventually come to regard them as mere commodities. To turn something into a commodity is, with time, inevitably to turn it into a mere commodity. It is the camel's nose in the tent. These critics may be right. But where is the evidence?

Before getting into specific complaints about how the market corrupts, we want to outline what it would take to make a successful Corruption Objection. To make a successful corruption-based criticism of the market, one needs to prove certain things and provide certain kinds of evidence.

First, one needs real evidence that the market in fact corrupts. Many people accuse the market of corrupting people's character without ever supplying or referencing the needed *empirical* evidence that it in fact does so. Or, if they do provide evidence, it is spotty, minor, anecdotal, unsystematic, or ambiguous, not enough to justify a strong condemnation of the market.

The Burden of Proof

This isn't some minor point. We need to keep in mind that people who advance the Corruption Objection bear the *burden of proof*. The two sides of this debate do not start off on equal footing. The people advancing the Corruption Objection assert a controversial empirical claim, namely, that certain kinds of exposure or involvement in certain markets cause certain kinds of bad character. They have to prove their hypothesis, the same way that, say, medical researchers who want to claim that a chemical causes cancer have to prove their hypothesis. Otherwise—in the absence of substantive empirical evidence—we are by default justified in being skeptical of the claim that markets cause bad character, just as we are by default justified in being skeptical of a claim that some chemical causes cancer.

Data, Not Anecdotes

Note that arguments from anecdotes won't do. Consider, as an analogy, that many people believe that drinking diet soda causes people to become overweight. They may be able to tell stories of friends who started drinking diet soda and, some time later, became overweight. But these stories don't isolate cause and effect and don't separate causation from correlation. We also don't know how representative these anecdotes are. These stories may provide us with leads for further investigation, but they do not suffice to make the case. We need instead to collect data, to observe correlations, to try to isolate causes and effects, to look for natural experiments, to perform artificial experiments, and so on. Doing so is hard—it's the kind of thing one learns in graduate school methods courses.

Causing Vs. Revealing Corruption

Critics must be careful here to distinguish between two claims:

A The market *causes* people to have worse character or preferences.
B The market *reveals* people's base character or preferences.

The Corruption Objection depends upon A, not B. But many times the critics use examples of B as if these were examples of A.

Consider: you might find some of the markets we described in the introduction, such as vending machines selling used panties, perverse or gross. Suppose you are right. But it's not so clear that the market here is perverting men so much as just catering to pre-existing perversions. Even if these "perversions" are cultural rather than innate or genetic, it's again not clear the market is causing this culture rather than just responding to it. Critics of the market might assert the market manufactured these wants, but, again, we need evidence, not assertion.

Consider again the issue of art sales. As we noted in Chapter 6, some people buy and sell art precisely because they regard the art as having serious non-instrumental value. Still, there may be some people who do regard objects of art as mere commodities, as use-objects for the sake of financial gain. Yet, even if so, this tells us nothing about the market's role in *causing* this attitude. In a society in which works of art are never for sale, many people will be indifferent to great art.

However, if art then goes on the market, and some of it acquires significant market value, some of the people who were indifferent to its aesthetic value might nevertheless decide to participate in the buying, trading, and selling of that good, since there is money to be made. They will indeed treat the art as a mere commodity—but that's not because the market corrupted them. They were already inclined to view art as nothing more than use-objects. Similarly, we assume that the people running iTunes do not appreciate the aesthetic value of *all* of the music they sell, but they sell it nonetheless. Still, this is not yet evidence that the market corrupted anyone.

On the contrary, they were *indifferent* to the art and music before, but the market *improved* them by getting them to regard the art and music at least as a mere commodity. In this case, the market induces people to treat things they don't care about as valuable because other people care about those things.

Markets Are Not Corrupting by Definition

Sometimes, those who advance the Corruption Objection substitute an a priori or conceptual argument in place of the needed empirical evidence. As an example, consider this argument:

1 The market, by definition, is a zone where people are supposed to pursue their self-interest.
2 Therefore, the market will make people more selfish.[1]

2 does not follow logically from 1. 2 really is an empirical claim, one that could in principle be demonstrated or refuted, and the people making this argument need to supply the relevant empirical evidence.

As an analogy, consider this parody:

1 In football, players are encouraged to pursue a win, without concern for the other team's desire to win.
2 Therefore, playing football will make people more selfish.

Again, 2 does not follow logically from 1. 2 is an empirical claim, that could be tested in principle. It could turn out to be true or false. It's possible that playing football instead encourages a team mentality and selflessness. It's possible that people are good at compartmentalizing, and so the ethos of football has little or no effect on people's character outside of football. It's possible that American football is corrupting, but football as played in Canada is not, and that equally competitive lacrosse tends to improve character. (In that case, the problem would not be football itself, but the way Americans play it.) We don't know unless we check.

As far as we can tell, the people who advance the Corruption Objection *almost never check*. For example, the Marxist philosopher G. A. Cohen, in his book *Why*

Not Socialism? and his other works, repeatedly claims that market society leads to a hypertrophy of greed. Is he right? He cannot rely upon Karl Marx's armchair speculations to find out. The only way to test the thesis is to test the thesis, that is, to do the kind of work social scientists do when they try to isolate causes and effects. Since the Corruption Objection relies upon empirical premises, its proponents owe us proper empirical evidence that such corruption does in fact take place. What proponents really need to do is supply us with the kind of sustained empirical analysis that would merit publication in a social scientific academic journal. Few critics of market society, from Rousseau to Marx to Cohen and Sandel, bother with this step.[2]

Might Markets Corrupt Us in Some Ways While Improving Us in Others?

Even if one does manage to show that participating in the market or in certain markets has a corrupting effect on character, one still needs to show that markets are corrupting on *net*, however one might balance different effects on character. After all, it's possible that the market degrades some norms or virtues but improves others. So, for instance, suppose conservative and communitarian critics of the market are right that the market tends to weaken familial bonds and the sense of filial duty. Even if so, it might also turn out that the market simultaneously increases people's tolerance and openness. We might determine, on net, that the tradeoff in terms of character alone is worth it—that the market reduces some desirable character traits but improves others, and the improvements outweigh the losses. If we're going to focus just on character, we need to focus on the whole character.

Might Corruption Be a Price We're Willing to Pay?

A critic arguing that markets corrupt our character should consider whether this corruption is outweighed or not by the other benefits of markets. So, suppose Barber is right when he asserts that markets infantilize adults. (As far as we know, he isn't, since he didn't supply any empirical evidence that this is so.) But, at the same time, markets also deliver greater happiness, greater wealth, longer lives, increased access to art and culture, and so on.[3] We might think the trade-off is worthwhile—it's worth sacrificing our character to get the goods the market delivers. So, for instance, Adam Smith agreed with Rousseau that the division of labor into ever more minute, routine tasks could stultify workers, but he also thought that the gains to their standard of living from the division of labor were worth that cost.[4] (He also thought we could overcome potential stultification through free public education.)

Corruption Isn't Strictly Speaking Wrong

It takes additional work to go from the claim "Markets in X corrupt" to the claim "Participating in markets in X is *wrong*." The latter claim doesn't follow straightforwardly from the former. The reason is that sometimes it can be permissible to do things that corrupt one's character.

We don't have any clear moral duty to have *perfect* character—we might instead only have a duty to have *pretty good* character overall, and a general duty to work, from time to time, on improving our character. So, for instance, if it turned out that playing football made people have slightly worse character overall, it's not obvious that playing football would therefore be *wrong*. It might be within people's prerogative to continue to play.

Or, we might think it's worth sacrificing some of our character if doing so is necessary to generate good outcomes. So, for instance, soldiers fighting in just wars might be so scarred by those wars—suffering from post-traumatic stress, anxiety, depression, and so forth—that they might thereby be unable to have perfect moral character. But it might still be right for them to fight even at the expense of their character.

These considerations become even stronger when we think about how our participation in the market affects *other* people. It might turn out that when we buy and sell certain things, this will tend to corrupt others, but that might be a problem with them, not with us. It can be—and usually is—permissible for a person to perform some action, even if performing it induces others to lose virtue, to become corrupted, or to perform wrongful actions. So, for instance, suppose a popular music band releases a clangorous, psychedelic dance song, which in turn induces a psychopath to murder some celebrities. This doesn't make releasing the song wrong. The problem is not with the musical performers, but with the people who reacted wrongly to the song.

Similarly, if we buy and sell certain goods, and this induces you to conclude all human relationships are merely instrumental and that others' lives have no intrinsic worth, it is a problem with you, not with our buying and selling. You have a duty to have more integrity and to be less easily influenced.

Summary

When you encounter a corruption objection, ask yourself:

1 Did that person provide empirical evidence that this corruption is widespread and is really caused by the market?
2 Did that person investigate whether (or at least acknowledge the possibility that) the market might corrupt character in some respects but improve it in others?
3 Did that person investigate whether (or at least acknowledge the possibility that) the market might harm our character on net, but deliver other benefits that make it worth losing some of our character?
4 If the person claims that the market is wrongful because it harms our character, did she show we have a moral duty to maintain our character at that level?

Our point here is that it takes a lot of work to make a successful Corruption Objection. In the next few chapters, we'll examine some of the major instances of the Corruption Objection, each of which falls short in some way.

Notes

1 E.g., Cohen 2009.
2 This problem plagues Radin 1997. Radin claims that if things are offered for sale, and if economists regard certain items as having potential market value, then this will degrade our moral attitudes. Yet, though this is an empirical claim, she provides no empirical evidence that this degradation would in fact occur.
3 See Schmidtz and Brennan 2010; Cowen 2008; Stevenson and Wolfers 2008.
4 See Rasmussen 2008.

11

THE SELFISHNESS OBJECTION

The Argument

The Selfishness Objection isn't just an objection to commodifying specific things, but to commodifying almost anything. It's a complaint about markets in general more so than a complaint about specific markets. It goes something like this:

The Selfishness Objection

1 Markets rely upon self-interest.
2 Therefore, markets cause people to be more selfish.
3 Therefore, markets make us more corrupt.

It's possible that the critics are right. But, as we keep stressing, we cannot settle this kind of issue from the armchair by doing a priori philosophical or economic analysis.[1] We need to conduct historical, sociological, and psychological research on what exposure to markets does to people, and what happens when markets are replaced by something else.

Do Markets Corrupt? On the Contrary

In fact, there are people conducting just this sort of research. Neuroeconomist Paul Zak says,

> ... market exchange itself may lead to a society where individuals have stronger character values. The clearest evidence for this is the studies of fairness in small-scale societies conducted by Henrich and his colleagues. They showed that *the likelihood of making fair offers to a stranger in one's society*

is more strongly predicted by the extent of trade in markets than any other factor they have found. Exchange is inherently other-regarding—both you and I must benefit if exchange is to occur.[2]

Zak concludes that, as a matter of empirically verifiable fact, market societies induce people to play fair. People from market societies characteristically know how to put themselves in their trading partner's shoes. People from non-market societies do not.

Economists like to conduct experiments (using large amounts of real money) in which participants have the opportunity to cheat and swindle each other or to play fairly. Joseph Henrich, Herbert Gintis, and other moral psychologists and behavioral economists have tested a large number of variables to see which factors tend to make people play fair or cheat. These studies disconfirm rather than support the thesis that markets make people more selfish overall.

Gintis further summarizes these studies:

> Movements for religious and lifestyle tolerance, gender equality, and democracy have flourished and triumphed in societies governed by market exchange, and nowhere else.
>
> My colleagues and I found dramatic evidence of this positive relationship between markets and morality in our study of fairness in simple societies—hunter-gatherers, horticulturalists, nomadic herders, and small-scale sedentary farmers—in Africa, Latin America, and Asia. Twelve professional anthropologists and economists visited these societies and played standard ultimatum, public goods, and trust games with the locals. As in advanced industrial societies, members of all of these societies exhibited a considerable degree of moral motivation and a willingness to sacrifice monetary gain to achieve fairness and reciprocity, even in anonymous one-shot situations. More interesting for our purposes, we measured the degree of market exposure and cooperation in production for each society, and we found that the ones that regularly engage in market exchange with larger surrounding groups have more pronounced fairness motivations. The notion that the market economy makes people greedy, selfish, and amoral is simply fallacious.[3]

As it turns out, empirically, the strongest *cultural* predictor that participants will play fairly with strangers is how market-oriented their society is.

Note that this is not just the result of one set of studies. Either studies produce ~~other~~ similar results. Zak and Stephen Knack have shown that market societies also tend to be high-trust societies, while non-market societies tend to be low-trust societies.[4] Omar Al-Ubayli, Daniel Houser, and colleagues have shown that "priming" people with words related to markets and trade makes them *more* (not less!) trusting, trustworthy, and fair in experiments.[5] That is, when we get people into the market mindset, they become *nicer*. Mitchell Hoffman and John Morgan found, contrary to everyone's expectations, that "adult populations deliberately selected from two cutthroat internet industries—domain trading and adult entertainment (pornography)" are "more pro-social than [undergraduate] students: they are more altruistic, trusting, trustworthy, and lying averse."[6]

Another study by Gabriele Camera and his colleagues finds slightly more ambiguous results. The BBC reported that the study discovered that "money can reduce trust in groups."[7] But that's misleading. A better summary is this. Camera and his colleagues played a series of experimental games in which people could choose to cooperate or not, and could choose to be generous or selfish when cooperating.[8] They found that introducing money into small groups made players more selfish and less cooperative, but that introducing money into large groups made them less selfish and more cooperative. As we discussed in Chapter 7, the negative half of this experiment is not so surprising—in our culture, introducing money into small-scale interactions signals estrangement. If you introduce money into a small-scale relationship, you signal a lack of trust and an intention to have a more instrumental relationship. Yet, the positive half of the results cohere with the other studies we've discussed, which find markets make strangers nicer to one another. In large-scale relationships, introducing money enables trust.

Markets and Trust

Institutionalist economics often argues that market exchange does not rely upon self-interest alone. It also relies upon—and at the same time tends to reinforce—mutual trust, reciprocity, and trustworthiness.[9] Market systems require a high degree of generalized trust and trustworthiness to function. As an example, note that we could fly to Hong Kong, flash a credit card in front of strangers, and rent a luxury car worth more than most people's houses, all on our promise to pay. Somehow, market societies make this promise mean something.[10]

According to the Fraser Institute, these are the top 10 most free-market, capitalist countries in the world, in order: Hong Kong, Singapore, New Zealand, Switzerland, Australia, Canada, Bahrain, Mauritius, Finland, and Chile. Denmark is ranked #16.[11] The *Wall Street Journal* and Heritage Foundation, in their Index of Economic Freedom, produce a similar ranking. Their top 10 are: Hong Kong, Singapore, Australia, New Zealand, Switzerland, Canada, Chile, Mauritius, Denmark, and the United States. We can break these overall rankings down in rankings on particular kinds of economic freedom. For instance, in the 2012 rankings, Denmark scores 99.1 in business freedom, 90.0 in investment freedom, and 90.0 in financial freedom. In comparison, the US scores 91.1, 70.0, and 70.0 respectively on these measures. (100 here = perfect freedom.)

Now, consider that, according to Transparency International, these are the top 10 least corrupt countries: Denmark, New Zealand, Singapore, Finland, Sweden, Canada, the Netherlands, Australia, Switzerland, and Norway.

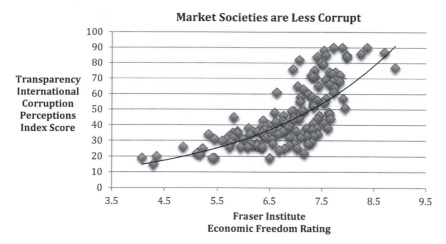

FIGURE 11.1 Economic Freedom vs. Corruption

You may notice quite a bit of overlap between the most economically free and the least corrupt countries. That's not a coincidence. As Figure 11.1 above shows, there is a positive correlation between countries' degree of economic freedom (as measured by the Fraser Institute's economic freedom ratings) and countries' lack of corruption (as measured by Transparency International's Corruption Perceptions Index[12]). Note also that the most marketized societies tend also to be significantly *above* the trend line. (For our statistically savvy readers, in Figure 11.1, correlation = 0.7267, and so R^2 = 0.5842.)

Benjamin Barber claims that markets corrupt politics, but in fact the most marketized societies are also the least corrupt. On the contrary, one of the most consistent findings of public choice economics, the subfield of economics that studies government behavior, is that politics corrupts markets. The more politicized an economy becomes, the more private actors try to rig regulations and the law to cheat consumers and competitors.[13] Instead of trying to keep the nasty market away from pristine politics, we should be trying to keep nasty politics away from the market.

In fact, whenever political scientists or economists plot trustworthiness, lack of corruption, trust, or citizens' generosity against economic freedom, they find a very strong *positive* correlation. So, for instance, people in market societies give more to charity and volunteer more than people in non-market societies.[14] Part of the reason they do so is that they are richer and so can afford to do so. (We don't know if that's supposed to be an objection or a point in our favor.) But even controlling for income, they still give more.

Pets: A Small Test Case

Let's consider some more mundane micro-examples. Consider again the question of commodifying pets, which we discussed in Chapter 6. People sometimes buy and sell pets from pet stores or shelters, they sometimes acquire pets as gifts, or they sometimes acquire pets through some other exchange not governed by market norms. Someone advancing the Corruption Objection should check to see whether otherwise identical pets belonging to demographically identical owners end up being treated worse if they were purchased rather than acquired through non-market means. Or we might want to test to see whether otherwise identical cultures treat pets better or worse if one marketizes pets and the other does not.

The Corruption Objection seems to predict that we should see differences in how people treat and/or regard their pets depending on the method or means by which they acquired those pets. In particular, we ought to see not just that people treat purchased pets less well than they treat pets acquired outside the market, but also that purchased pets are treated as mere use objects, while non-purchased pets are treated with respect. We ought to see a decline over the years in how well purchased pets are treated.

There may indeed be such behavioral differences, but this needs to be discovered through empirical research. Our own suspicion was that we would find no such differences, controlling for the antecedent attitudes of the people who acquire a pet. Put differently, we suspect that the means of acquiring a dog or cat has no independent impact on the behavior or attitude of those who acquire pets. Pets will or will not be cherished, cared for, loved, and so on, whether or not they are acquired through markets. Our suspicion may be wrong. However, the *other side*, the side advancing the Corruption Objection, bears the burden of proof. After all, they are making a controversial empirical claim about what markets do to our character.

Instead of just registering our suspicion here, we went and checked to see what research is out there on this very question. We found none that would support the Corruption Objection in this case. We found one paper that found that people who consider themselves "guardians" rather than "owners" of their pets tend to treat their pets better.[15] The authors of this paper were careful to say that they did not detect any causation from the "Guardian Campaign," which seeks to change the legal language and standing of pets to their keepers (from owners to guardians, in the legal sense) in order to produce more humane treatment. However, this paper did not test whether buying and selling pets resulted in worse treatment than acquiring the pet through other means. Most of the self-described "guardians" purchased their pets, while many of the self-described "owners" did not. So, this paper supports the hypothesis that thinking of your pet as mere property means you treat your pet worse, but it does not support and may even undermine the hypothesis that buying and selling pets causes us to think of them as mere property.

A special report in the *Journal of American Veterinary Medicine* tested a wide range of factors to see what determines the level of veterinary care pets receive.[16] In fact, purchased pets get better care than pets acquired from shelters, but, as far as we can tell from the paper, that is because people usually buy dogs but acquire cats for free, and dogs receive much more and better care than cats do. Not surprisingly, people with more money tend to give their pets better care—they can afford to do so.[17] At any rate, there's again no evidence here that marketizing pets leads to them being treated as mere commodities.

All this empirical work is not the final word. Further investigations might reveal that that Corruption Objection is correct. It's possible when all the evidence is in, it will come out in the critics' favor. But, at this point, the social science is on our side.

Markets and Tolerance: How Pricing Labor Ennobles

Economist Gary Becker argued in a 1957 book that the market tends to eliminate unjust discrimination.[18] He says, suppose that people have a "taste for discrimination"—they prefer to hire white workers instead of equally high quality black workers. This will tend to reduce blacks' wages. However, this gives firms willing to hire blacks an advantage. Black labor becomes a bargain. Firms can hire blacks at a lower rate, sell their products for less (because the labor costs are lower) and make higher profits. The more other people discriminate against blacks, the more a white factory owner would benefit from hiring them. The market thus *punishes* taste discrimination because it makes discrimination come at the expense of people's other selfish interests.

Becker's argument is not mere speculation. Economist Linda Gorman says South Africa provides a good test case. In the early 1900s, despite threats of violence and legal sanctions, white mine owners fired highly paid white workers in order to hire lower paid blacks. The South African government had to pass the apartheid laws to stop them from hiring blacks.[19]

Or, take Jim Crow Laws. The economist Jennifer Roback says the economics of the streetcar business weighed heavily against providing separate compartments. Jim Crow was expensive. Train companies lost money by having to run extra train cars. Lunch counters lost money by having to supply twice as many bathrooms. Southern states thus *required* private companies to mistreat blacks. The laws were there because many businesses did not discriminate until forced to do so. If you read old newspaper editorials from the Southern states under Jim Crow, you'll frequently find editors complaining about how greedy businessmen just chase the dollar and are unwilling to uphold the moral ideal of segregation.[20]

Roback adds that the Southern states had a wide range of laws designed to stop blacks from competing for work. Enticement laws forbade white farm owners from trying to hire black farmworkers away from other farmers during the planting or harvesting season. Black farmworkers who tried to leave their jobs for higher-paying jobs could be thrown in jail. Vagrancy laws required blacks to be employed at all times. Any unemployed black man was considered a vagrant and could be put on a chain gang. Thus blacks could not search for better employment; they had to stick with whatever job they had. Emigrant-agent laws forbade white recruiters from enticing laborers to leave their current cities or states to take jobs elsewhere. These and other laws and regulations were created in order to *stop* the market from helping blacks.

Capitalism gives people an economic incentive to overlook their differences and instead work together. And, once people work together, they tend to stop caring about those differences. This is why market societies are usually the most tolerant.[21] Competitive market pressures and the desire for profit push people to see past racial or religious divides. This explains Voltaire's observation that at the London Stock Exchange, people of all races and creeds came together to do business.[22]

A critic might respond here with a claim familiar to most Americans: "Women earn 77 cents to the dollar for what men earn." This sounds like a clear counter-example to Becker's thesis, but it's not. What's really going on is that the average working woman earns about 77% of what the average working man earns. However, as labor economists Claudia Goldin and Lawrence Katz explain, this doesn't mean that an otherwise identical man and woman working side-by-side at the same job get paid radically different amounts. Instead, women tend to work fewer hours (outside the home) than men, even when working full-time. Women tend to take more sick leave and time off to care for children. Women also tend to choose jobs that pay less. Once just these factors are taken into account, the wage gap closes to 91 cents on the dollar. This doesn't yet mean the other 9 cents is discrimination—there may be other factors at work, such as men being aggressive in negotiating and asking for raises.[23] Goldin says, for instance, that fresh out of an MBA program, men have only a small wage advantage over women, but after fifteen years, the gap widens.[24]

A critic might respond that women tending to choose different jobs that tend to pay less, or tending to take care of children more and thus working fewer hours outside the home, reflects sexism. Perhaps. Perhaps this results from contingent and therefore modifiable sociological relationships and gender roles. Perhaps it results from less modifiable gender tendencies that result from evolutionary selection pressures. We take no stance on this here. Instead, we just note, first, that the market can't always fix what isn't brought to market. We also note that just as market societies are the least racist and homophobic societies, they are also the least sexist. It's too bad markets don't completely fix the problem, just as it's too bad Advil doesn't cure all headaches. But it would be bizarre and backward to then blame markets for sexism, just as it would be to then blame Advil for headaches.

Notes

1 One example of an a priori argument that markets are corrupting is Bowles 1998.
2 Zak 2008, xv.
3 http://www.bostonreview.net/gintis-giving-economists-their-due
4 Zak and Knack 2001.
5 Al-Ubayli, Houser, Nye, Paganelli, and Pan 2013.
6 Hoffman and Morgan 2013.

7 http://www.bbc.co.uk/news/science-environment-23623157
8 Camera, Casari, and Bigoni 2013.
9 E.g., Ostrom 2003; De Soto 2000; Richerson and Boyd 2008; McCloskey, 2011; North 1990; Zak and Knack 2001.
10 For more on the role of trust, see Schmidtz and Brennan 2010.
11 Gwartney, Lawson, and Hall 2012.
12 Transparency International 2012.
13 Mueller 2003, 333–58.
14 For example, market-oriented societies tend to be the most giving and charitable. See the Charity Aids Foundation 2012.
15 Carlisle-Frank and Frank 2005.
16 Lue, Pantenburg, and Crawford 2008. For similar results, see Slater, di Nardo, Pedocini, dalla Villa, Candeloro, Alessandrini, and del Papa 2008.
17 Grier 2006 tells a story about how contemporary American attitudes toward pet stewardship came to be. An increase in wealth and leisure is a significant part of the story.
18 Becker 1957.
19 Gorman 2013.
20 Roback 1986.
21 E.g., see Berggren and Nilsson 2013; Jha 2013.
22 Jha 2013.
23 Bertrand, Goldin, and Katz 2010; Goldin and Katz 2008; Stevens, Bavetta, and Gist 1993; Kaman and Hartel 1994.
24 http://freakonomics.com/2010/01/28/superfreakonomics-book-club-goldin-and-katz-on-the-male-female-wage-gap/

12

THE CROWDING OUT OBJECTION

The Problem

Closely related to the objection that certain markets make us more selfish is the objection that certain markets crowd out or reduce our intrinsic motivation. The complaint is that people are motivated to do certain things for their own sake. However, the worry is that once we start paying them to do those things, their intrinsic motivation vanishes. Virtue stops being its own reward once we start rewarding virtue.

How do different modes of exchange affect our motivations? As we keep stressing, this is an empirical question. The field of research that tries to answer this question is still relatively recent and undeveloped. That said, there is a great deal of work that has already been done on the market for labor, and on different compensation schemes. In particular, a great deal of management research looks at the impact of quantity and type of pay on effort, job satisfaction, or performance.[1]

It seems like commonsense economics that as you offer workers more money, you should see an increase in the quantity of work effort supplied or in productivity.[2] Paying more for a particular behavior should result in more of that behavior.

But, it turns out, this result does not appear to always hold. What social psychologists call the "overjustification effect" and what economists call the "crowding-out effect" sometimes works against this expected result. Sometimes, researchers have to their surprise discovered, paying more leads to getting less. Sometimes, introducing an external financial reward where once there was none can lead to less of the desired behavior. What gives?

The Overjustification Effect

Many of us are intrinsically motivated to engage in some activities. We read books because we love to read, we work on puzzles because it delights us, and we sometimes donate blood because we're moved by the plight of others. When that is so, an external reward can sometimes short-circuit our enjoyment of the activity.

Suppose you see a sign at your workplace asking you to donate blood. The sign tells you that there is a shortage of blood, and that many people needlessly suffer for want of something that, as the Canadian Blood Services put it in a recent marketing campaign, "is in you to give." You put some thought into it, reflect on the good that you might do, and decide to make the trip to the local blood bank. At the blood bank, you notice that the staff are handing out checks for $25 to the people who donate blood.

"That's great!" some economists might say. You now have two reasons to give blood—you want to help, and you get $25. If the first reason isn't good enough for some people, maybe the second reason will be. Or if you are moved to donate blood just a little by a desire to do something good for others, maybe the $25 will push you over the line, and get you into the blood bank. We should see more people giving blood.

"That may be bad," some psychologists might say. When we have two reasons to do something, sometimes, instead of the two reasons adding up, we get one reason *replacing* the other. Sometimes external incentives, like money, do the opposite of what they're intended to do. Instead of more people giving blood, we might see fewer. If $25 is not enough to move you to donate blood, then you won't. This is so even if, prior to the offer of money, you were inclined to donate blood for altruistic reasons.

How could that be? Psychologists offer a number of reasons for this effect, most often called the overjustification effect, but occasionally referred to as the corruption effect. We can call them Control, Signal, and Frame.

Control: Imagine having the following internal monologue. "Why am I planning to give blood?" you might ask yourself. The answer you want to give is "because I'm moved by the plight of others, because I want to help, and because I've decided that this is a good thing to do." You want to say that you are internally motivated. You're not being pushed or prodded into doing it, you're acting of your own free will. But now you see someone waving a $25 check in front of your nose. You reason that that someone must think that they can push and prod you into giving blood. "If they think they can control me," you say to yourself, "they've got another thing coming!" And you get back in your Infiniti, and drive off without giving blood.

This kind of internal monologue is what self-determination theorists offer as an explanation for the overjustification effect. Self-determination theorists are so called because they believe that each of us places a high value on being self-determined, or self-directed. We value our autonomy, and we get prickly when others try to control our behavior by offering rewards or doling out punishments. An external reward can impair either our sense of self-determination, or our self-esteem. The external reward can be perceived as *controlling* our behavior. If we were to maintain our intrinsic motivation in the face of an external reward we would be overjustified, and so we adjust by lowering or eliminating our intrinsic motivation. If the value of the $25 check is not enough to overcome the value to you of being self-determined, then you won't donate blood, even if you would have but for the offer of $25.

Signal: One prominent alternative explanation is based on signaling. When we choose to do something like donate blood, or vote in an election, sometimes our reason is to signal to others that we are a certain sort of person. The kind of person who donates blood is an altruistic person, moved by concern for the well-being of others. The kind of person who votes is a civic-minded person, moved by gratitude for the sacrifices of those who fought for the right to vote, and moved by public-mindedness and concern for the common good. When we introduce an incentive, like $25, we introduce noise into the signal. We no longer clearly signal that we are altruistic or civic-minded, we may instead be interpreted as just wanting $25. We can imagine a skeptical inquisitor asking about our recent blood donation, or our trip to the local voting booth. If they were to find out that we were paid, or were threatened with a fine if we didn't do it, then they are likely to be skeptical about the purity of our motives. The goodness of our intentions is drowned out by the noise of money. So we are less likely to do the good thing, even if we intended to.

Frame: Psychologists (and survey-writers, marketers, and politicians) have long known that what people decide to do (or say, or buy, or vote for) depends on how they frame the question, on what words and terms they use to describe the issue, problem or decision. How we frame a decision can alter how we behave through the mechanism of engaging heuristics about what it is appropriate or fitting for us to do. So, rather than changing our motivation, which remains constant, the framing hypothesis seeks to explain the overjustification effect by suggesting that certain cues can alter what we take to be the appropriate method or procedure for making decisions. The relevant question becomes "what kind of a situation is this?" rather than, "who's in charge here?" or "what does this say about me?" It is not about the agent, but about the context the agent finds herself in.

Ann Tenbrunsel and David Messick have done a great deal of work using this approach. They suggest that different cues in our environment alert us to what considerations are relevant for making decisions. With frames that cue us to mind the well-being of others, we are more likely to engage in decision-making that is cooperative and conscientious. This view has empirical support. Some studies appear to show that presenting the Bible to subjects prior to an economic game results in players making fairer offers, or playing in less selfish ways.[3] Other frames cue us to pay more attention to ourselves, to calculate what is to our advantage, and to be more selfish. Some studies appear to show that at least in some contexts, the introduction of money functions as a frame that leads to more selfish and less cooperative behavior. This was so in small groups (but not large ones) in the study we discussed earlier by Gabriele Camera and colleagues. In a tragic real-world example, engineers at NASA raised worries about the safety of the ill-fated *Challenger*. They said it was too dangerous to fly. Instead of accepting their judgment, NASA asked them to think from the perspective of management, to think like managers would. Unfortunately, framing the question this way made the engineers overcome their reluctance, and they okayed the launch.[4]

Tenbrunsel and Messick call frames that make us more cooperative and conscientious "ethical frames," and those that make us more selfish and calculating "business frames." Within a business frame, standard economic cost-benefit analysis and calculation dominates. The profit motive dominates. This frame makes us behave more like homo economicus. The ethical frame, on the other hand, frames decisions in ways that make us aware of our obligations to others.[5]

The offer of money can be perceived as controlling. The offer of money can introduce noise into an altruistic signal. The offer of money can engage a business frame, cueing us to behave more like homo economicus, and less like intrinsically motivated, conscientious, and cooperative people. With these tools, we can now explain a number of worries about money and markets. Previously, we discussed the possibility of paying for reading. Sandel might worry that the overjustification effect may trump our intrinsic motivation to read. Offering money may undermine the process of coming to love reading for its own sake, or for the many and varied pleasures of reading. Sandel could also worry that use of money as compensation for reading can frame the reading as an instrumental tool in the pursuit of the real end, that of getting paid. And once we're in a homo economicus mood, we then might be less prone to enjoy reading for its own sake.

Richard Titmuss argued in *The Gift Relationship* that paying for blood donations would sometimes result in fewer willing donors, and would, at other times, result in worse quality blood. Titmuss argued that compensating for blood donations would substitute our altruistic motives for selfish financial ones; people would no longer be engaged in a gift relationship, but would, instead, be involved in a simple financial transaction, an exchange of commodities. Elizabeth Anderson[6] describes the siting of a nuclear waste facility as another example of the over-justification effect or a framing effect in action. Swiss citizens did not want to have a waste facility located near them because they no longer thought of themselves as fellow citizens engaged in the joint task of figuring out the best location for the waste, but as entitled property owners fighting about the reasonable compensation for the hassles involved in living near such waste, just as soon as an offer of financial compensation was added to the survey.

The overjustification or the crowding effect is widely regarded as a significant feather in the anti-commodification cap. Similarly, if money and markets engage a business, rather than an ethical, frame, then we might want both to play a less prominent role, at least in some domains.

In order for this research to count as a feather in the anti-commodification cap, we have to keep in mind what the anti-commodification thesis claims. The claim is not that there are better and worse ways of having a market in blood, reading, kidneys, and so on. If that were the claim, then it would merely be a claim within business ethics, compatible with commodification of blood, reading, kidneys, and so on. Instead, the anti-commodification thesis is the claim that there are some things that should not be bought and sold; that there are some things that ought not to be commodities *at all*. There are *domains* where money should not be used; there are *domains* where market exchanges should be verboten. The claim is not that there are better and worse ways to pay or compensate someone, or better and worse kinds of markets *within* some domains, but that some domains should be sealed off from money and markets entirely.

If we could show that there's a way of having a market in kidneys, for example, that avoids all of the objections anti-commodification theorists offer, then that would effectively undermine the anti-commodification view with respect to kidneys. We would reduce the anti-commodification thesis about how kidneys are not commodities at all, to a business ethics thesis about how best to sell a kidney. This is what we try to show below. We will try to demonstrate that the overjustification and business frame feathers in the anti-commodification cap are barbless; that the overjustification effect is underjustification for the anti-commodification thesis; that the ethical frame is not incompatible with the market.

Time, Place, Manner: What the Research Shows

Judy Cameron conducted two separate meta-analyses on the overjustification effect with a different co-author for each. One analyzed 96 experimental studies that compared subjects who received an extrinsic reward to those who received no reward.[7] The other assessed a quarter century of research on the overjustification effect. The result for the former meta-analysis was that, "overall, reward does not decrease intrinsic motivation." A small negative effect was obtained only when "expected tangible rewards are given to individuals simply for doing a task." In the case of the latter meta-analysis, the conclusion was that the crowding-out effect of extrinsic rewards, like money, on intrinsic interest and creativity was only observable "under highly restricted, easily avoidable conditions."[8] They also concluded that getting a positive effect on generalized creativity from extrinsic rewards is "easily attainable using procedures derived from behavior theory."

This work, however, has been challenged. In particular, Deci, Koestner, and Ryan took issue with the details of the study, conducted a meta-analysis of their own and found that, contrary to the results of the earlier meta-analyses, the overjustification effect held.[9] Since it makes our task harder, let's just stipulate that Deci is right, and that, at least with respect to whether or not the overjustification effect obtained to a significant extent, Cameron and her co-authors are wrong. Let us grant the anti-commodification theorists the strongest version of the overjustification effect. Is the strongest version of the overjustification effect avoidable by altering the participants, the means of payment, the mode of payment, the mode of the market, or the price? Put differently, does the overjustification effect function as an in-principle objection to markets and money as such within some domains, or is it merely another instance of a time, place or manner objection to markets?

Psychologists and economists working on these fields point out that the over-justification effect obtains under certain very specific conditions. Bruno S. Frey explains that we can expect a crowding-out effect when the external reward is regarded by the subject as "controlling" their behavior.[10] Within self-determination theory, scholars have abandoned talk of intrinsic versus extrinsic motivation in favor of a refinement of extrinsic motivation into autonomous versus controlled motivation.[11] The distinction here is between perceiving oneself to be guided by one's own free choice and volition even with an external reward as the object, as opposed to perceiving oneself to be controlled, seduced, or coerced by the external reward.

On this view, not all external rewards undermine intrinsic motivation. Verbal rewards can be perceived as informational (as applauding competence, for example) or as controlling. Grades can be "controlling" when a student perceives herself as studying and reading purely or primarily for the sake of the grade. But it is not a necessary feature of the fact that grades are awarded that intrinsic motivation is crowded-out. In classroom contexts where autonomy is supported and emphasized, students can internalize the reward system and thereby maintain or enhance their intrinsic motivation.[12] Grades can be regarded as a symbol of achievement, competence, or be regarded as part and parcel of the activity itself. David Rosenfield, Robert Folger, and Harold F. Adelman found that intrinsic motivation declined when presented with an external reward, unless the reward was seen to reflect competence.[13] It is not an external reward as such that generates the crowding-out effect, but only rewards given in a context where we either perceive ourselves to be motivated by that reward, or believe that we will be perceived by others as being so moved.

The overjustification effect is not a reason to stop grading students. At best, it's a compelling argument to grade them in ways that are sensitive to the effect, with some ways of grading students being better than others. But what's true of grading is true of compensating within a market. At best, it's a compelling argument to compensate people in ways that are sensitive to the effect. And just as there are many different ways of grading students and providing feedback, so there are many different ways of compensating someone and paying them. The crowding effect isn't evidence against grading, that would be overgeneralizing the point. At best, it's an argument against grading in this way or that way. The same is true of the anti-commodification thesis: at best, the crowding effect can support the view that we shouldn't pay people like this or like that, but it cannot underwrite the claim that we ought not compensate people for something or other at all. Unless there is no way of compensating someone without generating the crowding effect, this effect is merely a matter of business ethics, not a matter of the moral limits of markets.

The same holds for the research on the framing effect as well. So, for example, despite identical payoff structures, M. Pillutla and X. P. Chen managed to get more cooperation when a dilemma was framed in a noneconomic way, as compared to framing it in an economic way.[14] But how we frame what we're doing does not change what we're doing. It only changes what we take to be the appropriate calculation for determining what we will do. If we want to avoid the business frame, we need to make use of ethical frame cues. That we can do this while engaging in market activities should be obvious. Charities often attempt to loosen our grip on our wallets by making use of devices that put us in a charitable and caring frame of mind.

Anti-commodification theorists sometimes appear to overlook the fact that this literature is often geared towards those who operate in the market, particularly managers. The literature is supposed to guide how managers do their job. As guides for managers within a market context, this research is a contribution to business ethics, not a piece of evidence counting in favor of the anti-commodification thesis.

Despite it being called a "business frame," there is nothing about the nature of markets or money that requires the use of it. It may turn out to be the case that what it means to be an ethical manager is to use cost-benefit analysis less, or rarely, or not at all, and so they should be guided in structuring their employer–employee relationships in ways that avoid business frames.

When Money Isn't Money

What is true of verbal rewards and grades is true of money as well. So, for example, Mellstrom and Johannesson discovered that a sum of money paid to women for blood donation lowered willingness to donate blood.[15] But they also found that the effect disappeared when they paid in the form of a charitable donation to a charity of the subject's choice. The form the payment took did not cast doubt on the subjects' intrinsic motivations, and so did not crowd it out. In our parlance, the altruistic signal of blood donation was lost in the noise of a financial reward, but was regained when the option of charitable giving was introduced as a substitute form of payment.

Awards function similarly. For some kind of awards, a financial component may seem less than fitting. We can apply the arguments of anti-commodification theorists to explain this apparent incongruence between the nature of the award, and the nature of money. Consider several general kinds of possible awards: an award for exceptionally fulfilling one's civic duty, an award for excellence in undergraduate teaching, or an award to recognize the highest achievement in literature. In each of these cases, if the award is coupled with some kind of financial compensation, we can predict that the meaning of the award may be sullied or profaned.

While that is so, we have awards in each of these categories that do no such thing. So, for example, the Nobel Prize for literature comes with a cool one million dollars. And yet, no one believes this prize is less meaningful, less significant, or profaned by the inclusion of the financial component. In 1985, Michael Sandel received the Harvard–Radcliffe Phi Beta Kappa award for undergraduate teaching. Each year, undergraduate students select up to three professors at Harvard for this award. The award comes with a check for $100. It is hard to believe that the award is sullied by the money. If it were, Sandel would probably not highlight it on his publicly-available bio, but he does (and with good reason). Finally, and most illustratively, consider the Museum of the City of New York award for improving the quality of life of city residents. Carruthers and Espeland discuss the case of Ada Louise Huxtable, an architecture critic and historian, who received an award of $24 from the Museum of the City of New York on July 25, 1996. The award was delivered by the mayor, Rudy Giuliani at the time, in a ceremony full of pomp and pageantry, with many important and significant personages in the audience. The strange sum is the precise amount the Dutch gave to Native Americans in exchange for Manhattan Island.

In each of these cases, either the money changes the nature of the award not at all, or, if it does or were to, thoughtfully choosing the sum or its presentation can impact the meaning, and avoid profaning it. There is no overjustification effect by analogy at work here. The $24 Museum of the City of New York prize is comical. We can imagine that, for recipients of this award, the value of the awarded money is much greater than its economic value and its ability to purchase some object. Rather than spend it on any object at all, it would make sense if the check were never cashed, and was instead framed in Huxtable's office. The signal that is sent in the carefully planned ceremony for recipients of this award is clear to those present. It is not that the contribution of people like Huxtable should be understood as worth "merely" $24, the $24 is to be understood ironically, as signaling a value much, much greater.

If money just were an impersonal and fungible object, none of this would make much sense. Clearly, we are not always indifferent between $24 and objects we value at $24. Indeed, we are not always indifferent between a particular check for $24 and the same amount in any financial equivalent, like two tens and four singles, or two tens and two toonies, or a different check for $24. The restaurateur with a framed five-dollar-bill behind him isn't going to trade it for the five in your pocket. That five dollar bill is a "special" five dollar bill. To the restaurateur, its value is much greater.

If all that is true, then notice that Sandel's Oxford professor who objected to a monetary tip from a student applied one particular interpretive heuristic to the tip,[16] and concluded that the student thought of education and teaching as a mere commodity, although he could have done otherwise. When, in the movie *A Beautiful Mind*, John Nash is given pens from fellow professors at the Princeton Faculty Club, the ritual is suffused with meaning. The gift of a pen is a sign of respect. Princeton University has explained that there is no such actual tradition, and that this didn't really happen. But it doesn't matter, because the fictional portrayal in the movie is not so absurd as to strike us as deeply implausible or incoherent. A gift of money could also function as just such a sign, if only the Oxford professor's student had figured out how to do it, or if only the Oxford professor wasn't so stubbornly attached to his preferred interpretive schema. The very same can be done with a gift of money for reading, if it were surrounded by some kind of ritual or ceremony that helped the child see the significance of the reward as symbolically more meaningful than the sum.

Carruthers and Espeland explain that "[l]ike all other social objects, money has meaning that depends on its use and context. Such uses are not, however, idiosyncratic. Nor is context ad hoc. Both are socially structured in patterned ways we can discern."[17] Using Wittgenstein's views on language, they argue that, "[t]he meaning of money, like the meaning of words, cannot be reduced to that which it represents. Thus, it is misguided to try and identify universally representational properties of money and link these to its meaning. The meaning of money does not depend on some characteristic that is common to all money. Instead, its meaning depends on what people in a particular context do with it."[18] For Carruthers and Espeland, how we interpret money depends on its "flow"—where it comes from and where it eventually goes.

In the context of a labor market, Amy E. Mickel and Lisa A. Barron identify four variables for the creation of "symbolic meaning" that can generate more "bang for the buck."[19] They discovered that how much and when you are paid are not the only variables that can impact effort, satisfaction, and performance. According to them, "who distributes the monetary reward, why the reward is distributed, how the reward is distributed, and who receives it" all matter in creating symbolic meanings that can further motivate employees, and give them greater job satisfaction.

Thus, to say that money as such or markets as such commodify some good or practice is to ignore the fact that commodification only occurs when money is interpreted in some specific way. The same is true of the application of the overjustification effect to buttress the anti-commodification thesis. The effect simply cannot be used as support for the anti-commodification thesis. Instead, and at best, it can be used to help guide us in market design by pointing to instances or cases where the overjustification effect trumps the relative price effect. But if we alter the manner of payment, as we have argued, we can alter the associated interpretive schema, and thereby avoid a commodification attitude, or the implication that markets and money are somehow intrinsically tied to commodification. They are not.

Auctions

Viviana Zelizer has demonstrated that money can be regarded as a gift, as compensation, and as an entitlement. Her empirical work shows that we construct social meaning systems that define a particular act of receiving or giving money in different ways. Carruthers and Espeland, as well as Mickel and Barron furthered that view by demonstrating that altering the manner, altering how we are paid, can alter the symbolic meaning of that money. To claim that, in principle, there are some things that do not belong on the labor market is to claim that there is no manner of compensation—who, when, why, to whom, and how much—that overcomes whatever the moral objection is. Anti-commodification theorists have not done that work. They are not entitled to the claim that there are some things that money shouldn't buy in the market for services. They may, at best, be entitled to the claim that there are some services that ought not to be bought and sold in this or that particular manner. So they are entitled to a claim within business ethics, rather than to a claim at the level of normative moral or political philosophy.

In the market for labor, who, how, when, why, and how much each play a significant role in constructing a social meaning to money that may differ, sometimes sharply, from the common definition found in economics textbooks. In the market for goods, how they are sold may also impact how we regard the buyers, the sellers, and the object of sale itself. While employers may ritualize the payment of bonuses and make a ceremony of certain kinds of compensation, we have a set of different kinds of markets with long-standing histories and traditions.

One particularly interesting mode of market exchange is the auction. There are many different kinds of auctions. David Easley and Jon Kleinberg describe four popular types of auctions. The Ascending-bid auction, which is also called an English auction, involves a seller who "gradually raises the price, bidders drop out until finally only one bidder remains, and that bidder wins the object at this final price." Descending-bid auctions, also called Dutch auctions, involve a seller who "gradually lowers the price from some high initial value until the first moment when some bidder accepts and pays the current price." There are First-price sealed-bid auctions, where bidders write their bid and place it in an envelope, with the seller opening all of the envelopes at the same time, and rewards the highest bid with the item. Finally, they describe a Second-price sealed-bid auction, also called a Vickrey auction, which functions the very same as the First-price sealed-bid auction except that the highest bidder gets the item while paying the second-highest bid.[20] There are other kinds of auctions too, including an All-pay auction, where bidders submit a bid, the highest bidder gets the auctioned item, but all bidders pay. Easley and Kleinberg say that this "seems counter-intuitive" but they explain that this is how we can model political lobbying activities. Lobbyists are hired, bids are offered, and someone gets the lobbied-for contract or other item. But all of the companies had to pay for the lobbyists, and so all of the companies had to spend money even though only one company wins. Spending on lobbying can be considered a "bid."

Anti-commodification theorists depend on these claims. They tell us that people will exhibit rationally self-interested behavior in market contexts, that we will regard the objects for sale with a commodification attitude. On first blush, the auction appears to be a perfect illustration of the way markets can push us to focus more on ourselves, and how the structure of a market exchange can lead us to have a commodification attitude. Arjan Appadurai, for example, insists that "[a]uctions accentuate the commodity dimension of objects (such as paintings) in a manner that might well be regarded as deeply inappropriate in other contexts."[21]

A great deal of economic work on auctions appears to lend support to this view. Economists focus on what it is rational for actors to do in different kinds of auctions. They also try to figure out what we can expect from the different kinds of auctions by modeling people as rational, self-interested maximizers who know how much they value the objects put up for auction. Easley and Kleinberg do this. They assume that "each bidder has an *intrinsic value* for the item being auctioned," which they also refer to as the bidder's "true value."[22] These assumptions permit economists to go about their business. And much of their business is the business of modeling. What functions as a set of assumptions for purposes of modeling in the economic literature appears to function as an accurate depiction of what happens in real-world auctions for anti-commodification theorists.

But the homo economicus of economic models doesn't really appear in real-world auctions. Or so says Charles W. Smith,[23] an economic sociologist who produced the seminal work on the sociology of auctions. Perhaps for those of us on the outside looking in, as spectators, all we see is a crass battle of self-interested buyers trying to outbid each other. But for the participants to auctions, the kind of auction, the physical location, the particular participants, and how it's done all combine for a deeply meaningful performance, a performance that sometimes accentuates the commodity dimension of objects, but often times decommodifies those dimensions in the act of auctioning off an object.

Auctions "flourish," Smith tells us "in situations in which the conventional ways of establishing price and ownership are inadequate either because costs cannot be established, the item is old or used, there is something special or unusual about the item, ownership is in question, different persons assert special claims, or for some other reason." Although some insist that attaching financial values to special, unusual, or unique items is deeply controversial, as is the further question of who ought to have the object in their possession, Smith explains that participants in auctions see the auction as "socially acceptable" and "legitimate" both for figuring out how much it's worth, as well as who is to have it. "Put slightly differently, auctions serve as rites of passage for objects shrouded in ambiguity and uncertainty."

What Smith calls the "social structure" of auctions is similar to what we call the time, place, and manner of markets: " ... the influence of time, place, and situation, and the importance of past and ongoing practices, all play a role in establishing values."[24] This is unlike the assumptions of economics for modeling behavior in auctions, since economists assume away the causal influence of time, place, and manner, or the "social structure" of auctions in the outcomes of auctions.[25]

Rather than "accentuate the commodity aspect" of an item, auctions help us navigate deeply ambiguous and difficult translations of object to financial price.

Indeed, in the case of one-of-a-kind auctions, or art auctions, "[t]he secret in maintaining a high-flying sales auction is to ensure a steady flow of unique and rare items by emphasizing differences between items so that each item can stand on its own." In standing on its own, it defies description as a "commodity."

Participants in auctions sometimes form long-lasting relationships based on debts of gratitude and the obligation of reciprocity. So, for example, in some agricultural commodity exchange auctions, there is an expectation that the big buyers buy up stock of the commodity at a certain price despite the fact that market forces would drop that price lower. In good years, those big buyers benefit from reciprocal relations, since they can acquire more of the good at a special price.

What's more "[t]hese social, psychological, and environmental complexities of real auctions"—what we're calling the time, place, and manner of markets—"reveal the limitations and fallacies implicit within the neoclassical economic model" just as they do in revealing the limitations and fallacies of anti-commodification theorists. "Real auctions clearly do not support a view of human behavior, or even economic behavior, as either rational or individualistic. Real auctions rather support a conception of human behavior that is expressive, interpretive, and social and grounded in behavioral practices; they illustrate a multilevel social reality that incorporates individual beliefs, communal meanings, and patterns of social interaction and reflects a specific time and physical location."[26]

When anti-commodification theorists argue that something or other is incompatible with markets, they ignore the fact that there are many different ways of designing a market. At best, they are entitled to the conclusion that there are ways of structuring a market that undermine dignity or respect when dignity or respect are called for, but they have not demonstrated that there are some things that are flatly incompatible with any and all of the dizzyingly wide array and variety of possible market designs.

Gifts Vs. Commodities?

Anti-commodification theorists rest their case on a deep division between a gift and commodity exchange. The distinction is thought to track the difference between non-market and market exchange. "By and large," writes Alfred Gell, " ... gift institutions have had a favorable press in anthropology, and 'commodities' an unfavorable one ... 'Gift-reciprocity-Good/market-exchange-Bad' is a simple, easy to memorize formula." He adds, presciently, "But perhaps the tide is about to turn."[27] Whether or not it is, it should.

In 1954, Marcel Mauss argued that there exist two types or kinds of exchanges that grounded different kinds of relations—commodity exchange, and gift exchange.[28] Commodity exchange, Karl Marx argued, "is an exchange of alienable things between transactors who are in a state of reciprocal independence," while "non-commodity (gift) exchange is an exchange of inalienable things between transactors who are in a state of reciprocal dependence."[29] Commodity exchanges represent impersonal and distant relations between the exchanging parties. Social and personal relationships are irrelevant, only the price of the object of exchange matters. The exchangers come into the exchange owing each other nothing, and, once the exchange is complete, they walk away owing each other nothing. The exchange is clean, forming no social bonds, or obligations of gratitude or reciprocity. The object of exchange does not symbolize anything over and above its use-value, or its utility to the consumer. Commodity exchange does not ground a basis for personal relationships.

Exchanges based on gifts are appropriate and fitting when we want to form a relationship. "The purpose that [the gift] did serve was a moral one. The object of the exchange was to produce a friendly feeling between the two persons concerned, and unless it did this, it failed its purpose."[30] Gifts create entanglements. A gift, when accepted, forms the foundation of an obligation to reciprocate and a debt of gratitude. What's more, the gifted object takes on a unique identity, and is symbolically significant. "Unlike anonymous commodities," writes Andrej Rus, "gifts are held to be inalienable: a gift is not just 'a watch' but 'a-watch-that-my-father-gave-me-for-my-birthday'."[31] So, Rus concludes, social scientists take commodity exchange to represent "economic rationality and commercial profit making." Gift exchanges, on the other hand, are "carriers of social concerns and moral obligations." In summary, "'[c]ommodity vs. gift' is in this sense often used as metaphor for 'market vs. non-market.'"[32]

By now, it should be clear that the distinction between gift and commodity exchanges does not track the distinction between market and non-market exchanges. Earlier, we pointed out, relying on the work of Zelizer, that money can sometimes function as a gift. So an instrument most clearly associated with markets, although not constitutive nor necessary for market transactions, can have the social meaning we attach to gifts. Closer to the mark, however, bonuses and other modes of payment delivered in a particular manner can be regarded and perceived by recipients as calling for reciprocity and gratitude, rather than be understood as mere compensation or entitlement. Instead of "commodifying" and "de-personalizing" employer-employee relationships, certain forms of compensation can support and encourage social bonds and relationships, they can be perceived more as "gifts." The same can be said of the market in organs in Iran. Here in the west, many see the commodification of organs. In the eyes of the kidney sellers in Iran, however, they perceive themselves as acting altruistically, as performing a service to humanity, as making a gift of their kidney. This is why Sigrid Fry-Revere describes that market as "compensated kidney donation" rather than "kidney selling" or something similar. In certain kinds of auctions, the "social structure" or time, place, and manner of the auction can serve to maintain rather than undermine the uniqueness of an object.[33] Some auctions also rely on the expectation of reciprocity and gratitude between buyer and seller.

Changing the time, place, and manner of a market can change how we regard each other as buyer and seller, how we regard the objects for sale, and what we take to be our obligations to each other. A market exchange can involve elements of a gift exchange, a market exchange can build bonds of friendship between former strangers, a market exchange can result in the demands of reciprocity and the obligations of gratitude, a market exchange can be a building block of social relationships. There may be a useful distinction between gifts and commodities, but that distinction does not distinguish markets from non-markets. They may be ideal types. As ideal types, they may mark a sharp distinction between markets and non-markets, but real-world markets can be designed in ways that result in the attitudes and obligations associated with a gift, rather than a commodity exchange. Some believe the following conditional holds: "if kidneys are not commodities, then we cannot have a market in kidneys." But the truth of the antecedent does not establish the truth of the consequent. An Iranian can say to us, without making any kind of mistake, "kidneys are not commodities, I would like to sell my kidney." Someone who believes that kidneys are not commodities can, nevertheless, endorse a market in kidneys.

Paying Students for Good Grades

Economist Roland Fryer has conducted experiments in paying at-risk middle and high school students to get good grades: $50 for an A, $35 for a B, and so on. The results were mixed. Fryer hypothesized that perhaps the students didn't respond to the incentives because they didn't know *how* to get good grades. He thus tried an alternative. Rather than paying students directly for good grades, he tried paying them for engaging in good study habits. He also tried setting out small, concrete goals that students could reasonably reach in a week, and then paid students, teachers, and parents when the students met these weekly goals. Here the results were much more positive. Students who received money did over twice as well as those who did not. The more money they got, the better they did.[34]

In an earlier study co-authored with David Austen-Smith, Fryer discovered that black and Hispanic students had a strong social disincentive against performing well in school.[35] White students tend to have *more* friends and be *more* popular as their grades go up. (This may surprise you, given the stereotype that "nerds" are loners.) For whites, there is a persistent positive correlation between good grades and popularity. But for blacks and Hispanics, getting *above average* grades tends to cause them to become *less* popular. Black students who get good grades are often stigmatized for "acting white."

We regard Fryer's work as heroic. He sees that students, through no fault of their own, face bad circumstances, lack social and human capital, and face strong social disincentives against learning. He takes an entrepreneurial and scientific approach: let's experiment, find what works, figure out why it works, and then scale it up.

Sandel no doubt admires Fryer's goals, but he sees Fryer's *methods* as corrupting.[36] Sandel worries that paying students to read will "crowd out, or corrupt the love of reading for its own sake."[37]

In response, we'd invite Sandel to identify a single one of Fryer's experimental subjects who had a deep love of reading, but who, as a result of the payment scheme, lost that love and started to read only for money. On the contrary, what Fryer is doing is trying to improve students who—thanks to their disadvantaged circumstances—are unlikely to have a love of reading for its own sake. There's little here for the market to crowd out or corrupt. If Fryer's experiments work, at best, he'll get students to learn to love reading for its own sake. A second best result is that he'll at least *get them to read*. And if the experiments don't work, we'll at least learn that they don't work and why, and can try something else. (Though, we hasten to add, as we are writing with more up-to-date information and results than Sandel had access to, that Fryer is finding methods that work.)

Notes

1 See Mitchell and Mickel 1999, 570.
2 In fact, this isn't even commonsense economics. As a typical economics textbook would say, paying a worker more for his labor might result in less labor, not more. After all, money has diminishing returns, and as a worker gets paid more, he might decide to work fewer hours in order to enjoy spending his higher pay on leisure.
3 For example, see Shariff and Norenzayan 2007 (showing that religious primes make participants more generous in dictator games), or Mazar, Amir, and Ariely 2008 (showing a decrease in cheating and increase in prosocial behavior in dictator games).
4 Tenbrunsel and Bazerman 2011.
5 It is lamentable that this is the contrast, precisely because it conceals an important controversy. It is not difficult to believe that using a business frame is at least occasionally the ethically right thing to do. Put differently, on some views about ethics, cost-benefit analysis is all there is, on others it is at least occasionally what one ought to do. Most plausible ethical theories insist that cost-benefit analysis and calculation is a necessary instrument in the ethical toolbox. So, sometimes the business frame just is an ethical frame. The contrast between an ethical frame and a business frame is a way of begging many important questions. But we will treat these frames as technical terms of art, where "business frame" does not mean a non-ethical frame, and "ethical frame" does not mean ethical frame.
6 Anderson 2000b, 197.
7 Cameron and Pierce 1994.
8 Eisenberger and Cameron 1996.
9 Deci, Koestner, and Ryan 1999.
10 Frey 2002, 69–70: "Crowding-out effects are due to people's perceptions of being *controlled* by external intervention. The resulting marginal shift in the locus of control from inside to outside the person tends to undermine intrinsic motivation."
11 Vansteenkiste, Lens, and Deci 2006, 19.
12 Deci, Koestner and Ryan 1999, 22: " ... the more autonomy-supportive the social context the more it maintains or enhances intrinsic motivation and the more it facilitates the internalization and integration of extrinsic motivation ... "
13 Rosenfield, Folger, and Adelman 1980.
14 Pillutla and Chen 1999.
15 See Mellstrom and Johannesson 2008, 857: "Our results ... suggest that the skepticism towards monetary compensation for blood donations seen in many countries is warranted. But our results also suggest that the potential problem of introducing monetary payments can be resolved by simply adding an option to donate the payment to charity."

16 Sandel 1998.
17 Carruthers and Espeland 1998, 1386.
18 Carruthers and Espeland 1998, 1387. They continue: "Different kinds of money, like tools, can look superficially alike although they do and mean very different things. The same piece of currency, like the same tool, can be used in a dazzling array of contexts to do very different things. There are some places where money does not or should not go and some functions for which it is inappropriate." (At p. 1387.)
19 Mickel and Barron 2008.
20 Easley and Kleinberg 2010, 250.
21 Appadurai 2005.
22 Easley and Kleinberg 2010, 226.
23 C. W. Smith 1990, 162: "Unfortunately, the auction paradigm presented by economists has little relationship to the dynamics of real auctions."
24 C. W. Smith 1990,163.
25 C. W. Smith 1990, 162: "Participants act in terms of their own known interests and resources with minimal external constraints. The prices and exchanges that result are merely products of the pursuit of individual economic self-interest and preference. The practices, places, participants, and conventions of the auction itself—what could be called its "social structure"—are seen to have no direct causal influence on the auction process and its outcome."
26 C. W. Smith 1990, 175.
27 Gell 1992, 142.
28 Mauss 1954.
29 Gregory 1982, 12.
30 Mauss 1954, 18.
31 Rus 2008, 83.
32 Rus 2008, 83: " ... we have on one side commodity exchange, which is prevailing in our capitalist societies, where exchange of goods is devoid of almost all social or personal considerations. On the other side, there is gift exchange, which creates or reinforces social relationships between individuals. In social science, commodity-exchange usually stands for economic rationality and commercial profit making, while gifts are acknowledged to be carriers of social concerns and moral obligations. 'Commodity vs. gift' is in this sense often used as metaphor for 'market vs. non-market'."
33 Fry-Revere and Basanti 2014.
34 Allan and Fryer 2011.
35 Austen-Smith and Fryer 2005.
36 Sandel 2012a, 51–56, 61.
37 Sandel 2012a, 61.

13

THE IMMORAL PREFERENCE OBJECTION

The Argument

As we discussed in Chapter 7, an information market is a stock market in which people place bets on whether certain events will occur. Stock prices range from $0.00 to $1.00, such that the going stock price reflects the market's view, as a whole, of the probability that the specified event would occur. Information markets aggregate dispersed knowledge by allowing people to bet on what will or will not happen. They "tax bullshit" because they punish people for making bad predictions and reward them for making good predictions.

In Chapter 7, we discussed a semiotic objection Sandel raised against information markets. Sandel was especially vexed by the proposed Policy Analysis Market, which would have allowed people to make bets on things like wars and terrorist attacks. In his view, these information markets commodify life and death, and are for that reason inherently disrespectful. We explained back in Chapter 7 why semiotic objections to such markets are unsuccessful. However, Sandel also had a Corruption Objection to these markets, which we put aside in order to focus on semiotic questions. We return to this objection now.

One of Sandel's major objections to PAM is that it might corrupt us. If you place a large bet that a terrorist attack will occur tomorrow, you might thereby acquire an immoral preference that the attack occur. Right now, I prefer that terrorists do not attack Boston. But if I bet $10,000 that terrorists will attack Boston tomorrow, I would—because I have so much money on the line—start to desire (at least somewhat) that terrorists attack Boston. And so, the argument goes, information markets corrupt us by giving us a stake in bad outcomes.

This argument can be generalized as follows:

The Immoral Preference Objection

1   In information markets, people sometimes bet that certain bad things will happen.
2   If a person bets that a bad thing will happen, she will come to have a stake in that bad thing happening, proportional to the size of the bet.
3   If a person comes to have a stake in a bad thing happening, she will come to prefer that that bad thing happen, proportional to the size of the bet.
4   To prefer that a bad thing happen shows flawed character; a perfectly virtuous person would not have such a preference. If an environment or context induces a person to have worse character, it is corrupting.
5   Therefore, information markets are corrupting.

This is a powerful argument—perhaps the best version of a Corruption Objection we've seen. It's not quite a conceptual argument—it does rely upon empirical claims—but to make this argument, Sandel needn't do much additional research. Rather, he's relying only on the very psychology that the defenders of information markets themselves accept. Advocates of information markets agree and assume that placing a bet gives people a stake in the outcome. Information markets would not really work otherwise. So, Sandel can just say, "If information markets work, they will corrupt; if they do not corrupt, they won't work."

Now, Sandel concludes his criticism of the Policy Analysis Market by saying that if the market really does save lives, we might decide it's worth having, all things considered. He thinks that PAM and other information markets will tend to corrupt us, but says that the benefits might be worth the costs to our character.[1] So, on Sandel's behalf, we can say that he followed the outline we gave earlier about what it takes to make a successful Corruption Objection.

Do All Negative Predictions Corrupt?

That said, though this is the best version of a Corruption Objection we've seen, we find it much less damning of the market than Sandel does. In response, we begin by noting that a similar kind of objection can be raised *outside* of information markets. Consider these cases:

A   An oncologist tells a patient, "You should get your affairs in order. You most likely have only a few months to live."
B   An economic forecaster (on television, working for government, or working for an investment firm) predicts that there will be a severe recession by the third quarter.
C   An executive tells the board that the company is likely to suffer $20 million in losses next quarter.
D   A weather forecaster predicts that the hurricane will cause $10 billion in damage along the coast.

E A parent tells her daughter that drinking an entire bottle of booze will give her a hangover and make her sick.

F A prominent "Big Data" statistician develops a model of the US electorate, which predicts that the worse candidate will win by 30 Electoral College votes.

G An intelligence officer briefs the president that he expects terrorist attacks on US embassies in the Middle East and North Africa over the weekend.

H An epidemiologist at the Centers for Disease Control informs the public that even if governments undertake immediate action, the current strain of bird flu will kill at least 200 million people worldwide.

I A government professor tells his students that unless they study, they will get bad grades.

J An environmental activist claims that GMOs and a lack of crop diversity will lead to illness and famine.

K Karl Marx claims that capitalism will immiserate the proletariat.

L The president says on TV, "If we don't invade Syria, hundreds of thousands of innocent people will die."

M A psychologist predicts, in front of her graduate students, that a certain priming treatment will induce subjects to cheat more in the matrix task.

In each of the cases above, someone predicts that something bad will happen. Some of the predictions are conditional; some are not. But each involves someone making a prediction.

In each of these cases, a decent person would prefer ex ante that the bad thing not occur. However, in virtue of having made the prediction in public or in front of others, the person making that prediction acquires a *stake in being right*, and thus acquires a stake in that bad thing happening. In each of these cases, the people making the prediction are supposed to be experts, and experts are supposed to make accurate predictions. Their reputations are at stake here. Also, for many of them, their jobs and livelihoods are at stake. Soi-disant experts who continually make false predictions can lose their status, reputation, and income.

If a doctor tells a patient she has only a few months to live, the doctor most likely hopes that the patient will be one of the lucky ones who beats the odds. But if the doctor tells a thousand patients they each have only a few months to live, but all of them "miraculously" beat the odds, then the doctor looks incompetent, like she doesn't know what she's talking about. If people knew that she had been wrong so frequently, they would (or at least *should*) stop seeking her opinion, and she'd lose her practice. So, even a doctor—someone who wants to cure people—starts to prefer that bad things happen when she predicts these bad things will happen.

Consider that Philip Tetlock did a long-term study of experts' ability to make predictions on hard questions. (He purposefully did not test their ability to make predictions on what the experts considered easy questions.[2]) He found that they were typically not much better than chance. Many experts, especially foreign policy experts, find Tetlock's results embarrassing. The reason: when a person, especially an expert, predicts that X will occur, she acquires a stake in X occurring, and thus acquires some preference that X will occur. Tetlock showed that they were incompetent at making such predictions.

Whenever you make a negative prediction, you acquire some stake in that bad event occurring, especially if it is your job to make predictions or if your reputation and credibility are on the line. If Michael Sandel is worried that betting on PAM is corrupting, he should similarly be worried about his own character when he manages his retirement stock portfolio.[3] So, the problem here in the first instance is not the *market* in the information market, but rather the fact that people are making predictions at all. When people put money where their mouths are, this gives them a further stake in having a bad thing occur, but even if people aren't betting on their predictions, they often still acquire a stake in bad things occurring.

Sandel could just agree with these points, but then respond that the problem is that information markets will draw more people into the inherently corrupting prediction game. But he would then be in an uncomfortable position of having to say that getting more people employed in the professions or roles listed in A–M—all of which sometimes involve making negative predictions—would be in that respect corrupting.

Bets and the Instrumental Value of Life

The problem Sandel sees in information markets is even more general. It has to do with how making bets changes the instrumental value or disvalue to us of certain bad occurrences. Consider, for instance, life insurance. We now expect responsible spouses or parents to buy life insurance. But many people opposed life insurance, when it was invented, because they believed it would be corrupting.

To illustrate why, we'll tell a story about a famous economist named Jim:

> Back in the 1950s, Jim was working at a university in one state, while living in another. He would teach all day on Mondays, and then drive home overnight. One night his car broke down in the middle of the night. He was unable to call his wife, since there were no payphones nearby. When he finally got home late the next day, she said, "My God, Jim, I was worried you'd died!" He responded, "Really? I guess I haven't purchased enough life insurance!" (The next day, he bought more.)

The joke here reflects just why people thought life insurance was immoral and corrupting. Jim believed that the optimal amount of life insurance would, by definition, be whatever amount made his wife indifferent to whether he lived or died.

With that in mind, consider five scenarios:

A I take out no life insurance.
B I take out life insurance equal to six years of my current yearly income.
C I take out life insurance equal to my entire expected lifetime income.
D I take out life insurance equal to twice my entire expected lifetime income.
E I take out life insurance equal to five times my entire expected lifetime income.

Now consider how A–E would affect my wife, the primary beneficiary of my life insurance policy. My wife may—I hope!—love me so much that she wouldn't want me to die, even for $75 million dollars. But, regardless, as I move from A–E, her desire that I avoid death will probably *weaken*. She may want me to keep living, but if she's at all rational, her desire that I live should be stronger in situation A than in E. After all, she needs me to live so I can provide her with financial support. Yet the more insurance I buy, the less she needs me to live. So, by buying life insurance, I corrupt my wife, in the sense that I weaken the strength of her desire that I live.

We might thus conclude, as Sandel does about information markets, that life insurance is the "devil's bargain," that the consequences outweigh the gains, but that we should "remain alive to its repugnance".[4] But we doubt most people would want to pass this judgment.

Instead, an alternative spin on life insurance is this: Sure, it reduces the strength of people's preferences for good things, but it isn't thereby automatically *corrupting*. Yes, we all have heard stories of people killing their partners or elderly parents to get their life insurance. But, aside from cases like that, most people continue to love their spouses and parents just as strongly even when they have insurance. The market here corrupts, if we want to call it that, only in the sense that it *reduces the instrumental value* of someone's life.

Life insurance doesn't change the intrinsic value of someone's life, but it does *lower* the instrumental value of that person's life. Something like this happens with information markets, too. If I bet $40 that the Queen of England will die tomorrow, this doesn't change, from my perspective, the intrinsic value of her life. I still see her as a bearer of Kantian dignity, an end in herself, and all that. But, sure, in virtue of having spent $40, the instrumental value of her life to me, whatever that value was antecedently, is a little lower. Or, another way to put it, is that the instrumental value of her death to me becomes higher.

Insurance changes the instrumental value of someone's life or death, but that might have no effect on how people regard the intrinsic value of a person's life. It might even have a positive effect. When my spouse realizes that I have purchased enough life insurance to support her and our family should I die, she has less of an instrumental stake in me living. But, in virtue of my having acted so responsibly, she might value my life even more for its own sake.

All Things Considered Preferences

Sandel might worry that when we bet on death, the instrumental value of death might trump the intrinsic value of life. We know of cases where that happens— where people kill their spouses to obtain insurance money. But these kinds of cases are rare, even among people who have lots of insurance and who have a chance to get away with murder.

Consider: if a genie said to me, "I'll pay you $40, but the Queen dies," I'd say no thanks. If a genie said to me, "I'll cause a terrorist to attack Boston, maiming and killing hundreds, and pay you $100 million," I'd say no thanks. Maybe some people would take the offer. But many of us would refuse. If so, then it's not like placing bets in information markets really does make us all things considered want the bad things to happen.

Sandel might respond by asking, "How can you assume that most people would refuse? After all, there's no such genie making offers like that."

Here we turn to the work of moral psychologist Dan Ariely.[5] Dan Ariely's main research finding is that most people will lie, cheat, and steal on the margin, but only if doing so is compatible with them thinking of themselves as overall good people. So, for instance, Ariely finds that most people will cheat to win a few extra dollars in a game, but they won't cheat to win a large amount of money. Ariely calls this the "fudge factor." We set ourselves a moral score we want to maintain, and we allow ourselves to do things only if it's compatible with maintaining that score. If saints get an A+ in ethics, the average person wants a B. This person will lie a bit here and there, compatible with having B-level character, but she won't let herself slip down to a C or D. Given how robust Ariely's findings are across a range of experiments and cultures, and given how often they've been duplicated, we doubt most people would take the genie's offer.

People placing bets in information markets *already believe* that bad things will happen—they wouldn't bet otherwise. Given that these bad things are happening, they'd prefer to get money than not. So, consider these three options:

A. A terrorist attacks Boston, and I get $50.
B. A terrorist attacks Boston, and I get $0.
C. A terrorist does not attack Boston, and I get $0.

Sandel's complaint about information markets would be really damning if he could show that these markets cause people to prefer A to C. But information markets work because people prefer A to B. (These markets don't need people to prefer A to C.) But preferring A to B is not bad, immoral, or corrupt.

Consider: I definitely don't want my kids to die of cancer. I wouldn't want them to die of cancer, even for $20 billion. But at the same time, I'd much prefer A) they die of cancer and I get $20 billion than B) they just die of cancer. Don't misread this: I'm not saying I want $20 billion as a payment for their death. I'm not saying I'd be willing to have them die for $20 billion. Instead, I'm making the very boring claim that I'd rather have $20 billion than not. And this is all that information markets trade upon.

When Pricing the Priceless Ennobles

So far, we've only discussed how putting a price on someone's life affects the *instrumental value* of that person's life. But Sandel might be surprised to learn that there's empirical evidence that putting a monetary price on a person's life, whether through life insurance or through damages awarded in a wrongful death tort case, can cause us to see people as possessing greater *intrinsic value*.

Consider: if someone kills me in a car accident, my wife can sue that person for the loss of my future income. When I buy a term life insurance policy, I'm insuring against the loss of future income should I die early. It's an easy arithmetic problem to estimate what my lifetime income is likely to be.

But now consider: how do we think about wrongful death torts or life insurance for children? If a drunk driver kills my kids, he *saves* me money. Should he therefore not be made to pay anything if I sue him? Similarly, if my kids get sick and die, I'll save money in the long run. How should that figure into life insurance for children?

Sociologist Viviana Zelizer, in her book *Pricing the Priceless Child*, says that these became important questions in the late 19th century. Children started working less (on the farm or in factories). They thus stopped being economic assets to their parents and started being net economic burdens. How, then, would courts price the life of a child—an economic burden—in a wrongful death tort? How should life insurance deal with their deaths?

As Zelizer documents at length, what happened was that, in deciding to put a price on children's lives, people started to think of children as "priceless," as possessing a special kind of value not shared even by adults. The current attitudes we have towards children—seeing them as in some way sacred—developed *as a result* of trying to price children once we stopped seeing them as an economic asset.[6] So, contrary to what Sandel might expect, putting a price on things is sometimes the very thing that makes us come to see those things as priceless.

Conclusion

All this leaves Sandel's main objection somewhat intact, but what's left intact is not all that worrisome. If Bob places a bet that a disaster will occur, then it becomes to that extent instrumentally valuable to him that the disaster will occur, and his desire that the disaster not occur will be diminished. But it turns out this problem is not special to information markets. Instead, it exists in many situations in which people make negative predictions, even if they have no money at stake. And, finally, even if Sandel is right that these bets *lower* our desire to avoid the bad outcomes we've wagered will occur, he has not shown us that these markets actually make us desire all things considered that the bad outcomes occur. What's more, extant moral psychological work suggests that most people would not develop an all things considered preference that bad things occur, even if they bet that something bad would occur. Finally, we noted research that shows that pricing things sometimes is what causes us to regard those things as priceless, that commodifying things sometimes causes us to regard those things as being more than mere commodities.

Notes

1 Sandel 2012a, 154.
2 Tetlock 2005, 244.
3 After all, if Sandel chooses to invest in Fund A rather than Fund B, he acquires a stake in A outperforming B, and so acquires a stake in B performing badly relative to certain competitors.
4 Sandel 2012a, 154.
5 Ariely 2013.
6 Zelizer 1994.

14

THE LOW QUALITY OBJECTION

The Argument

One version of the Corruption Objection holds that certain things should not be for sale because selling those things leads to lower quality versions of those things. In the abstract, the argument goes something like this:

The Low Quality Objection

1   When X is sold on the market for profit, there will be less of X or lower quality X than if X is provided for free, not for profit, via gifts, or from the government.
2   If so, then X should not be provided on the market for profit.
3   Therefore, X should not be provided on the market for profit.
4   If X should not be provided on the market, then selling X on the market for profit is wrong.
5   Therefore, selling X on the market for profit is wrong.

Now just insert for X whatever good someone claims the market shouldn't provide.

Examples

Consider: Harvard, Stanford, Georgetown, and the University of Michigan—the universities where the people in the debate about commodification work—are not-for-profit universities. The University of Phoenix, Kaplan University, DeVry University, and Strayer University are for-profit businesses. The former are some of the finest universities in the world; the latter are, well, not. The former receive some of the highest spots in *US News and World Report*'s college rankings; the latter are unranked. So, one might be tempted to conclude, for-profit colleges are rather crummy. (We—authors of the present book called *Markets without Limits*—wouldn't stoop to work for any of the for-profit colleges we've heard of.) For-profit education is poor education.

Or, consider how globalization has affected Hollywood movies. As Hollywood tries to appeal to a wider global audience, reaching across more cultures with differences in taste and language, it has minimized dramatic subtlety, irony, and linguistic tension, and instead relied more on action and special effects that appeal to people everywhere. But in trying to appeal to such large and diverse audiences, though, Hollywood has lowered the aesthetic value of its films. Or so many people believe.

Or, to bring this closer to home in this debate, consider the market for books criticizing commodification. Debra Satz, Margaret Jane Radin, and Elizabeth Anderson published their books with university presses. They wrote the books for scholarly audiences. Michael Sandel and Benjamin Barber, on the other hand, published their books with trade publishers for popular audience, may have hired publicists to help get them on *The Daily Show* or *The Colbert Report*, and are trying to make as much money as they can from book sales. Satz's and Anderson's books are clearly much better works of philosophy, with substantially more rigor than Sandel's, and especially much more value than Barber's. In working to write best sellers, Sandel and Barber cut corners on their arguments in a way Satz and Anderson would refuse to do.

Not a Moral Argument

For the sake of argument, let's assume that there are a range of things where selling those things for profit tends to lower the quality of those things. Instead, suppose those things tend to be higher quality when sold not-for-profit (the way Harvard and Stanford sell education, or Oxford University Press sells books), or provided "for free" by governments and private foundations.

Even if so, this has little *moral* sting. Even if selling certain items for profit lowers the quality of those things, it does not follow that it's *morally wrong* or *morally bad* to sell those things for profit. After all, there's no general moral duty to produce only the highest quality things.

So, for instance, suppose you decide to experiment with a new way of organizing and paying the labor force in your bakery, and the result is that you end up producing lower quality cupcakes. This is a good reason to go back to your old business plan, but it's not, thereby, a *moral* reason. You did something that turned out badly from a strategic point of view, but didn't do something *morally* wrong.

Or, imagine that a foundation, Community Spirit Motors, decided to start a not-for-profit car factory. But suppose that all of their cars are bad quality—not dangerous, but just lower quality than what for-profit companies such as Honda produce. If it turns out that not-for-profit car companies tend to stink, that gives us strategic reasons to refrain from creating not-for-profit car companies. But it doesn't give us *moral* reason to refrain. It's not *wrong* or *evil* to produce cars this way.

And the same goes vice versa. If it turns out, empirically, that certain goods are *better quality* when produced by not-for-profit organizations than for-profit businesses, then that's a reason to prefer having them produced by not-for-profit organizations. Still, that wouldn't make it wrong or evil to produce these things for profit.

Now, consider the issue of for-profit education again. Critics of for-profit education will often point to corrupt business practices at places like the University of Phoenix. We agree with many of these criticisms. We think the University of Phoenix is a corrupt institution. But the problem here isn't that the University of Phoenix is selling something that's not meant to be sold for profit, but that it sells it the wrong way, using manipulative and deceptive sales techniques. As we noted in the introductory chapter, the debate over commodification is not a debate about business ethics. Yes, the University of Phoenix violates norms of business ethics, and it may even turn out that all for-profit schools do, especially since they cater only to the segment of the market that has not already been captured and dominated by the pre-existing not-for-profits. But that doesn't mean it's inherently wrong to sell education for profit. Also, for what it's worth, while we agree that the University of Phoenix has bad business ethics practices, we also think that Harvard, Stanford, Georgetown, and the University of Michigan have bad business ethics, if not *as* bad. (For instance, Brennan has complained numerous times that many philosophy departments in the United States use deceptive or manipulative advertising techniques to convince students to major in philosophy. We also know first-hand that Georgetown sometimes violates Title VII in its hiring practices.)

You might think that government should provide education, including higher education, "for free." (We put "for free" in scare quotes because there's no such thing as a free lunch. Someone has to pay for it.) Let's assume you are right. Even if you are, it doesn't automatically make it wrong for someone to also provide that good for profit. Government provides you "free" protection via the police, but that doesn't make it wrong for you to hire a bodyguard. Government provides you "free" education via public schools, but that doesn't make it wrong for you to buy language courses from for-profit institutions. Government provides "free" courts to settle disputes, but that doesn't make it wrong for you to use for-profit arbitration services. So, the question of whether government should provide education for "free" has little direct bearing on whether it's wrong to sell education, whether for profit like Kaplan or not for profit like Georgetown.

Rejecting the Assumption

So far, we've been taking it for granted that selling some things for profit results in lower quality versions of those things. We've shown that even if this is true, there's no clear *moral* upshot to that—it doesn't make it wrong. So, we've shown that premise 4 of the Low Quality Objection is false. That's enough to kill the Low Quality Objection. But now we want to challenge premise 1 as well. We dispute that the market corrupts the way critics say it does.

Consider: Rousseau asserted that commercial society teaches people to be vain, stupid, and philistine. The economist of culture Tyler Cowen would respond that yes, markets produce boy bands and pop princesses, but they also produce Mozart, Beethoven, Michelangelo, and Shakespeare—each of whom, Cowen documents, was a businessperson trying to make money.[1] Our culture is more commercialized than Rousseau's, but at the same time, a child born to poor parents in our culture is much more likely be exposed to and enjoy high culture—or read people like Rousseau, for that matter—than his counterpart in Rousseau's time and culture.[2] After extensive research, Cowen concludes that there's little evidence that the market is dumbing down people's tastes in art and music. Rather, at worst, it's supplying philistines with the culture they already want. And, at its best, the market is producing plenty of high culture. It's no coincidence that a society's commercial centers tend to be its cultural centers as well, and no coincidence that if you want a good philosophical critique of commercial society, you'll find these are being produced in Boston, New York, and London, not Pyongyang, Moscow, or Havana. You might lament that as Hollywood tries to reach a broader audience, movies are being dumbed down. But, at the same time, for-profit premium channels such as HBO and Showtime are producing the best film drama available.

Part of this has to do with the size of the market. As Deirdre McCloskey explains, the potential market for art and music is something like 255 times larger now than it was in Beethoven's time: "That's 255 times more music, painting, and the rest, good and bad, glorious and corrupting."[3]

School Choice

Allison Benedikt, an editor at *Slate*, recently wrote a "manifesto" in which she argued, "If you send your kids to private school, you're a bad person."[4] Her main claim is that when richer, higher human and social capital parents withdraw their kids from bad public schools, they thereby remove their good influence on those schools and on the low human and social capital kids left behind. Putting your gifted kid in a bad school is bad for your gifted kid, but it's good for the other kids in the school. Benedikt sees the rush to private education as elements of a corrupted market mentality, in which people all strive to get as much as they can for themselves and their loved ones, rather than focusing on the common good.

There are a number of problems with this argument. First, it glosses over a complicated moral problem about how much we are obligated to sacrifice our own interests or our children's interests for the sake of other people's interests. Most moral philosophers who have grappled with this question conclude that while we have rather strict negative duties to avoid harming others or violating their rights, our positive duties to help others are weaker, more open-ended, and can be discharged in a wide range of ways. So, consider that I (Brennan) give to charity. In virtue of doing so, I buy fewer toys for my children than I otherwise might. Thus, I sacrifice some of my children's interest for the sake of strangers. However, even if I think I'm obligated to sacrifice some of their interests, it doesn't follow that I am obligated to impose massive sacrifices on my children for the sake of others.

A further problem with the argument is that it relies upon what are likely to be false empirical assumptions. First, it assumes that putting higher quality students in with lower quality students will help the latter rather than hurt them. But the research on this question yields mixed results.

Second, it assumes that in order to improve low quality schools, it's better for everyone to keep their kids in those schools than for people to threaten to leave. But that's not obviously true—in fact, that's counterintuitive from an economic point of view. Benedikt assumes that if high human and social capital parents decide they'll keep their kids in a local public school, they will probably use their influence to improve that school. She may be right. However, as economist Alex Tabarrok notes, generally speaking, the "power of exit" beats the "power of voice," and the power of voice is usually weak unless backed up by the power of exit.[5] That is, when people are free and willing to leave, this has a stronger tendency to induce others to behave better than when people just have the power to express their opinion. Tabarrok says this is why restaurants are more likely to respond to your complaints than the DMV—the fact that you can walk away makes your bark have some bite. When we can walk away from bad suppliers, this means that suppliers can and must compete, and so we generally find higher quality products supplied.

It's ECON 101 that creating monopolies tends to produce poor quality goods. But that's just what Benedikt is asking us to do—to treat our local school system as a monopoly. Imagine a world in which people decided they would allow only one restaurant per town, and that they would only eat at their town's local restaurant. In that world, we'd expect restaurants to be much lower quality than what we find in the real world. Benedikt needs to explain to us why education is different, why monopolies in education are good when monopolies in almost every other good are awful.

Contrary to Benedikt, economist Caroline Roxby finds that competition and the power of exit *helps* rather than hurts public schools. As she summarizes her findings:

> The most intriguing evidence comes from three important, recent choice reforms: vouchers in Milwaukee, charter schools in Michigan, and charter schools in Arizona. I show that public school students' achievement rose significantly and rapidly in response to competition, under each of the three reforms. Public school spending was unaffected, so the productivity of public schools rose, dramatically in the case in Milwaukee.[6]

The empirical work on charter schools often seems mixed in its results. Sometimes studies of charter schools find they improve test results. But sometimes critics of school choice and charter schools will cite studies in which introducing charter schools or school choice did not improve test or learning results. However, these critics overlook that even in these cases, school choice doesn't *hurt* test or learning results. Instead, school choice generally produces, at worst, *equally good results for less money*. That's a *positive* result, not a negative one. It's a reason to celebrate school choice, not to dismiss it.

Consider, by analogy: suppose privatizing and commodifying roads didn't improve the drive quality or reduce traffic one iota, but it did reduce the cost of providing these roads by 30%. That would free lots of money to be spent on other valuable things. If a private road system produced the same quality roads as a public road system, but for less money, then we should prefer private roads.

Since most people who write about school choice aren't trained in economics, they often focus too much on test results without thinking about the *cost* of delivering those results. But that's a mistake. We all prefer to find a way to improve students' learning outcomes. But we should also prefer to find ways to produce current outcomes for less money.

Ilya Somin notes that Benedikt's complaint overlooks some of the civics benefits of private schools. Certain studies have shown that students in private schools, especially Catholic schools, receive better civics education and retain more civics knowledge than students in public schools, even once we statistically control for demographic factors. (That is, private schools do better than public schools, but not just because they have richer students with more highly educated parents.)[7] Since many of the people—such as Sandel and Barber—who advance variations of the Corruption Argument are worried about civics, they should at least for this reason welcome rather than condemn the retreat from public schools. Somin also says that it's potentially dangerous to have all students attend government-run public schools, as this increases the likelihood that students will just be indoctrinated into pro-government and statist points of view. (We doubt Sandel or Barber are much worried about that, though.)

Markets in Blood: What You Think You Know Is Wrong

Critics frequently cite the market for human blood as an instance of the Low Quality Objection. Richard Titmuss argued in his 1971 book *The Gift Relationship* that it is better from a consequentialist point of view not to have markets in human blood, but instead to rely only upon blood donations.[8] He argued that paying people for blood 1) reduces the actual amount of blood received, and 2) lowers the quality of the blood received. More people give blood, and healthier people (who have better quality blood) are more likely to give blood, when giving blood is seen as an altruistic gift than a mere exchange for cash. Part of the reason is that people have an aversion to selling parts of their bodies. Healthy, affluent people might give blood, but they wouldn't be willing to sell blood for the low market price—they see that as beneath them. However, homeless people and others who tend to be sick might be willing to take that price.

If Titmuss is right, that's worrisome, but it's not clear his empirical claim is right. The evidence suggests Titmuss is wrong. Researchers Nicola Lacetera, Mario Macis, and Robert Slonim have done a series of scientific experiments on what affects blood donations. They find, contrary to Titmuss, that economic incentives such as gift cards do in fact increase blood donations and do not affect the quality of the blood received.[9] They complain that the World Health Organization has for forty years advised against paying for blood, but the WHO, like Titmuss, was using data from uncontrolled experiments and non-scientific surveys. Titmuss's complaint is based on bad data, they claim.

Cécile Fabre notes that blood selling is legal in the United States but illegal in England. Despite that, she notes, more or less the same percentage of Americans and English donate blood (and they donate with the same regularity), though some Americans also sell blood.[10] In a comprehensive study, sociologist Kieran Healy found that what determines the quality and quantity of blood given is *not* whether blood is bought or sold, but a wide range of other factors in how blood is produced, on the marketing strategies of blood procurement groups, and so on.[11]

Even if Titmuss were right, though, it's not clear that this would make paying for blood *morally wrong*. It would just make it inadvisable. If markets for blood don't work as well as blood donations, great, we should go with donations over markets. But, as we explained previously, this isn't a moral "should."

Whether there are certain goods—such as education, museums, healthcare—that are best provided through not-for-profit means is a big topic. We cannot discuss here the pros and cons of commodifying each of these goods. However, we have done enough to undermine the Low Quality Objection. One problem with the Low Quality Objection is sometimes that it rests on an empirical mistake—the market in fact delivers the good better than the alternatives, or the market does not in fact corrupt the good in question. But, even when the critics are right that commodifying the good for profit produces a lower quality product, it doesn't thereby make buying and selling it *wrong*. The Low Quality Objection has no *moral* force.

Buying Admission to Ivy League Schools, Part I

Harvard University (where Sandel and Radin work) has an undergraduate admission rate of 6.3%. Stanford (where Satz works) admits 7.1%. Brown (where Brennan had his first job and Jaworski visited as a research professor) admits 8.9%. Georgetown (where we work) admits 17%. These are among the most selective universities in the country—there are only about 30 universities and colleges in the US with admissions rates below 20%. Michigan (where Anderson works) admits 40%, low for a state university.[12] (Michigan's graduate programs are among the very best in the country and are much more competitive.) Most of the students at these schools have SAT scores far above the national average, and a fair number of them get perfect scores. In addition, they typically excel in a range of activities besides academics—they have impressive résumés full of sports, service, music recitals, and clubs when they apply. In short: it's extremely difficult to gain admission to a name-brand college.

However, there is *another* way, a way available to those blessed not with brains or talent, but with the right last name. The open dirty secret of these universities is that they have much lower admissions standards for "legacy" applicants, especially *wealthy* legacy applicants. (A "legacy" is the child of an alumnus.) As Sandel explains, legacy admissions are "a form of affirmative action for the affluent."[13] Sandel notes that universities will also sometimes relax standards for the children of rich parents, even if those parents are not alumni, because the universities expect that the parents will make "substantial" donations to the schools.[14] When I (Brennan) worked at Brown, I noticed the university went out of its way to woo the children of Hollywood superstars.

Sandel admits there is a possible moral justification for these practices: these donations allow elite universities to offer financial aid to needy students. As of 2013, Harvard's total attendance fees are about $55,000 per year. Yet, an applicant from Northern Virginia (where we the authors live) whose parents make less than $70,000 per year is expected to pay *nothing*—tuition, room, and board are free, paid for through Harvard's massive endowment and from alumni donations.[15] Many elite universities, such as Harvard or Chicago, spend more money per student than they take in through tuition. This money has to come from some-where, and so perhaps, some people think, this justifies allowing a few wealthy people to buy their children admission to elite schools.

Sandel worries that this will be corrupting. He says,

> The corruption objection is about institutional integrity. [H]igher education … embodies certain ideals—the pursuit of truth, the promotion of scholarly and scientific excellence, the advancement of humane teaching and learning, the cultivation of virtue. Although all universities need money to pursue their ends, allowing fund-raising needs to predominate runs the risk of distorting these ends and corrupting the norms that give universities their reasons for being. That the corruption objection is about integrity—the fidelity of an institution to its constitutive ideals—is suggested by the familiar charge of "selling out".[16]

This objection needs some unpacking.

We could interpret Sandel as saying: "As a matter of fact, lowering standards for legacy students (or the children of the ultra-rich) tends to make the schools worse as measured by their overall intellectual quality." This is in principle a testable empirical claim. But, if this is Sandel's claim, we would expect that the optimal level of legacy admissions would be greater than 0% but less than 100%. Allowing *some* students in who will pay full tuition and whose parents will donate buildings or to the endowment probably aids universities in maintaining their high quality. In effect, these students pay a massive premium that benefits the other students— or the faculty—by allowing the school to have better quality faculty and research facilities than it otherwise would. The rich dumb students pay for the poor smart students. This is why universities have reduced standards for legacies in the first place, as Sandel acknowledges.

But Sandel probably means that allowing any legacy admission is intrinsically corrupting, a sort of "devil's bargain," as he is fond of saying. Harvard wants to have the best student body, as measured along a variety of ways of achieving excellence, and so admitting a less-than-excellent-but-rich student intrinsically goes against this standard. Maybe it's worth the bargain, but it's a sacrifice of integrity.

Sandel might be right about this, but we think the upshot is not troubling for our thesis. Consider two different models of Harvard University:

A *1926 Harvard:* A fancy school for average intelligence rich kids who can pay full tuition.
B *1963 Harvard*: A fancy school intending to be the leader in research in every field, with the most gifted student body anywhere.[17]

Harvard was always an elite university, but it wasn't always a university with an intellectually elite student body. As Charles Murray notes, the average IQ among graduates from Harvard in 1926 was about 117, only 2 points higher than the average IQ among all college graduates in the country. But in the decade from 1950 to 1960, Harvard's leaders changed the nature and mission of the university. The president of Harvard transformed the university, moving from what we call the 1926 model to the 1963 model. Harvard actively sought to recruit the best and brightest students in the world. As a result, the average 1950 Harvard freshmen would be in the lowest 10% of the entering class of 1960.[18] The typical freshman entering Harvard in 1950 would be deemed unworthy of admission today.

We support Harvard's decision to recruit an intellectually elite student body, though this is not without its downsides.[19] So, we support Harvard's decision to move from the 1926 model to the 1963 model. But, that said, that doesn't make the 1926 model morally wrong. It's not inherently corrupt to offer rich students a good but expensive education. Consider: imagine that someone today decided to create a new university along the 1926 Harvard model, that is, an expensive institution with elite professors and facilities, but with relatively low admission standards. Regardless of whether you *like* the idea of someone doing that or not, it wouldn't be *morally wrong* to do, any more than it is wrong for BMW to make luxury cars or for Qantas to offer first-class seating.

Now, given that Harvard decided to move to the 1963 model—a move that was not morally required—Harvard's leaders now face difficult questions about just what it takes to maintain that model, and whether it is permissible to move away from that model toward a different vision of what the school will be. This is a problem all leaders face. They inherit a tradition and a vision of their organization. Under some circumstances, they have obligations to maintain those traditions and visions. But they also are responsible for deciding whether to substitute a different vision or to break tradition. Leaders should take these questions seriously. But, without here going into a fifty-page discussion of the ethics of organizational integrity and the ethics of respect for tradition, we will note that it's not at all obvious that leaders cannot substitute a new vision in light of new circumstances. If Harvard decided to move back to the 1926 model, that would not automatically be *wrong* or *corrupt*.

Also, Sandel's complaints about legacy admissions would be stronger if universities were admitting higher percentages of legacy applicants each year. However, as far as we could discover in researching this issue, elite universities like Harvard, Yale, or Georgetown are *reducing* rather than *increasing* the number of legacy admissions over time.[20] And, also, even though these schools maintain lower standards for legacy applicants, they are simultaneously increasing these standards over time. Being a legacy applicant to Harvard in 2013 gives you a big boost in your chances of admission, but not as big a boost as you would have gotten in 1993 or 1973. So, even if we agreed with Sandel that legacy admissions are corrupt, it's strange for him to use them as an example of his overall thesis that commodification is corrupting society. After all, in this case, by his standards, things are getting better, not worse.

So far, we've just assumed that Sandel is right to regard legacy admissions as a kind of compromise. But he's not obviously right about this.

Consider: Ivy League universities and their peers do not simply admit students on the basis of academic achievement. Instead, they admit students who have other kinds of achievements, such as excellence in music or sports. They do not simply select individual students on their individual merits, but also aim to create a student *body* with a particular kind of character. Admissions counselors want a diverse student body, where students will encounter other students who have different backgrounds and life history. The hope is that students will grow in their human, social, and cultural capital as a result. Much of what Harvard is selling to its students is *the other students*.

Now consider the role of legacy admissions again. Legacy students—students whose parents and grandparents went to these elite universities—usually have a certain degree of cultural and social capital. They're usually upper or upper-middle class. They were raised in environments where they learned the manners, modes of speech, and behaviors of the elite. They are, in a sense, aristocratic in their behavior. One reason why elite universities might admit such students is that they want their *other* students to learn these elite manners, modes of speech, and behaviors, or to at least be exposed to them. Harvard grooms its students to become the new elite, and one way it does this is by socializing them with the current elite. It's a product most students want to buy.

Conclusion

It's worth repeating here in closing a basic lesson from microeconomics: normally, for-profit market competition leads to higher quality, not lower quality. In competitive markets, firms have to win customers, customers who are free to walk away from a bad deal. Firms compete by trying to raise quality while reducing prices. Normally, when we see low quality, this is either because people don't value quality much, or because the products are not being produced in competitive for-profit markets. Twentieth-century socialism was supposed to bring production for use rather than for profit, but the hard-learned lesson was that production for profit is production for use. During the Cold War, consumer goods made in the capitalist West were cheap but high quality, while goods made in the socialist East were expensive but low quality. There may be cases where certain goods are best delivered by non-profits—we'll remain agnostic about that here—but these are going to be special cases, not the norm.

Notes

1 Tyler Cowen has written a series of books (e.g., Cowen 1998) tracing the positive impact of commerce on art.
2 This follows Schmidtz and Brennan 2010, 127.
3 McCloskey, 2008.
4 See http://www.slate.com/articles/double_x/doublex/2013/08/private_school_vs_public_school_only_bad_people_send_their_kids_to_private.html
5 See http://marginalrevolution.com/marginalrevolution/2005/09/the_tragedy_of_-2.html. Tabarrok draws upon Hirschman 1970.
6 This quotes the abstract from Hoxby 2003a. See also Hoxby 2003b.
7 Somin 2013, 176. He cites Campbell 2001.
8 Titmuss 1971.
9 Lacetera, Macis, and Slonim 2013.
10 Fabre 2006.
11 See also Healey 2006.
12 http://colleges.usnews.rankingsandreviews.com/best-colleges/rankings/lowest-acceptance-rate
13 Sandel 2012a, 109.
14 Sandel 2012a, 109.
15 http://npc.fas.harvard.edu
16 Sandel 2012a, 110.
17 Murray 2012, 31, 54–55, notes that the transformation from Harvard as a school for rich kids to the Harvard we know today occurred largely over a decade in the 1950s. In the 1920s, Harvard students were no more intelligent on average than state university students.
18 Murray 2012, 54–55.
19 See Murray 2012. Murray argues that similar transformations by other elite colleges actually contribute to, rather than undermine, classism in America, such that white people in the US are now divided into two classes much more so than they had been 100 years ago.
20 http://thechoice.blogs.nytimes.com/2011/04/29/legacy-2/?_r=0

15

THE CIVICS OBJECTION

The Argument

Benjamin Barber claims that markets are dangerous for a country's civic life. Capitalism's need to sell sell sell induces a cultural change in which citizens are concerned only with procuring consumer goods for themselves, and not concerned about their common civic life. Markets draw people away from the public forum and toward the market.[1] Barber's main argument appears to go something like this:

The Civics Objection

1 Markets encourage citizens to think of freedom as the ability to fulfill their own desires rather than to think of freedom as political autonomy.
2 Therefore, markets encourage citizens to retreat from common civic life.
3 Therefore, markets undermine civic virtue.[2]

We reject the premises of this argument for a number of reasons, including:

- *Against premise 1*: Barber doesn't actually give us any evidence that markets *succeed* in getting people to think this way.
- *Against premise 2*: We don't see any empirical evidence from Barber that market societies actually undermine citizens' participation in democracy. On the contrary, there is evidence that markets do not have this effect.
- *Against the hidden premise*: Though not explicit in the argument above, Barber assumes what we will argue is an overly narrow view of civic virtue.

Do Markets Cause People to Adopt an Ideology?

Most people think freedom is good, but what exactly is freedom? In premise 1, Barber claims that markets encourage a particular conception of freedom—freedom is the absence of interference or domination by others. However, Barber says, there is an alternative conception of freedom, where "freedom" connotes not the absence of interference, but the presence of political autonomy and the power to shape society through political means.

Barber is right that these are alternative conceptions of freedom. However, to be frank, he does not provide much evidence that markets actually *cause* people to adopt one conception over another. What Barber mostly does, instead, is cite a range of political philosophers and economists who are friendly to markets, and who themselves advocate thinking of freedom as the absence of interference.[3] He also notes that many people living in market societies accept this conception of freedom. However, Barber does not show us that living in a market society *causes* people to think this way. For all we know, consistent with the evidence he provides, people adopt market institutions because they already think this way. Or, perhaps A) people accepting the idea of freedom as the absence of interference and B) people being friendly to markets have a common cause, C.

Away from the Forum and to the Market?

Many people believe market societies tend to draw people away from public, civic life. In principle, this is a testable hypothesis, something that can be studied by the social sciences. However, it's a *hard* question to study, because one needs to find a way to operationalize the degree to which a society is market-oriented and also what counts as political participation. In addition, one needs to look for and control for other possible variables that affect political participation.

One quick measure would be to see if the more marketized countries worldwide also have lower rates of political participation. Figure 15.1 charts major democratic countries, showing the relationship between their degree of economic freedom (as measured by the Fraser Institute) and their voter turnout for elections for a

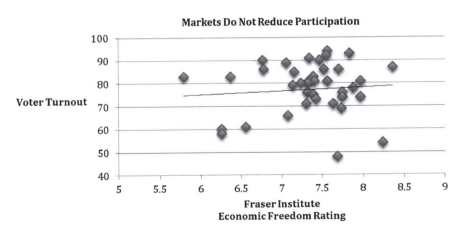

FIGURE 15.1 Market Societies and Voter Turnout

country's lower national legislative house.[4] In fact, the relationship is weakly positive, rather than negative, as Barber would predict. (Here, $R^2 = .008$.)

Of course this is not the final word on the matter. It's just a piece of a larger puzzle. In fact, the question of what determines turnout is quite complicated, and there is a large literature on this.[5] However, we have found no empirical literature showing that market societies tend to have less political engagement, or that commodification causes disengagement.[6]

Civic Virtue through the Market

So far, we have taken Barber's view of civic engagement for granted. Barber has a *narrow* conception of citizenship, in which being a good citizen means being engaged in political and quasi-political activities, such as voting, deliberating, running for office, serving in the military, and volunteering. But there's an alternative, *broad* conception of citizenship, in which being a good citizen can instead mean working at a productive job, creating art, being a good parent, or pursuing knowledge. We favor the broader view over the narrow view.

Consider, by analogy, two views of "courage." The archaic Greeks (that is, the Greeks who lived at the time the *Iliad* was supposed to have taken place) had a narrow view of courage. For them, courage was largely a martial and manly virtue, a virtue that could properly be exercised only by men, and only during conflict and battle. However, most of us now reject this narrow conception of courage. We instead subscribe to a broad view of courage. To be courageous is to have an appropriate recognition of danger and risk, and to be willing to confront that danger and risk. Once we realize that this is what courage is all about, we recognize that courage can be exercised by both men and women, and it can be exercised almost everywhere, not just on the battlefield. A woman can exercise courage in childbirth just as much as a man can exercise courage in war. (And, also, a man can exercise courage in childbirth just as much as a woman can exercise courage in war.) Just as we have adopted a broad conception of courage, we should also adopt a broad conception of civic virtue, or so we will briefly argue here.

Philosophers almost universally define civic virtue as the disposition to promote the common good of society over purely private ends.[7] But this leaves open just *how* and *where* one can exercise civic virtue. Civic virtue is the disposition to promote the common good. Political participation can promote the common good, and so it is one avenue for exercising civic virtue. However, lots of other things can promote the common good as well. Michelangelo contributed to the common good of society by making art. Thomas Edison promoted the common good by making light bulbs. Marie Curie promoted the common good with her scientific discovery. And, in our view, a typical baker does much more to promote the common good by baking and selling bread than he does by voting or writing letters to his elected officials.

While Barber sees the move from the forum to the market as a loss of civic virtue, we see it as a potential gain. In our view, the market is as good or better a place to exercise civic virtue than the forum. We will illustrate this point with a thought experiment.[8]

Imagine you could wave a magic wand that would instantaneously make everyone fifteen times richer, and to that extent dramatically improve everyone's standard of living. Most people would conclude that this counts as promoting the common good.

Now suppose your magic wand's power is not instantaneous, so that it takes 200 years for incomes to increase fifteen-fold. While this second magic wand is not as good as the first, it is still in the common good.

Now suppose the slow-acting magic wand is imperfect. Though it systematically improves conditions over time, it causes some important problems, people sometimes get hurt, and it needs to be supplemented by government activity to really maximize its contribution to the common good and to correct the problems it causes. Even then, the magic wand serves the common good, just imperfectly.

Suppose instead of the slow-acting magic wand, we have a noble philosopher-queen, who determines that if we work together, divide up various tasks, and so on, we can increase our incomes by fifteen times over the next 200 years. The philosopher-queen issues various instructions and offers some rewards for good work and punishments for bad work. Unfortunately, the queen is imperfect in exactly the same way the magic wand was. Even then, the philosopher queen serves the common good. More importantly, those of us who follow her directives and work for her would, in general, be helping to serve the common good. If any of us have the goal of serving the common good, one strategy would be to work for the philosopher-queen, to do whatever job she recommends you do.

Now suppose instead of the imperfect philosopher-queen, you have a market economy that issues the same directives, offers the same rewards and punishments, and has the same results. While the queen might have had written or verbal commands, the market economy uses prices instead. While the queen might have issued monetary rewards or fines, the market economy offers profits/consumer surpluses and losses. Yet, otherwise, the system is the same. Again, as with the queen, the market economy serves the common good. In a sense, the market economy *just is* the philosopher queen. Thus, those of us who follow its directives and work for it would, in general, be helping to serve the common good, just as we would have been in working for the philosopher-queen. If any of us have the goal of serving the common good, one good strategy for satisfying that goal would be to work for the market economy.

Mainstream economic theory claims the market economy is, fundamentally, the same as the imperfect philosopher-queen or the slow-acting, imperfect magic wand.[9] If so, then productive work in the market—including for-profit business activity—will generally promote the common good. In the hypothetical land governed by the wise philosopher-queen, a person with a high degree of civic virtue would just ask the queen how he could be most useful, and do what the queen asks. Since the market just is the philosopher-queen, a person of civic virtue in a market society can similarly do what the market deems useful.

Now, Barber might respond with any of the following objections:

A Most market activity has only a tiny marginal impact on the common good.
B For market activity to serve the common good, it needs to be imbedded in the proper, well-functioning regulatory institutions.
C For market activity to serve the common good, agents need to behave rather well, practice some degree of social responsibility, and so on.
D Market activity sometimes undermines the common good, sometimes greatly so. It can be difficult for a market agent to determine whether she will serve the common good, undermine it, or have no effect upon it.
E To have civic virtue, it's not enough that you promote the common good, but you must also have a sufficiently strong desire to promote the common good. Many people on the market are motivated only or predominantly by selfishness.

A–E may seem like strong objections, but they miss the mark. The problem is that none of these objections give us any reason to endorse Barber's narrow view of civic virtue over our broader view. A–E each apply to political activity just as much as they apply to activity in the market. So, for instance, most political activity has only a tiny marginal impact on the common good. Political activity needs to be imbedded in the right institutions to serve the common good. Political activity can harm rather than promote the common good. And, political activity doesn't count as an exercise of civic virtue unless political actors have the right motives. A–E are not objections to our view, but, rather, further elaborations on what civic virtue requires, whether exercised through politics or through the market.

Economists have long understood that in a market economy, the systematic effect of private citizens' pursuit of private ends is to create background conditions of wealth, opportunity, and cultural progress. Each of us does as well as we do because of the positive externalities created by an extended system of social cooperation. This extended system of cooperation explains why each of us in contemporary liberal societies has our high standards of living and easy access to culture, education, and social opportunities. We are engaged in networks of mutual benefit, and we benefit from other people being engaged in these networks. When we go to work in the market, we help create, sustain, and improve these networks of mutual benefit. When things are going well—and overall they tend to go well—we create a series of positive externalities through our innovations, through the division of labor, and by helping to create economies of scale.

If a person is motivated to promote the common good and to serve others, it thus does not follow that she must pursue political activities or must avoid the market. Rather, each of us will have a unique set of options in how we can contribute to the common good. For some of us, that means specializing in political or quasi-political activity. For some, it means specializing in non-political activities. For others, it means doing a mix of political and non-political activities. Contrary to Barber, then, we cannot automatically treat a reduction in political participation as a reduction in citizens' civic-mindedness.

Now, one final response to this is to insist that to exercise civic virtue is, by definition, to participate in politics. This contradicts the definition of civic virtue that other philosophers and political theorists have been using, but the person making the objection could just say that these philosophers and theorists have been using a bad definition.

This objection has little force. If one insists that, by definition, civic virtue requires political engagement, our response is that one can be a good community member by engaging in public-spirited non-political activity. A public-spirited person who promotes the common good through non-political means might lack civic virtue, but instead have "schlivic" virtue. Let us say that schlivic virtue is the disposition and ability to promote the common good by non-political activity. If one insists that it is not an open question whether civic virtue involves political engagement, our response is that this just makes it an open question whether, in order to be a good community member, one should have civic virtue, schlivic virtue, or some combination of the two. So, if Barber insists that the market undermines civic virtue, then we can just respond that it instead promotes schlivic virtue, which is sort of like civic virtue, but *better*.

Notes

1 Barber 2008, 118–65.
2 Barber 2008, 131–32.
3 Note that pro-market philosophers can and do adopt alternative conceptions of freedom. See, e.g., Schmidtz and Brennan 2010.
4 Turnout rates taken from Franklin 2001, 83–100.
5 For a review of this literature, see Birch 2009.
6 See, e.g., Norris 2000.
7 Burtt 1990, 24; Dagger 1997, 14; Galston 2007, 630; Crittenden 2007; Brennan and Hamlin 1995.
8 This argument follows Brennan 2012b.
9 See, e.g., Krugman and Wells 2009, chapters 1, 2, 4, passim; Mankiw 2008, 8–12, Part III; Weil 2009, chapters 2, 10–12, 17; Ekelund, Ressler, and Tollison 2006, chapters 1–4 and 12–13; McConnell, Brue, and Flynn 2014, chapters 1–4, 7, 9, 11, passim.

PART IV

Exploitation, harm to self, and misallocation

16

ESSENTIAL AND INCIDENTAL OBJECTIONS

Most Complaints About Commodification Aren't Fundamentally About Commodification

Recall that there are many questions one might ask about the morality and justice of markets:

1   How much should governments intervene in and regulate the market?
2   What is the best way to structure property rights and background legal rules?
3   How much should governments provide social insurance or other welfare programs to protect citizens from misfortune on the market?
4   What are the proper norms of business ethics? How should businesses conduct themselves?
5   What sorts of things should be and should not be for sale?

The commodification debate is supposed to be concerned with question 5.

While there is a lively debate over the last question, one of our goals in this book is to show that this debate is misplaced. Instead, much of the time, when anti-commodification theorists intend to complain about the buying and selling of some good or service, their problem is not fundamentally with the buying and selling, but just with the goods or services, period. For example, child pornography shouldn't be for sale because it shouldn't be possessed, period. A market in child pornography might make things even worse, but the fundamental problem with the market in child pornography is the pornography, not the market. Other times, critics' real problem is not with the fact that goods and services are sold, but with *how* the goods and services are sold. Their complaints aren't about commodification, but about business ethics, or about background considerations of distributive justice and the structure of the market. For example, the problem with buying laptops from Apple isn't that laptops shouldn't be bought and sold, but that Foxconn employees are mistreated.

Thus far, we've attacked semiotic and corruption objections to markets in everything, the two most important kinds of arguments in the debate about commodification. However, three major kinds of objections remain:

1 *Exploitation*: Markets in some good or service might encourage the strong to exploit (to take unjust advantage of) the vulnerable.
2 *Paternalism*: Markets in some good or service might cause people to make self-destructive choices.
3 *Misallocation*: Markets in certain goods and services might cause those goods to be allocated unjustly.

Yet, when we examine complaints in these three categories, we find that most of the complaints aren't really about commodification per se. Consider:

Exploitation: Suppose someone claims that organ sales are wrongful because they involve unjust exploitation. The poor in the third world will, out of desperation, sell their organs for low prices. Because they operate in malfunctioning legal environments, or because organ sales are illegal, they might lose their organs, but then never receive payment, and have no legal means to sue those who defraud them.

These are all legitimate worries with existing organ markets. But these problems aren't essential to kidney sales. Instead, these are problems that could in principle be overcome with better regulations and better laws within better-functioning legal systems. If we're worried that desperately poor people will be taken advantage of, then we could require that kidney sellers have a certain income before they are eligible to sell. If we're worried that kidney sellers will be defrauded in the black market, then we could fix that by *legalizing* kidney sales, so that kidney sellers have recourse to proper law courts. If we are worried that kidney sellers won't understand the harm they might cause themselves, we could require them to pass a series of tests on the dangers before licensing them to sell their kidneys. And so on. Such reforms might be difficult. Still, the point here is that these kinds of worries don't show that kidneys are not the kind of thing that must not be for sale, but merely that kidneys are not right now being sold the *right way*. It's the how, not the what.

Note that we are not actually advocating that the kidney market be regulated in any of these ways. We do not actually advocate forbidding the poor from selling kidneys. But our point here is that we do not need to argue one way or the other. People who object to kidney markets on the grounds that they involve exploitation, harm, or information asymmetries are at most objecting to contingent features of the kidney market. They at most object to exploitative kidney sales, not kidney sales per se. We should all agree that kidneys may be bought and sold, even if we might disagree about just how lenient or stringent the conditions are for properly buying and selling them.

Paternalism/harm to self: Sarah Conly makes a powerful case for paternalism in her book *Against Autonomy*.[1] She argues that people tend to be irrational, and so tend to choose actions that undercut rather than promote their own goals. At least in principle, and often in practice, she thinks people would be better off *by their own lights* if some choices were taken away for them or made for them. She concludes, "We should, for example, ban cigarettes; ban trans-fats; require restaurants to reduce portion sizes to less elephantine dimensions; increase required savings; and control how much debt individuals can run up."[2]

Since Conly opposes cigarettes, trans-fats, and KFC's Double Down, she thereby opposes markets in cigarettes, trans-fats, and oversized chicken, bacon, and cheese sandwiches. But her problem isn't fundamentally with the market. Rather, it's with the goods themselves. She thinks it's wrong to consume cigarettes, period. So, her fundamental opposition to markets in cigarettes is covered by what we called, in Chapter 2, the Principle of Wrongful Possession.

There are some things that people inherently should not have—indeed, that should not even exist—and, as a consequence, people should not buy or sell.

The commodification debate concerns whether there are goods, services, and activities that are permissible to possess, use, and exchange with others, but which may not permissibly be bought and sold on markets. As far as we can tell, paternalistic complaints about the market are covered by the Principle of Wrongful Possession. Paternalists think markets in bad things might make things worse, but they haven't identified any cases where the things in question would in their view be rightful to possess and use, so long as we don't sell them. So, for example, Conly doesn't want people to have cigarettes at all. For her, commodifying cigarettes is bad because cigarettes are bad; commodification does not transform something good into something bad.

Misallocation: Sometimes people oppose markets in certain goods because they believe markets won't distribute the benefits and burdens of social cooperation fairly. So, for instance, we both know people who oppose private education because not everyone can afford high quality private education. However, this isn't obviously a reason to forbid markets in private education. Consider, in parallel: the market does an excellent job producing high quantities of food. Yet, for various reasons (including a wide range of bad government policies), some people cannot afford food. We don't thereby decide that we should shut down markets in food. Rather, a more obvious solution is for governments to give the desperately poor food stamps—vouchers to purchase food on the market. Why not do the same for education?

The Exploitation Argument

To exploit someone is to take unfair or pernicious advantage of that person's vulnerability. For instance, consider the following paradigmatic case:

> *Drowning Man:* Bob's boat capsizes in the ocean. As hungry sharks circle him, his strength gives way, and he realizes he will soon drown. Just then, Charlie appears in a fishing boat. He says to Bob, "I'm willing to save your life, but only if you give me 90% of your life savings and 90% of your future earnings." Bob would rather be poor than dead, and agrees.

In the case above Bob was going to die, but Charlie offers him another option that didn't previously exist. Charlie makes Bob's situation better, not worse. Bob agrees to the deal because he expects to profit from it. It may even be, depending on the background circumstances, that Bob actually profits much more from the deal in absolute terms than Charlie does. Still, despite this, almost everyone except the most hardcore libertarians judge that the transaction in Drowning Man is unconscionable and exploitative.

We concur with the commonsense view here. We think Charlie is taking pernicious advantage of Bob, and that the transaction is immoral.

Some anti-commodification theorists say that many markets are objectionable in the way Drowning Man is objectionable. They claim that the sale of certain goods or services leads to widespread exploitation. They conclude that certain markets are immoral, and they sometimes even demand that governments outlaw some of these kinds of markets. In the abstract, their argument simply goes as follows:

The Exploitation Argument

1 Markets in X involve widespread exploitation.
2 If so, then it is morally impermissible to purchase X.
3 Therefore, it is morally impermissible to purchase X.

Now, to construct an exploitation argument, just insert different contested commodities for X: organs, sexual services, paid surrogacy, sweatshop labor, wage labor in general, chocolate, diamonds, or whatnot. Surely, critics say, some markets are wrongful because they involve exploitation.

Essential Vs. Contingent Exploitation

Let's take it for granted for the sake of argument that many markets do involve widespread exploitation and that such exploitation is wrong. This leaves open, though, whether such markets are essentially and necessarily exploitative, or whether they are only incidentally and contingently exploitative. As we discussed in Part I, many times the opposition to markets is not actually about the thing being sold, but about the *way* that it's being sold.

Take any good X that you think it is normally permissible to sell. We can imagine an instance of buying and selling X where one of the parties to the trade exploits the other. Doing so is easy: just modify the Drowning Man thought experiment above. Imagine one party, due to misfortune, desperately needs to buy or sell. Imagine that the other party knows the first party is desperate and takes advantage of this when they make a deal. So, for instance, it is normally permissible to buy and sell apples. But now imagine you're drowning, and we offer to save you, but only if you sell us next year's apple harvest at pennies per bushel.

But it does not follow from this, of course, that it is inherently immoral to buy the good in question, as that good is not the kind of thing that should be bought or sold. Rather, all that follows is that in this particular instance buying the good involves exploitation. In other cases, where there is no exploitation, there is no objection to buying the good.

So, with any particular good or service that some person claims is being sold or produced in an exploitative way, we need to know whether the person thinks that it's possible to sell or produce the good in a non-exploitative way, or whether she believes that buying and selling the good necessarily leads to exploitation. As explained in Chapters 2 and 3, anti-commodification theorists intend to show that there are inherent limits to markets. Their view is that some things may permissibly be possessed, and can even be given away, but may not be bought or sold. Thus, they need to identify classes of goods that it is permissible to have, but selling or buying those goods always introduces wrongful exploitation where there previously was none.

Prostitution

Consider the example of prostitution. In real life, it's possible that most sex trading has been exploitative. However, if so, it's not, as far as we can tell, because sexual markets are inherently exploitative. The problem with extant sexual markets is that people often beat and rape prostitutes, that traffickers sometimes enslave them, that police officers often abuse them, and that people often sell sexual services only because they are in dire economic circumstances. But that none of this implies prostitution is inherently exploitative. If prostitution is often or even always exploitative, it is exploitative only due to the presence of certain conditions that in principle could be absent. (In Part V, we'll argue that our negative attitudes toward prostitution markets are part of what make them so bad.)

Consider the character Belle in the TV series *Secret Diary of a Call Girl*. Belle is a college graduate. She chooses to be a high-class prostitute because it pays well and she enjoys sex. She isn't desperate and could get another job. Belle hasn't been beaten, raped, enslaved, or exploited. She hasn't experienced mental illness, addiction, or childhood trauma. Selling sex does not traumatize her; rather, she enjoys it. Some people might find her behavior distasteful, repulsive, or undignified, but that doesn't make it wrong. Buying sex from someone like Belle isn't inherently wrong. (Recall that we have already dealt with semiotic and corruption objections in previous chapters.) It's a mutually enjoyable, mutually beneficial exchange with an autonomous, consenting adult. Buying sex from Belle is roughly on par, morally speaking, with paying a musician to play you a song.[3]

Now, perhaps no actual prostitutes have been like Belle. (The show is based on a real person, Brooke Magnanti, who is now a research scientist at the University of Bristol.[4]) If so, then perhaps all actual payments for sex have been wrong. Still, that wouldn't show that buying sex is inherently wrong. It would at most just show that the conditions under which it's not wrong to buy sex haven't occurred.

In summary, prostitution may often or usually be exploitative, but it is not essentially exploitative. The imperative to avoid exploitative sex markets does not translate into an imperative to avoid sex markets, period.

Wage Labor

Almost all Marxists used to believe, and many still do believe, that for-profit wage labor is essentially and necessarily exploitative. Their argument went as follows:

The Marxist Exploitation Argument

1 *The Labor Theory of Value*: The price of a good on a market is determined by the value of the labor that produced those goods.
2 To produce a product, a capitalist must buy raw materials on the market, for price \$RM.
3 The value \$RM of these raw materials is determined by the labor it took to produce them. (This follows from the Labor Theory of Value.)
4 The workers will add their socially useful labor to these raw materials. Let's say their labor is worth \$L.
5 Therefore, their finished product will sell for \$RM +\$L on the market. (This follows from the Labor Theory of Value.)
6 *The Definition of Profit*: A capitalist can make a profit only by selling the goods he produces in his factory for less than what he paid to produce them.
7 Since the goods will sell for \$RM +\$L on the market, and since the capitalist already paid \$RM for the raw materials, the only way for the capitalist to make a profit is to buy labor from his workers at a wage \$W, where W < L.
8 Therefore, for a capitalist to make a profit, he must pay his workers less than the actual value of their labor.

According to Marx, the reason workers put up with this bad deal is that they have few other options. They are like Bob in Drowning Man—they either have to accept the bad deal, or die. The capitalists own all the land and productive property, so workers must either sell their labor for less than their labor is worth, or die of starvation.

There are two serious problems with the Marxian exploitation argument. First, it relies upon the Labor Theory of Value, which economists definitively refuted in the 1870s. In fact, prices are set by supply and demand, not by the value of the labor that went into producing the good. Marx conflated two separate claims, A and B:

A In order to transform materials into something more valuable, one usually has to work or labor on those materials.
B The value of materials sold on the market is determined by the value of the labor that went into producing them.

The reason the Labor Theory of Value seems attractive, intuitively, is because A is true. But B, not A, is the Labor Theory of Value, and B does not follow logically from A.

Marx actually got things backwards. Marx thought that the value of the product was determined by the value of the labor that went into the product. On the contrary, it's closer to the truth that the value of the labor that goes into the product is determined by the value of the product.

Second, Marx did not seem to realize that in a normal market transaction, both parties profit. Suppose Alice sells Betty a candy bar for $1. Normally, this doesn't mean that Alice tricked Betty into paying more than the candy is worth, or that Betty tricked Alice into accepting less than the candy's objective value. Rather, there's no such thing as the objective value of the candy. Instead, the candy has a different value for Alice than it does for Betty. Alice values the candy for less than $1, while Betty values it for more than $1. Alice and Betty both are better off after the transaction than before.

Some contemporary Marxists will respond that even if Marx was wrong about the details of the exploitation argument, it remains true that many workers are underpaid, because capitalists take advantage of their desperation to pay them a wage less than they could earn under better bargaining circumstances.

We note that this new argument implies that at worst wage labor is only contingently exploitative. The original Marxist argument, based on the labor theory of value, said that it was impossible both to 1) make a profit and 2) pay workers what their labor is worth. This new argument instead says that workers in fact tend to get less than what their labor is worth, but only because they have a bad bargaining position. At least in principle, even the most diehard contemporary Marxist must admit that it is possible to pay a laborer the full value of her work, without exploiting her, and still make a profit.

Anderson on Surrogacy

Elizabeth Anderson claims that paid surrogacy exposes women to exploitation. The problem, she says, is that women who serve as surrogates are often "oriented toward the exchange of 'gift' values, while the other party operates in accordance with the norms of market exchange."[5] What Anderson means by this is that the surrogate mother is often not acting solely in her self-interest, but instead works from a desire to help promote others' welfare. In contrast, Anderson claims, those who purchase surrogacy services treat the surrogate mother as a mere means to producing a baby—they have their own self-interest at heart, and do not intrinsically care about the woman who carries the baby. Anderson claims the contract between the surrogate and her employers ends up being exploitative. The parents who employ the surrogate, or the agency that finds the surrogate on their behalf, take advantage of the surrogate mother's kindness in order to secure the best deal they can for themselves. Surrogacy agencies manipulate potential surrogate mothers, telling them that if they really were generous and loving, they would not be "so solicitous about securing their own interests."[6] She also claims that many women who become surrogates do so because they feel guilt over having had abortions or because they are trying to work through other emotional issues. Only 1% of surrogate mothers do so entirely for the money.[7]

Suppose Anderson were correct. Suppose surrogate mothers tend not to bargain for maximal compensation because they are oriented in part by altruistic motives. Suppose, however, that the parents who employ surrogates always drive a hard bargain. According to Anderson, the parents then take advantage of and exploit these mothers. But if this is a reason to forbid markets in surrogacy, it is a reason to forbid many or most markets in nursing, medical practice, teaching, counseling, protection, childcare, many forms of training, and a wide range of other markets as well. It is a reason to forbid Michigan from hiring Anderson. The problem is that many people who sell goods or services have partly altruistic motives, while many of their customers are selfish. People who are attracted to care professions want to help people, but people who want care often just want, in that moment, to help themselves. Anderson would have difficulty showing that her complaints about surrogacy apply especially or particularly to surrogacy.

However, we are not sure Anderson's argument is correct. On behalf of the claim that surrogacy agencies try to take advantage of women, she uses a collection of essays published in 1984 by Pandora Press, a "women's" or "second-wave feminist" book publisher. On behalf of the claim that only 1% of surrogate mothers are motivated entirely by the money and that many of them have emotional issues, she cites one peer-reviewed psychiatry article from 1983. Paid surrogacy was uncommon in the early 1980s; it's more common now. Who is willing to participate in that market has changed, and the motives and attitudes have probably changed as well.

At any rate, even if Anderson were right, it would not show that surrogacy is *essentially* exploitative. It may turn out that most parents take advantage of potential surrogate mothers' generosity in order to secure the best deal they can for themselves. If so, then we could just agree that those transactions involve some level of exploitation. (Whether it is wrongful exploitation is another matter.) However, this doesn't imply that surrogacy is *always* or essentially exploitative. If it is exploitative, it is exploitative because of conditions that do not always obtain. Even according to Anderson's weak sources, at least 1% of surrogacy contracts that obtained before 1983 did not involve this kind of exploitation. If there is an imperative to avoid exploitation, this doesn't translate into an imperative to avoid surrogacy contracts. Instead, at most it translates into an imperative to avoid exploitative surrogacy contracts.

We note in passing that similar responses undermine Anderson's other complaints about paid surrogacy. She worries that some women enter into such contracts in ignorance of the intense emotions involved. Surrogate mothers don't really know what they're getting into. But, if so, this doesn't show that paid surrogacy is wrong. At most, it shows that we should only hire women as surrogates who have previously given birth, because these women will be able to make informed decisions about the emotional costs of surrogacy. Similarly, Anderson worries that many surrogacy contracts do not allow surrogates to back out if they want to keep the baby. Without here entering into a discussion of whether such surrogates really should be allowed to keep the baby—itself a complicated question—we can just say even if this is a problem, it doesn't show that paid surrogacy is inherently wrong. At most, it just shows that we should have surrogacy contracts that give surrogate mothers more power. Finally, Anderson complains that commercial surrogacy asks women to undermine their natural bonds with the babies they carry. But, if so, then this is not essentially a problem for paid surrogacy. It also implies that unpaid surrogacy for one's family or friends is morally problematic, if perhaps not *as* morally problematic.

Are There *Any* Essentially Exploitative Markets?

In looking through the academic literature on exploitation or brainstorming this issue ourselves, we cannot locate any markets that are essentially exploitative. Instead, the markets that people claim are exploitative are only contingently so. Markets in organs, human hair, diamonds, T-shirts, and sex may involve massive exploitation, but if so, that's just because of the way the current markets happen to be organized. At least in principle, there can be markets in these goods that do not involve any exploitation. So, if there is value to be gained from markets in these goods—e.g., if it turns out that markets in organ sales really would save lives—then we should not try to eliminate such markets, but instead try to make them less exploitative. In the following chapters, we will discuss some proposals on how to do that.

In Part I, we explained that the debate about commodification is not about business ethics. Business ethics concerns what moral norms businesses must abide by, such as principles forbidding dishonesty, coercion, exploitation, and harm, and perhaps principles requiring businesses to seek to promote the common good or the interests of certain affected groups. Perhaps, when certain businesses violate these norms, we acquire a duty to boycott those businesses. But none of that means that the products they sell are inherently the kinds of things that cannot be for sale. So, for example, it might turn out empirically that all chicken nugget sellers illegally dump waste products in schoolchildren's drinking water. If so, we should refrain from buying chicken nuggets. But it's not because chicken nuggets aren't the kind of thing that should be bought or sold, but just because the existing sellers happen to run their businesses wrongly.

So it goes with other exploitative markets. It may be that buying sex from the prostitute on the corner involves exploitation, but that doesn't mean buying sex necessarily is exploitative.

In addition, it's not merely enough that the product be essentially exploitative. The main philosophical debate about commodification is about whether *markets introduce wrongness where there wasn't any to begin with.*

When people complain about commodification, they mean to complain that *making something a commodity* is morally problematic. Thus, consider the market in child pornography. In one sense of "exploitation," these markets always involve exploiting children. And, as we said in the introduction, it is wrong to buy and sell child pornography. However, the fundamental problem is not with the buying or selling of child pornography, but with the possession of it in the first place. One should not buy or sell child pornography because one should not have it. The problem isn't the *market* in child porn; it's child porn. In contrast, the debate about commodification is about things which one may permissibly possess and acquire, but which cannot be bought or sold. Complaints about commodification are supposed to be complaints about commodification.

Of course, commodifying bad things, things people shouldn't have or do anyway, might make things even worse. Child pornography is bad, period, but industrializing the production of it would probably be even worse. But, as explained in Part I, that's not the issue that the anti-commodification theorists are concerned with.

This is a point that matters. The burden of proof is on critics of commodification to say why exchanging certain goods and services is wrong. In some cases—such as organ sales and information markets—their opposition to commodifying certain goods and services might literally be *killing* people. In other cases—such as prostitution, drugs, or surrogacy—their opposition might be driving people onto black markets, where they are harmed and exploited.

As far as we can tell, no anti-commodification critic has identified any essentially exploitative markets, we could just end our discussion of exploitation here. Our thesis in this book is that if you can have it for free, you may buy it, and if you may give it away, you may sell it. There are no inherent limits to markets, only incidental limits.

Essential Vs. Incidental Objections

Since this is a book about whether commodifying certain goods and services introduces evil where there wasn't any to begin with, here in Part IV, we limit our discussion of exploitation, harm to self, and misallocation to cases where others claim that the market really is the source of the problem. We will examine various cases where anti-commodification theorists claim it is permissible to buy and sell the goods and services in question, but, they claim, markets in those goods and services cause wrongful exploitation and misallocations, and there is no way to design or regulate that market that would overcome these problems.

Notes

1 Conly 2013.
2 Conly 2013, 1.
3 Someone might claim that by selling sex, Belle debases herself, even though she doesn't regard it as debasing. But if Belle doesn't see herself as debased and you do, who's right? (Since I don't resent selling my labor, does that mean selling my labor doesn't debase me, but perhaps it does debase an orthodox Marxist?) The answers to these questions aren't obvious.
4 See also Levitt and Dubner's 2009, 49–56, description of Allie.
5 Anderson 1990, 84–85.
6 Anderson 1990, 85.
7 Anderson 1990, 85.

17

LINE UP FOR EXPENSIVE EQUALITY!

Recently, I (Brennan) had to fly out of Reagan National right after class. When I arrived at the airport, there were a hundred people in line at the security checkpoint. The forty-minute wait might have made me miss my flight. But I had a first class ticket. I skipped the line and went through security immediately. Later, I purchased TSA Pre-Check, so I skip the line even when I fly coach.

Some might think this is unfair to the other passengers, those stuck in the long line. Would it have been more just or fair to make everyone stand in line together, regardless of ability or willingness to pay?

Markets Vs. Queues

Economists don't much care for having people stand in line. In their eyes, a long line is a sign something has gone wrong. They regard queues as inefficient, for reasons we will discuss further below.

But one anti-commodification theorist thinks we overlook the virtues of queues. Sandel claims that it is sometimes better to distribute some goods via queues rather than through markets.[1] Consider the following case:

- *Shakespeare in the Park*: New York City's Public Theater produces outdoor performances called "Shakespeare in the Park". It distributes tickets for "free" (we'll explain the scare quotes in a moment) in the early afternoon before the performance. A line forms hours before the ticket booth opens, full of people eager to get tickets. Thus, to get a ticket, most people need to queue for a few hours. But some people have advertised on Craigslist that they are willing to be paid to stand in line to collect tickets for others. According to Sandel, some line-standers received as much as $125 for this service.[2]

It's easy to regard this as a kind of cheating. The Public Theater wanted to give the tickets away, but some people are getting tickets without having to stand in line for them. It seems to violate everything we learned in Kindergarten.

Sandel worries that line-standing services change the composition of the audience in undesirable ways. The Public Theater wanted the tickets to be available to all, regardless of ability to pay. But if people start paying others to stand in line, then the tickets will tend to go towards those who can afford to pay $125 for a ticket. Once a large market in line-standing services develops, it will be almost as if the Theater itself were charging prices. Many low-income people who were willing to stand in line will no longer get tickets. Sandel concludes: the problem with markets in line-standing services is that they end up putting a price on things that were meant to be free. And, in doing so, they end up putting goods in the hands of the rich rather than the poor.

Sandel thinks that this worry generalizes. In his view, queuing is egalitarian, while markets are not. His argument goes like this:

The Queues are More Egalitarian Argument

1 Queuing distributes goods equally—everyone is on par.
2 Markets distribute goods according to willingness to pay.
3 People's willingness to pay is dependent not merely on how much they value something, but how much money they have to pay for it.
4 If so, then distributing according to willingness to pay tends to favor the rich over the poor. People have unequal ability to pay.
5 At least in some cases, it is unfair or undesirable for a good to be distributed unequally.
6 So, at least in some cases, it is preferable for a good to be distributed by queues rather than by markets.

In short, Sandel believes that queues treat us as equals, while markets favor the rich over the poor.

Let's take a closer look at premise 2. Many economists favor prices over queues because, they say, putting prices on things tends to ensure that those who want the thing more are more likely to get it. Consider, say, the market in ice. Suppose there are three consumers, Bob, Charlie, and Daniela, each of whom wants ice. Bob wants ice just so he can watch it melt. He is only willing to pay $1 per bag. Charlie wants ice to keep his beer cold. He is willing to pay $2 per bag. Daniela wants ice to keep her insulin cold. She is willing to pay $10 per bag. On a market, as ice becomes more scarce, the price of ice will increase. As the price increases, people who get low value from ice (such as Bob) leave the market, but people who get high value from ice (such as Daniela) remain in the market. So, if ice started selling for $5 a bag, Daniela would buy the ice she needs (making a hefty $5 profit on the first bag she buys), while Bob and Charlie would not buy any. And so, economists claim, market prices tend to help ensure that products go toward their most valued uses. This is one reason economists favor markets over queues or rationing.

Now let's take a close look at premise 3. The problem, Sandel says, is that people's demand doesn't simply depend on how much value they get from the thing they consume, but also on how much money they have to spend. Consider: the famous 1789 restaurant in Georgetown serves a fine 14 oz. cut of aged Shenandoah Valley rib eye for $55. Now, consider two people: Jason is an upper-middle class professor. Etienne is a hungry child from Haiti. Etienne *needs* the steak more than Jason. Etienne would get much more value from the steak than Jason would. But the steak will go to someone like Jason, not someone like Etienne. You, the reader, almost certainly have more food and clothing than you need. Some of it is of no real value to you. But, a critic of markets can complain, this clothing went to you, rather than a ragged refugee, because you have more money. (We should pause here to note that food and clothing gets produced in the first place in anticipation of someone being willing and able to buy it, not in anticipation of someone merely needing it.)

Sandel notes, with unease, that there is a trend of markets in "line-jumping." Many airlines offer people the right to jump the queue at security (or go through a dedicated fast-track line) for a fee. Commuters can sometimes buy access to express lanes with lower traffic. "Concierge" medical services allow the rich to buy immediate access to doctors while average people are stuck waiting for appointments. Line-standing services allow lobbyists to pay for homeless people to stand in line for them at Capital Hill, thus helping lobbyists gain an advantage over common people in bringing matters before Congress. Sandel worries that all such services do is produce greater inequality. The rich, who already have so much more than everyone else, get yet further advantages over others.

Are Queues More Egalitarian in the Short Term?

Queues are not really egalitarian. As Sandel himself acknowledges, premise 1 of his argument isn't strictly speaking true. Substituting a queue for a market just substitutes the currency of time for the currency of money. Sandel is right that there is no guarantee that markets will, in the short run, distribute goods to those who value those goods the most. But there is little guarantee that queues will either. He's worried that markets might in the short run crowd out the poor, but he understates the worry that queues might crowd out the busy. Sandel says that the goal of Shakespeare in the Park is to "make Shakespeare freely available to everyone."[3] But deciding to distribute tickets via a queue doesn't achieve this goal.

We all have 24 hours in a day, but we are not equally rich in time. Some of us have massive opportunity costs for our time, and some of us do not. Queuing favors the retired, the unemployed, those with few responsibilities, the idle rich, and the irresponsible. It disfavors busy workers, parents, those with many responsibilities, and those who take their responsibilities seriously. High school students have time to stand in line, but high school teachers do not. People collecting disability checks have time to stand in line, but the nurses who treat them do not. Queuing is not essentially egalitarian or fair. Markets may in some sense favor those with disposable income, but queuing favors those with disposable time. Some of us really can't afford to get in line at 10 am to get "free" tickets from a box office that opens at 1 pm. When the Public Theater decides to give away tickets, it prices busy people out of the market.

Queuing tends to punish productive and hard-working people, but tends to reward those who do not take on such burdens. This may seem like a classist or snobbish thing to say. But it need not be interpreted that way. We can illustrate our point by comparing our current selves to our past selves. When we were 20 years old, we contributed hardly anything to society or to others. We were typical self-centered, hedonistic college students. We were net tax-consumers rather than net-taxpayers. But we had plenty of time to stand in line for "free" tickets to Shakespeare in the Park. We both contribute far more to society now than we did when we were 20. We have plenty of responsibilities. We are net taxpayers rather than net tax-consumers. But neither of us now has time to stand in line. When the Public Theater chooses to make tickets for a special performance available for free, it thereby decides to reward our irresponsible younger selves at the expense of our responsible adult selves.

Insofar as queues are egalitarian or fair on one dimension, they are inegalitarian and unfair on others. If a theater company decides to give away tickets via a queue, it doesn't really give everyone equal chance. Instead, it decides to favor some people over others. Deciding to distribute tickets via a queue may help to get tickets in the hands of some poor Shakespeare lovers who could never afford to buy a ticket. But at the same time, it will mean that many busy working people who could have afforded to buy a ticket now can't afford the time it takes to acquire one.

The Public Theater's underlying goal is to make the tickets as widely available as possible. If so, then perhaps they should welcome line-standing services. After all, some people are short on time to stand in line for tickets, while others are short on money to buy tickets. If so, then a mixed system, in which some people with lots of free time stand in line to get tickets for themselves, but in which others without free time pay people to stand in line for them, helps to ensure that both the idle and the busy, the poor and better off, can have access to the tickets.

If Sandel is worried that most people can't afford $125 for line-standing services, he should welcome rather than condemn further commodification of line-standing. As line-standing services become more common, competitive pressures should push the price of line-standing services down, such that not only the rich, but other busy working people can afford to hire line-standers.

There are people who are genuinely disadvantaged whether we have a market in line-standing or not: the busy poor. A poor person working full-time doesn't get a ticket to Shakespeare in the Park, regardless of whether we forbid line-standing services or not.

Time Vs. Money

There is massive inequality in wealth. According to the Giving What We Can's "How Rich Am I?" calculator, I (Brennan) have an income, adjusted for my local cost of living and my household size (two adults, two kids), that is over 65 times that of the typical person worldwide.[4] However, my life expectancy is not 65 times that of the typical person worldwide. The distribution of time is in some sense far more equal than the distribution of wealth. One might be tempted to make the following argument:

Queues are More Egalitarian, Part II:

1 Time is distributed more equally than money, even once we account for the opportunity cost of time.
2 Therefore, if we want equal outcomes, it is better to distribute via time than via money.
3 Queuing distributes via time, while markets distribute via money.
4 Therefore, if we want equal outcomes, distributing via queues is better than distributing via money.

This argument seems plausible on the surface. But when we dig deeper, we will see we should be wary of spending time instead of money.

According to Angus Madisson, real GDP per capita worldwide, in 1990 Geary-Khamis dollars, increased from $467 in 1 AD to $6516 in 2003.[5] Brad Delong claims that real GDP per capita worldwide went from about $130 in 5000 BC to over $8000 by 2002.[6] Economists dispute the exact numbers, but they agree that average and median incomes have each risen by a factor of at least 20 in the past few hundred years.

At the same time, as people have gotten richer, they are living longer. Life expectancy doubled in the past century. The average person born in England today has a life expectancy at birth almost four times that of a person born in England 1000 years ago.[7]

The average (and median, and modal) person is getting richer in both time and wealth. But she is getting far richer in wealth than she is in time. This is one reason to want to distribute things as much as possible through markets rather than through queues. We are in some sense more equal in the amount of time we have than the amount of wealth we have, but time is in general much more scarce and precious than wealth. We should be extremely wary of distributing anything via time. When Sandel favors distribution via queues, he in effect says we should make the price of tickets to Shakespeare in the Park extremely high.

Now, that said, there are people who can spare cash more easily than time, and those who can spare time more easily than cash. Markets in line-standing help both kinds of people—those relatively rich in time can trade time for money; those relatively rich in money can trade money for time.

The Unseen Third Party

When Sandel decries line-standing services, he focuses on two parties: first, the (usually richer) person who paid for someone else to hold his place, and, second, the (usually poorer) person who ended up missing out or having to wait longer because the first person paid someone else to stand in line. But Sandel does not talk much about how line-standing services affect a third party—the person who is paid to stand in line. Line-standing services may in some cases make it more likely that a rich person rather than a poor person will have access to whatever good is being distributed via queues. However, at the same time, line-standing services transfer money from rich people who can afford to pay for line-standing to poor people who benefit from standing in line.

So, line-standing services don't simply cause rich people to snag theater tickets from college kids, but also transfer cash from rich people to poor people. Sandel himself says that people are more equal in time than in money. If so, then for this reason, Sandel should perhaps *favor* rather than oppose line-standing services. After all, when a rich person pays a poor person to do something for him, they become more equal in wealth.

Henry Hazlitt once said, "The art of economics consists in looking not merely at the immediate but the longer effects of any act or policy; it consists in tracing the consequences of that policy not merely for one group but for all groups."[8] When economists want to discuss the consequences of different policies, they consider all of those involved or who potentially could be involved. They consider not just the seen, but the unseen. Consider, then, two situations:

> *Situation A:* Busy Bob wants theater tickets, but can't afford to stand in line. Idle Ira wants tickets, and stands in line to get them. Homeless Harry wants food, but doesn't get any.
> *Situation B:* Busy Bob wants theater tickets, but can't afford to stand in line. He pays Homeless Harry $100 to stand in line for him. Homeless Harry now has $100 to spend on food and other necessities. Idle Ira, who was behind Harry, doesn't get a ticket.

The Public Theater might well prefer Situation A to Situation B. But it's not at all clear that the rest of us should share this preference. When economists say that markets tend to ensure goods go to their highest valued uses, they want us to consider all the goods involved—money, time, tickets, etc.—and all the users—Bob, Ira, and Harry. Suppose that Busy Bob enjoys Shakespeare less than Idle Ira. Even if so, situation B might well be preferable to situation A, because Homeless Harry probably enjoys the $100 even more than Idle Ira enjoys Shakespeare.

John Tomasi responds to Sandel that once we look at how markets in queue-jumping affect everyone, it's not so obvious that such markets are unfair. Tomasi asks us to consider two competing ways of thinking about fairness:[9]

1 *Nobody Cuts*: First come, first served. According to the principle, no one should be allowed to pay for an expedited trip through security. Instead, everyone should get in the same line, based on the order she arrives, and wait her turn.
2 *Social Justice*: According to this principle, inequalities are to be allowed if, in general, a policy of allowing inequalities benefits everyone, especially the worst off.

When it comes to airport security lines, Tomasi asks, which principle is better?

The problem with Nobody Cuts, as we discussed previously, is that while it's egalitarian in some ways, it's inegalitarian in others. First come, first served doesn't favor the rich buyer over the poor buyer, but it does favor the less busy over the busy. Nobody Cuts means I couldn't teach a class and then fly shortly after, but people on vacation can fly at their leisure.

Let's consider the second principle, the Social Justice Principle. According to this principle, we should allow inequalities when allowing such inequalities tends to benefit all, especially when such inequalities benefit the worst off. The idea here is that—if we are rational and not envious—it is better to each have unequal but big slices of a big pie than to have equally small slices from a small pie.

Tomasi asks us to consider: when someone pays for the expedited line at the airport, what happens to everyone else? The people who pay for extra amenities, first class tickets, queue-jumping, and so on, enable airlines to "lower their fare, compensating customers for slightly slower security lines, and luring new customers."[10] Industry business consultant Michael Boyd estimates that "premium first-class passengers account for 75 percent of the revenue on cross-country flights."[11] He says, "Pandering to business traffic is a lot more important than getting [coach class] volume." Full-fare first and business class travelers in effect subsidize everyone else.

Also, when the price of airfare decreases, bus and train prices must also decrease to remain competitive. So, Tomasi says, when a person pays to jump the queue, she isn't just inconveniencing those who didn't pay. She is instead helping to reduce their airfare and helping to reduce the cost of transportation for those taking the bus or train.

Tomasi doesn't say that literally everyone is made better off by queue-jumping. There may be some people who are unwilling to pay to jump the queue themselves, but who would prefer slightly more expensive tickets and a slightly shorter wait time. But, here, Tomasi says, we need to ask people to be a little public-spirited rather than purely selfish. If a market benefits the vast majority of people but causes you an inconvenience, an inconvenience you are unwilling to pay to avoid, the decent thing to do is shrug your shoulders and put up with it.

The Static Vs. the Long Term

So far, we have focused only on how queuing and market prices affect the distribution of goods in the short run. We've found serious flaws in Sandel's argument even with our focus so limited. But once we consider how markets and queuing fair in the long run, we see that the case for queues is even weaker.

Suppose there is a shortage of a needed good, say, gasoline. The government might decide that it is unfair to distribute gasoline via markets, and instead impose a rationing or a queuing system. Perhaps this will lead to a more equitable distribution of gasoline in the short term, during the crisis. But the problem is that distributing gasoline this way tends to ensure we'll be stuck in that crisis for the long term.

Consider what happens when we allow the market to deal with the shortage. When there is a supply shock—when the amount of gasoline available suddenly declines—the price of gasoline will rise. In the short term, as we discussed earlier, we expect low value users (people buying gas to ride ATVs on weekends) will drop out of the market faster than high value users (governments buying gas to fuel ambulances).

But, beyond that, a high price on gasoline acts as a lure, drawing *more suppliers* into the market. When the price of gasoline becomes higher, this incentivizes potential suppliers to start producing gasoline. So, for example, it might be unprofitable to extract oil from shale when oil sells for $20/barrel, but profitable when oil sells for $100/barrel.

More importantly, when the price of a good becomes high, this also induces potential suppliers to *find and supply alternatives* to that good. If the price of gasoline suddenly rose to $20/gallon, then anyone who could produce an alternative cheaper power source could make a fortune. Right now, one reason why there are few alternatives to gasoline is that gasoline is rather inexpensive. However, as the price of gasoline increases, so does the potential gain from finding substitutes. As any particular good becomes more scarce, the market automatically increases the reward to anyone who can develop a substitute. This is one way markets encourage innovation.

Similarly, consider what would happen if there were a shortage of ice after, say, a hurricane strikes Louisiana.[12] The Red Cross might decide to hand out ice for free, using a queuing system, giving each person in the line two bags until the ice runs out. But suppose in addition we allow a market in ice to emerge. With such a shortage of ice, ice might start going for $20 a bag. At first glance, that seems terrible. Rich Frat Boy Frank might buy the ice to keep his beer cold, while Poor Diabetic Diane can't afford the ice to keep her insulin cool. But consider what happens when Price-Gouger Pete in New Jersey hears that he can sell ice for $20 a bag in Louisiana. He decides to rent an ice truck, buy all the local cheap ice he can, and then drive down to Louisiana to sell it. When he arrives, he helps reduce the shortage, and also helps cause the price of ice to fall. At the same time, Entrepreneurial Edith in Virginia hears that ice is still selling for $15/bag in Louisiana, and does the same thing Pete did. The shortage is lessened even further, and the price of ice falls even more. As long as the price of ice stays elevated in Louisiana, more and more people like Pete and Edith will have an incentive to bring much-needed ice to Louisiana. And so, if we just let the market do its thing, the market will end the shortage and bring prices back down. All this might seem exploitative, but as long as people can make higher-than-normal profits from selling ice, they will have an incentive to supply ice where it is most scarce.

What Sandel and others miss is that markets and queuing not only affect how existing supplies of a good are distributed, but also affect whether new supplies will be produced, whether substitutes will be produced or created, and how those goods will be distributed into the future. Sandel extols the virtues of queues only because he limits his focus to how queues affect a small number of people in the short term. When we consider how queues affect everyone in the long term, the argument for queues becomes much weaker. As Matt Zwolinski concludes, "From a purely static perspective, there's a case to be made for queuing in certain circumstances, but there's almost nothing to be said for it from a more dynamic perspective."[13]

Over the long run, markets drive the prices of most goods we want to consume way down. This means that all of us are in a real sense spending less time in getting those goods, more of us are getting them, and we are getting more of them. It is basic economics to say that our standard of living is higher now because the costs of pretty much everything in terms of time and labor are much lower now. For instance, between 1835 and 1850, the price of light in Britain in terms of average labor hours was cut in half. Between 1850 and 1890, it was further cut by about 97%. Quite literally, we can now buy more light with 10 seconds of labor than a caveperson could have bought with 60 hours of labor.[14]

What Sandel Neglected to Mention

Sandel complains about five cases where people can buy the "right to cut in line":

1 Lines at airport security
2 Express lanes on freeways
3 Lines for lobbying Congress
4 Lines to get tickets from New York City's Public Theater
5 Doctors' appointment times in Beijing's hospitals.[15]

For someone who wants to expose the evils of overmarketization and overcommodification, this is an incongruous list. In each case, the market that Sandel decries arises in response to badly administered government services and goods, services and goods the government provides at low quality or in insufficient amounts. In each case, the market is responding to government-failure and government-made scarcity.

Airport security lines are long because governments administer airport security in invasive, ineffective, and counterproductive ways. We will not belabor this point here, but instead just invite readers to examine peer-reviewed social scientific analyses of the problems with airport security, such as Harvey Molotch's *Against Security: How We Go Wrong at Airports, Subways, and Other Sites of Ambiguous Danger*.[16] John Mueller and Mark Stewart argue that to justify the expense of the Homeland Security Administration, the HSA would need to prevent nearly 1700 major terrorist events per year.[17] Steven Levitt and Steven Dubner claim that airport security lines effectively kill people:

> The beauty of terrorism—if you're a terrorist—is that you can succeed even by failing … Let's say it takes an average of one minute to remove and place your shoes in the airport security line. In the United States alone, this procedure happens roughly 560 million times per year. Five hundred and sixty million minutes equals more than 1,065 years—which, divided by 77.8 years (the average U.S. life expectancy at birth), yields a total of nearly 14 person-lives. So even though Richard Reid [the attempted shoe-bomber] failed to kill a single person, he levied a tax on time equivalent to 14 lives per year.[18]

Similar remarks apply to how the state provides public roads. Traffic congestion means there is a shortage of roads (and alternatives to roads).

This congestion is killing people both literally and figuratively. It kills people by causing more accidents, causing more pollution, and by causing higher blood pressure. But it also kills people the way that having to remove shoes at the airport kills people. The average commute in the DC metro area is 34.5 minutes,[19] with approximately half a million people commuting each workday.[20] Let's make the generous supposition that DC-area governments are within 50% of the ideal amount of roads, that realistically, the best they could do if they were maximally competent would be to reduce the average commute to 22.75 minutes. If so, then inefficient public transportation is, in effect, wasting 2793 years' worth of life each year in the DC area. When the DC-area governments fail to provide sufficient roads, they are in effect killing 33 people each year, but they spread this death out among all commuters.

Now consider the issue of lobbying. Lobbyists are generally engaging in what economists call *rent seeking*. "Rent seeking" refers to when corporations, unions, or special interest groups lobby the government to manipulate the legal or regulatory environment in their favor. As the Nobel Laureate economist James Buchanan says, "If the government is empowered to grant monopoly rights or tariff protection to one group, at the expense of the general public or of designated losers, it follows that potential beneficiaries will compete for the prize."[21] A high degree of rent seeking is a sign of serious government failure. Economists estimate that the welfare losses from rent seeking in the United States might be as high as 50% of gross national product.[22] So, again, it is somewhat strange for Sandel to complain about markets here, when the problem to which markets are responding is caused by poor government design.

Notes

1 Sandel 2012a, 16–41.
2 Sandel 2012a, 21.
3 Sandel 2012a, 33.
4 Calculations according to http://www.givingwhatwecan.org/why-give/how-rich-am-I, and Milanovic 2007.
5 Maddison 2003, 70.
6 Delong 2002, 120.
7 McCloskey 2008, 18.
8 Hazlitt 1998, 17.
9 Tomasi 2012.
10 Tomasi 2012.
11 Credeur and Schlangenstein 2013.
12 Cf. Zwolinski 2008
13 In conversation.
14 Nordhaus 1996, 46–48.
15 Sandel 2012a, 16–27. Sandel also complains about "concierge doctors," but we see these doctors more as a luxury service than as an issue in line-jumping, and so we will consider this in the next chapter.
16 Molotch 2012.
17 Mueller and Stewart 2011.
18 Levitt and Dubner 2009, 65.
19 http://wamu.org/news/13/03/20/how_long_is_your_commute_an_interactive_map_of_the_dc_metro_region
20 http://www.wtop.com/41/3342484/DC-experiences-largest-commuter-surge-in-nation
21 Buchanan 2003, 15.
22 Mueller 2003, 355.

18

BABY BUYING

A famous photograph published in 1948 in the Valparaiso *Vidette-Messenger*, shows four unkempt, bewildered children, ages 2–6, sitting beside a sign: "Children for Sale: Inquire Within". Their mother, Lucille Chalifoux, stands above them, covering her face in shame. Perhaps the photo was staged. The original caption explains that Chalifoux and her husband—who, by all accounts, were irresponsible, neglectful, and abusive parents—decided to sell the children after years of economic desperation. A recent news report claims that the children were, in some sense, sold—the Chalifouxes did indeed give up their parental rights, at least de facto, in exchange for money. Some of the children went to abusive and exploitative homes; some did not.[1]

Was it wrong to "sell" the children? If so, was the problem the actual "selling," or was it rather the negligent way the parents gave up their parental rights?

This chapter discusses allocation objections to different kinds of markets in babies. We've already discussed worries about paid surrogacy in previous chapters, so we will not examine this issue any further. Instead, we'll start by examining the question of whether it is wrongful to pay for a "designer baby." We'll then discuss markets in adoption rights.

Hooray for Designer Babies

According to the *Wall Street Journal*,

> A personal-genomics company in California has been awarded a broad U.S. patent for a technique that could be used in a fertility clinic to create babies with selected traits, as the frontiers of genetic enhancement continue to advance.

The patented process from 23andMe, whose main business is collecting DNA from customers and analyzing it to provide information about health and ancestry, could be employed to match the genetic profile of a would-be parent to that of donor sperm or eggs. In theory, this could lead to the advent of "designer babies," a controversial idea where genes would be selected to boost the chances of a child having certain physical attributes, such as a particular eye or hair color.[2]

Some will regard this kind of technology as morally problematic.

There is a legitimate worry that we will botch the technology, and in the process end up hurting people. But this is a question of technological prowess, in principle no different from the questions we face with any drug or technology. If someone develops a cancer vaccine, we have to consider questions of side effects, effectiveness, and safety, and the same goes for technology for designer babies. So, let's just agree that there is some threshold of safety that baby designer technology—like any technology—must meet. This is not the issue that concerns us here. As we said in the introduction, the debate about commodification is not a debate about business ethics.

Another legitimate worry is that if people are allowed to design their own babies, this could result in dangerous sexual selection. In some countries, parents prefer male over female infants. If parents are allowed to choose their babies' sex, this could lead to undesirable and dangerous imbalances in sex ratios when the children reach maturity. But this isn't on its face a reason to forbid the market in designer babies—it's just a reason at most to regulate one aspect of that market.

The issue that interests us here is whether designer babies would lead to inequalities of ability. As the *Wall Street Journal* article reports, "Some people say it is unethical to bioengineer children because better-off parents could use it to give their children a competitive edge, widening societal divisions."[3] The argument goes something like this:

The Inequality Argument against Designer Babies

1 If markets in designer baby technology are allowed, these markets will be expensive.
2 If these markets are expensive, then only the rich will be able to afford designer babies.
3 The rich will use the technology to give their children greater health, intelligence, and other desirable traits, creating even further inequality.
4 Causing further equality would be wrong.
5 Therefore, allowing or participating in markets in designer babies is wrong.

This argument can be modified to argue that such markets should also be illegal.

Our response to the Inequality Argument against Designer Babies is to remind the anti-commodification theorist of the normal trend in technological development.

F.A. Hayek argues,

> Our rapid economic advancement is in large part a result of inequality and is impossible without it. Progress at a fast rate cannot proceed on a uniform front, but must take place in an echelon fashion ... At any stage of [the process of growing knowledge] there will always be many things we already know how to produce but which are still too expensive to provide for more than the few ... All of the conveniences of a comfortable home, of our means of transportation, and communication, of entertainment and enjoyment, we could produce at first only in limited quantities; but it was in doing this that we gradually learned to make them or similar things at a much small outlay of resources and thus began to supply them to the great majority. A large part of the expenditure of the rich, though not intended for that end, thus serves to defray experimentation with the new things that, as a result, can later be made available to the poor.[4]

Hayek would say that the reason we're richer now than we were in the past is of course not because we have more resources—if anything, we have less. Instead, it's because we are more knowledgeable about how best to employ existing resources. But, typically, when we learn how to make something new, such as a cellular phone, it is very expensive to produce it on a per-unit basis. The rich buy the first units, get all of the benefits at first, but then also pay all of the upfront costs. They thereby pay for the basic infrastructure that makes it available for all. The rich pay for experimentation, innovation, and fund entrepreneurs in finding ways to market to the poor, though this is not the intention of the rich. The reason wealthy countries today can provide what used to be luxuries (TVs, electricity, flush toilets) for all is because in the past those countries allowed that such goods be provided for just a few, rather than prohibited because not all can have them.

Allowing people to purchase status through markets has a unique feature—it generally causes status goods to become standard goods available to everyone. According to the US Census, 80.9% of US households below the poverty line have cell phones, 58.2% have computers, 83% of them have air conditioning, 68.7% of them have a clothes washer, 65.3% of them have a clothes dryer, and nearly 100% have refrigerators, stoves, and televisions.[5] When most of these items first appeared, only the rich could afford them. The rich buy them in part to have something no one else can afford. But in choosing to purchase such goods, the rich pay for the initial development of these goods, and in turn pay to make those goods available to a wider market. Those who want to buy status must then buy ever newer and fancier things, and the cycle repeats.

Economists have long recognized that when a new technology develops, it is usually expensive, and available at first only to the rich. But, as the rich pay for the initial development of that technology and enjoy the initial benefits, the rich also pay to make the technology available to all. This has been true of, say, dishwashers, washing machines, air conditioning, electric stoves, microwaves, personal computers, landline telephones, cellular phones, smart phones, laptops, air flight, automobiles, furnaces, electric lighting, electricity in general, toilets, sanitation, the ability to bath daily, having enough food to eat, having large houses, having lots of clothing, video games, and pretty much everything else. Perhaps designer baby technology would go against this trend, but that seems doubtful. After all, consider that the cost of sequencing one human genome dropped from over $100 million in 2001 to about $7 thousand in 2013.[6] The available evidence strongly indicates, if not guarantees, that designer baby technology will eventually be in the hands of almost everyone in developed countries.

Imagine a world like ours, but in which the overwhelming majority of people had extremely high IQs, were extremely healthy, had low risks of cancer or other diseases, lived long lives, had few behavioral problems, and were generally leading better lives. This is a world to aim for, not a world to avoid. The premise of the Inequality Argument against Designer Babies is that technology for designing happier, healthier, smarter people will eventually exist, but will be in the hands of the few. Our response is to say that we should welcome it going into the hands of the few, so that it may one day be available to the many.

One might object that such technology will not be available literally to everyone. Perhaps the very poor will never be able to afford to ensure their children are genetically blessed. If so, then undesirable inequalities would persist. We have two responses to this objection.

It remains unclear to us why this would call for closing the market, rather than subsidizing the poor. Consider: right now some people in the United States cannot afford to feed their children. No sensible person thinks this shows we should eliminate markets in food. Instead, at most, it means we should keep having markets in food, but use food stamps to subsidize the poor so that they can buy food. Similarly, if it turned out that designer baby technology forever remained too expensive for the bottom 5% of stable households (the kind of households where we would want children to be raised), then this doesn't on its face call for eliminating the market in designer baby technology. Instead, it at most calls for giving such households tax-funded vouchers for designer babies, in the same way that we subsidize food or health care.

Inequality: So What?

We object to the view that inequalities in talent and ability are inherently undesirable. Implicit in this objection, and in the Inequality Argument against Designer Babies in general, is the assumption that we live in a zero-sum world, where if some people are more talented than we are, this comes at our expense. But whether other people's greater talents come at our expense or help us is a contingent matter, dependent on the kinds of institution we find ourselves in. For people living in small, warlike hunter-gatherer communities, it really is a disaster if the tribe across the river is stronger and smarter than you. But for people living in market societies, it's not only not a disaster, but *good* to encounter people who are stronger and smarter than you.

Markets are not (generally) a zero-sum game. Markets make it so that the way extraordinarily talented people become rich is by offering goods and services to others at prices they can afford to pay. Few of us are as talented as, say, Steve Jobs, James Watt, Edwin Land, George Westinghouse, or Norman Bourlaug, but at the same time, few of us would be better off in a world where they never existed.

Imagine a genie cast a spell so that everyone was less talented than you. The genie makes you the most talented person not by raising your talents, but by making everyone less talented than you. There are two versions of this thought experiment:

1 Assume for the sake of argument there is such a thing as "natural talent", where natural talent refers to our potential under favorable circumstances in light of our genetic endowments. Imagine the genie makes it so that everyone has less natural talent than you. But the genie will allow that some of these less naturally talented people have better skills than you in some things. That way, if you decide to specialize in plumbing and utterly neglect learning carpentry, the genie will allow that some people know how to do carpentry. However, had you decided to do carpentry, you would have been better than any other carpenters, thanks to your greater natural talent.

2 Imagine an even more extreme case in which the genie makes everyone else literally worse than you at everything you can currently do.

In both cases, the genie is an evil genie, not a good genie. The overwhelming majority of people would be much worse off in the situations described in 1 and 2 than they are in the real world.

David Schmidtz summarizes this issue well:

> One way (the only way I know of) to rationalize the idea that *Jane's* being more talented entitles *Joe* to compensation is to suppose that life is like a zero-sum poker game in which the more talented Jane is, the less chance Joe has of winning. If Jane is more talented, Jane captures more of the pie, and captures more at Joe's expense. However, it is Rawls's point, after all, that society is not a zero-sum card game, but a cooperative venture in which the pie's size is variable. Almost all people can have a better life than they could have had on their own, and the reason is simple: Other people's talents make all of us better off. Talented bakers don't just capture pie. They *make* it. The rest of us have more pie, not less, when talented people put their talent to work.[7]

One reason why people struggle with basic economics is that we have a natural tendency to see the world in zero-sum terms. But we need to overcome this tendency. Market economies do involve competition, and sometimes, we would personally benefit from our competitors being less talented than we. But the market economy as a whole is not much like 100 people applying for the same job. Instead, in a market economy, there is far more cooperation than there is competition. For a job at Georgetown, I might compete with 400 applicants, but I type my application on a computer in which literally tens of millions of people had a hand in making. Georgetown Cupcake might prefer that competitor Baked and Wired go out of business, but when you by a cupcake from either place, you eat something that literally tens of millions of people had a hand in making.

A good way to think about this is to consider what might happen if the planet Earth began trading with the Vulcans from Star Trek. Suppose a few hundred years from now, Earth is vastly more productive and technologically advanced. Suppose we Earthlings discover how to build starships. Shortly after we test our first warp drive, the Vulcans make contact with us. Suppose, for the sake of argument, that all Vulcans are more talented than all Earthlings. The dumbest Vulcan is smarter than the smartest Earthling, the weakest adult Vulcan is stronger than the strongest Earthling, and so on. Suppose the Vulcans are also better at doing everything—growing corn, making computers, designing fashion—than Earth is. Everything we can do, they can do better, and they can do things we can't do, too.

To those with little background in economics, it might seem like Vulcans would have no reason to bother to trade with us. Or, to others with little background in economics, it might seem that trading with Vulcans would just put us all out of work, because everything we can do, they can do better.

But economists understand that's a mistake. In fact, except in unusual circumstances, both the Vulcans and Earthlings would gain immensely from interplanetary trade. Each planet should specialize in its comparative advantage—that is, the form of production for which it has the lowest opportunity cost.

To illustrate, suppose Earth needs to use 12 million Earthling workers to produce 1 starship per year, or it needs 2 million workers to produce 1 trillion tons of food per year. Suppose the smarter, stronger, and more logical Vulcans are far better at making things than we are. They need only 1 million Vulcan workers to produce 1 starship per year, or 1 million to produce 1 trillion of food per year.

To see how trade will affect the standard of living on both planets, we need to start by imagining that the planets don't trade, and just decide to produce everything they need themselves. Suppose each planet decides this year to have 12 million of its workers manufacturing starships and 12 million growing food. (To simplify this illustration, we ignore any other goods other workers might produce.) Table 18.1 shows the most they can produce and consume without trade:

TABLE 18.1 Production on Earth and Vulcan without Trade

Planet Labor Allocation (Starships, Food) in billions	Starships	Food, trillions of tons
Earth (12, 12)	1	6
Vulcan (12, 12)	12	12
Total Production	13	18

TABLE 18.2 Production on Earth and Vulcan with Specialization in Anticipation of Trade

Planet Labor Allocation (Starships, Food) in billions	Starships	Food, trillions of tons
Earth (0, 24)	0	12
Vulcan (14, 10)	14	10
Total Production	14 (+1)	22 (+4)

TABLE 18.3 Consumption on Earth and Vulcan after Trade (Vulcan trades 1 starship for 3 trillion tons of food)

Planet	Starships	Food, trillions of tons
Earth (0, 24)	1	9 (+3)
Vulcan (14, 10)	13 (+1)	13 (+1)
Total Consumption	14	22

Now suppose, in anticipation of trading, both planets decide to specialize in their comparative advantage. Earth stops making starships, and all 12 million former starship workers start producing food instead. The Vulcans don't specialize quite as much: they just shift 2 million of their food workers toward producing starships. As Table 18.2 illustrates, the total production of each good now increases as a result of specialization. But this doesn't yet mean that the Vulcans or Earthlings are better off.

Now imagine the Vulcans decide to trade 1 starship for 3 trillion tons of food. Table 18.3 shows that this will make everyone better off than they had been under autarky, when there was no specialization or trade. We don't need to know how much Earthlings and Vulcans value food for this exercise, because, as Table 18.3 shows, after trade, both planets have at least the same or more of both goods after trade.

Now let's examine how trade will affect Earthling and Vulcan wages. Assume that a starship sells on the interplanetary market for $3 trillion dollars, while a trillion tons of food sells on the interplanetary market for $1 trillion. (This is consistent with the Vulcans trading one starship for 3 trillion tons of food.) We can then calculate what the average yearly salary of the workers will be. The average wage in each planet is given by the following formula:

Average Wage = Value of Total Consumption/Number of Units of Labor

In light of that, we can make the calculations in Table 18.4.

In summary, trading with the smarter, stronger, genetically superior Vulcans is a windfall for the relatively dumber, weaker, inferior Earthlings. Vulcans benefit from trading with dumb, weak, and irrational Earthlings, but Earthlings benefit even more from trading with smart, strong, and rational Vulcans.

TABLE 18.4 Average Yearly Wages for Workers

Before Specialization and Trade:

Average Yearly Salary$_{\text{Earth}}$

$$\frac{(1\ \text{starship} \times \$3\ \text{trillion}) + (6\ \text{trillion tons food} \times \$1\ \text{trillion})}{24\ \text{million workers per year}}$$

$375,000

Average Yearly Salary$_{\text{Vulcan}}$

$$\frac{(12\ \text{starships} \times \$3\ \text{trillion}) + (12\ \text{trillion tons food} \times \$1\ \text{trillion})}{24\ \text{million workers per year}}$$

$2,000,000

After Specialization and Trade:

Average Yearly Salary$_{\text{Earth}}$

$$\frac{(1\ \text{starship} \times \$3\ \text{trillion}) + (9\ \text{trillion tons food} \times \$1\ \text{trillion})}{24\ \text{million workers per year}}$$

$500,000
(25% increase)

Average Yearly Salary$_{\text{Vulcan}}$

$$\frac{(13\ \text{starship} \times \$3\ \text{trillion}) + (13\ \text{trillion tons food} \times \$1\ \text{trillion})}{24\ \text{million workers per year}}$$

$2,166,667
(8.33% increase)

Now let's apply this to the argument about designer babies. We can simply repeat the previous exercise, except imagine that the trade occurs not between genetically superior Vulcans and inferior Earthlings, but genetically superior designer humans and the on average inferior humans produced by a genetic lottery. We would get the same results. In normal, well-functioning markets, designer babies' talents are not a curse, but a boon to others. If we can't find the Vulcans, we can design them instead.

Leveling Down

Here's a final objection to opposing designer babies in the name of equality. Suppose only rich parents can afford to engineer their children to have unusually high talents or to be resistant to various diseases. Some might see that as a reason to forbid the practice. But proponents of a ban would then seem to advocate "leveling down egalitarianism": they prefer that everyone be equally badly off rather than allow some but not all to be well off.

Imagine someone developed a vaccine for the common cold, but the vaccine only works on a quarter of people—it had no effect on most. Suppose, by bizarre coincidence, that the vaccine just happened to work on the top 25% of income earners and their families. Now suppose someone said, "It's not fair that the rich will be even better off than the rest of us! In addition to all their other advantages, now they, and only they, will be cured of the common cold. In the name of equality, we should forbid this vaccine."

If somehow vaccinating the rich against the common cold came at everyone else's expense, they'd have some grounds for concern. But here, that's not happening. It's hard to see this as anything other than pure malicious envy.[8]

Markets in Adoption Rights

Now let's turn from the easier question of whether it's permissible to pay for designer babies, to the harder question about whether it's permissible to buy and sell rights to parent babies.

Babies are not the kind of thing you can own. They are not property, the way a guitar or even a dog can be property. One might say that it follows straightforwardly that babies cannot be bought and sold.

However, the question of "baby selling" is not really about whether we can buy and sell babies as if they were property. Instead, the interesting question in the commodification debate is whether it is permissible to buy and sell *adoption rights*.

Biological parents generally have some sort of presumptive guardianship rights over their biological children. Parents have the right to live with their children, raise them as they see fit, and so on, within certain limits. These rights are of course not absolute. Parents who are abusive or negligent can and should forfeit their guardianship rights, that is, their rights to parent their children. Guardianship comes with responsibilities and limits: parents must provide adequately for their children, and they cannot just do anything they want to their children.

Note that guardianship rights are not only something one can forfeit, but something one can relinquish. Parents can voluntarily relinquish their guardianship rights over their children. Moreover, they usually have wide latitude to instead imbue others with those rights. So, for instance, in the hit movie *Juno*, pregnant teen Juno not only decides to relinquish guardianship rights over her baby, but specifically chooses Vanessa. However, even here, almost everyone accepts that there are limits to whom we can choose as adoptive parents. It was permissible for Juno to give Vanessa the baby, but it would not be permissible for her to give the baby to a known pedophile.

Our thesis, recall, is that if you may give something to someone, you may sell that thing to him or her. If you may take something from someone for free, then you may buy that thing from him or her. Let's apply that kind of reasoning here. Some people object to markets in adoption rights. But, for their objection to genuinely be about *markets* in adoption rights, they need to hold that 1) there are cases where it is permissible to transfer adoption rights for free, without the exchange of money, but 2) it would be inherently wrong in those cases to transfer adoption rights for money.

We think the interesting moral questions about markets in adoption rights aren't really about the *markets* per se. Instead, we see two major moral questions:

1 When, if ever, is it permissible for a person to relinquish, voluntarily and without compensation, his or her parental rights over a child?
2 What conditions and factors, independent of the willingness and ability to buy adoption rights, make a potential parent *fit* to adopt a child?

In our view, the ethics of adoption markets just reduces to the answers to these questions. Markets themselves play no explanatory role in explaining when it is wrong to buy and sell adoption rights.

We don't ourselves have an answer to the first question, and it's not essential that we do. Suppose you think parents may voluntarily relinquish their parental rights only if they are in distress. Our response would be that if that view is correct, then only parents in distress may sell parental rights. Or, suppose you think, as many of our left-liberal colleagues do, that new biological parents may always voluntarily relinquish their parental rights, provided they can find a suitable home for their children, or find a suitable governmental or non-governmental agency that will in turn ensure their offspring's welfare. Our response would be that if that view is correct, then any parents meeting those conditions may sell their parental rights. Or, suppose you think that parents may *never* voluntarily relinquish their parental rights. Our response would be that, if so, then they may never sell rights to adopt, but that's not because *selling* per se is wrong. Rather, it's because they may not *give* these rights away, period.

As for the second question: some potential parents are unfit and so should not be allowed to adopt or care for children. Others are fit and should be allowed to adopt or care for children. We do not ourselves have any fully developed theory of parental fitness, though there are philosophers and others who work on explaining this distinction. We accept commonsense ideas, such as that pedophiles should not be allowed to adopt or care for children. We also accept the commonsense idea that we ourselves are fit enough to be parents—our children should not be taken away from us, and we should be allowed to adopt. But beyond uncontroversial claims like these, we do not have a fully worked out theory.

However, let's just say that there is such a theory, the Correct Theory of Fitness, that explains which would-be parents are fit to adopt, and which are not. We don't ourselves know what the Correct Theory of Fitness is, and we don't ourselves know if anyone else knows what it is. However, presumably there is some truth of the matter here.

Now, according to the Correct Theory of Fitness, some would-be parents are fit to adopt. Others are not. Our view is that the question of who may *buy* adoption rights reduces to this Correct Theory of Fitness. It is permissible for you to buy adoption rights, so long as you are a fit parent, as judged by the Correct Theory of Fitness. If, according to the Correct Theory of Fitness, you are fit to adopt a child for free, then, we hold, you may pay as much as you'd like to adopt that child.

Our main concern for markets in adoption or guardianship rights is just that babies not go to unfit parents. But this is a question of the design and regulation of the market, not an inherent problem with the market that can never be solved.

Landes and Posner on Adoption Markets

Economist Elisabeth Landes and legal theorist Richard Posner famously defended a freer market in adoption rights.[9] Landes's and Posner's article is widely criticized, especially by people who haven't read it, as advocating "baby selling." But, Landes and Posner claim, as a matter of fact, there already is a kind of market in babies. As legal theorist Kimberly Krawiec elaborates, it's a dangerous "pretense" for governments to pretend that no such markets exist.[10] Landes, Posner, and Krawiec claim that, thanks to badly designed government regulations, this existing market is highly dysfunctional and inefficient. They claim that a freer market would be better for the suppliers of babies (mothers who wish to relinquish their guardianship rights), for the customers (potential parents who wish to acquire guardianship rights), and for the babies themselves.

According to Landes and Posner, here are some of the main dysfunctional aspects of adoption markets, at least as of 1978:

- There is a massive shortage of healthy white babies. That is, the quantity of white babies demanded by would-be adopters far exceeds the quantity of available white babies supplied by biological parents. However, there is a glut of unhealthy and minority babies.

- Since outright baby selling is illegal, this pushes many baby sales to the black market. However, as one might expect, black market baby selling suffers from many problems, just as all black markets have problems. The quality of the "product" is lower and less reliable. Sellers are less reliable and trustworthy. Some of the babies are obtained via kidnapping or coercion. And the price for the babies is made very high.
- Parents who wish to adopt a stranger's baby outside the black market typically must go through highly regulated adoption agencies. These adoption agencies are permitted to and do in fact charge fees, but they do not compensate mothers who relinquish their babies. Mothers receive some money to defray their medical costs, but not enough to compensate for the full costs of carrying a baby to term, let alone for their emotional costs. Moreover, because mothers receive such low fees, this causes a large queue—too many would-be parents are willing to "buy" at that low price, but not enough mothers are willing to "sell" at that price.
- Almost all adoptions (among strangers) are brokered by licensed not-for-profit adoption agencies, who have a near monopoly on the market. They suffer from the typical problems of non-profits and monopolies, and so their services are low quality.

So, in short, there are pre-existing markets in babies. However, the legal market is dysfunctional because the legally mandated price of white babies is artificially low. This leads, predictably, to a shortage of babies, with long, inefficient queues. At the same time, it also leads, predictably, to a black market in babies, with artificially high prices, and all the other undesirable and dangerous consequences of black markets.

Landes and Posner think that a less restricted market would reduce many of the problems with the existing market. They think it would reduce the shortage, eliminate or at least significantly curtail the black market, reduce the time parents spend waiting to acquire babies for adoption, and also lead to a better allocation of babies, an allocation more likely to serve the babies' interests. By pricing adoption rights, it becomes more likely that older or less desirable children will be adopted. If I see that the price of a newborn is $25K, but the price of a 10-year-old boy is $2K, I might well decide to adopt the older child, even though I'd prefer the newborn if the prices were the same. A less regulated market might allow both would-be sellers and buyers to contract with one another to ensure certain health or safety outcomes.

Note, finally, that Landes and Posner are *not* saying that babies should just go to the highest bidder, regardless of anything else. Of course, bidders should be fit parents. Known pedophiles, etc., should not be allowed to buy children.

Landes and Posner do not claim that further commodification of the adoption process will solve all problems. Nor do they need to. Instead, their position is just that further commodification would be an improvement.

It's worth noting, too, that alternatives to adoption are already heavily marketized. In-vitro fertilization costs tens of thousands of dollars. Good quality sperm from screened donors costs hundreds of dollars. Eggs cost thousands of dollars. Surrogate mothers charge tens of thousands of dollars.

Objection: Would Only the Rich Get Babies?

Whenever someone proposes to distribute something via a market, one of the first objections is that the rich will have a special competitive advantage in obtaining whatever is on that market. Just as Michael Sandel favored queues in the distribution of tickets to Shakespeare in the Park, he presumably would favor a lottery rather than a market in the distribution of adoption rights. The worry here is that if we allow adoption rights to be bought and sold, then fit rich would-be parents will snatch up all the babies, leaving no babies for the fit but not-so-rich. Or, perhaps, fit rich would-be parents will tend to buy adoption rights to the healthiest, most genetically advantaged, etc., babies, while fit but not-so-rich would-be parents will be stuck with the less desirable babies on the market.

One response, available to us, would be to grant this complaint, but then ask if it has any moral weight. Few viewers of *Juno* complained that Juno gave her baby to rich, successful Vanessa, rather than a fit but less successful would-be mother. As it stands, most people seem to accept that, in those cases where parents may voluntarily relinquish their children, these parents may relinquish their children to any fit parents of their choosing. When people are free to choose, some will have more advantages than others. But that isn't necessarily wrong. At any rate, we need to be supplied here with a moral argument showing that all fit parents merit an equal chance of getting the same babies.

A second response is to note that the supply of babies available for adoption is not fixed. It is endogenous to the market. If adoption rights can be sold, then some people who would otherwise not have relinquished their parental rights will choose to do so. A market in babies will increase the supply of babies. Think, for example, of the typical college student who accidentally gets pregnant. Right now, many (perhaps most) such students choose abortion over A) carrying their fetuses to term and raising the babies themselves or B) carrying the fetuses to term and then giving the babies up for adoption. However, if these college students could receive a monetary reward for choosing option B over an abortion, more of them would choose to do so. It's tempting to think that markets in adoption rights would simply raise the price of adoptions and thus make babies even more unattainable. However, right now, most of the money spent in acquiring adoption rights goes to adoption agencies, rather than to the mother providing the child. But, as Landes and Posner argue, in a more deregulated market, mothers relinquishing their parental rights would be allowed a higher payment themselves for those rights. The middleman adoption agencies would see their role and their payments diminished. If so, then it's quite possible that in a less regulated system, because mothers who supply babies would receive more money, the supply of babies would increase, even as the total cost to would-be parents of acquiring babies would decrease.

Objection: Immoral Preferences

A final objection to markets in adoption rights is that prices would reflect underlying racial biases. After all, most people prefer to adopt someone of their own race, but white people tend to be richer than black people, and so the effective demand for white babies will be higher. At the same time, there are more black children available for adoption than white children. White babies will thus fetch a higher price than black babies. This seems unsavory, at the very least.

Our response here begins by noting that in the existing adoption market, in which parents pay adoption agencies but only offer token compensation to mothers, white babies already cost more than black babies. Also, the queue and waiting times for white babies are longer than for black babies, meaning that the non-pecuniary costs of white babies are already higher. Unless the objector could show a less regulated market would exacerbate these problems, then the objector should have no real complaint against a less regulated market.

As far as we can tell, the market here does not *introduce* any immoral racial preferences, but simply reflects underlying racial preferences. It also reflects other underlying issues and inequalities, such as that, thanks to historical injustice, blacks have less income than whites. The problem here, then, isn't with the market. The market does not introduce a problem where there wasn't any to begin with.

Notes

1 http://azstarnet.com/news/local/sold-as-kids-their-lives-now-converge/article_f4fe5e61-f226-5a63-96f9-270154a02545.html
2 http://stream.wsj.com/story/latest-headlines/SS-2-63399/SS-2-345438/
3 http://stream.wsj.com/story/latest-headlines/SS-2-63399/SS-2-345438/
4 Hayek 1960, 42–44.
5 http://www.census.gov/hhes/well-being/publications/extended-11.html
6 http://www.genome.gov/images/content/cost_per_genome.jpg
7 Schmidtz 2006, 218–19.
8 Cohen 2009 argues that inequalities cut people off from one another. Inequalities reduce people's ability to empathize with one another, since they lack common life experiences. They thereby cause rifts that prevent people from being in complete community with one another.
9 Landes and Posner 1978; Posner 1987.
10 Krawiec 2010.

19

VOTE SELLING

The Ethics of Vote Selling Just Is the Ethics of Voting

For $50, would you vote Republican? Most people would recoil at such an offer. They believe it's inherently wrong to buy or sell votes.[1] In fact, of all the "contested commodities" we've discussed over the past 18 chapters, markets in votes might be the most contested. We can imagine Michael Sandel changing his mind about kidney sales, but he'll draw the line at votes.

When it comes to buying and selling votes, as with everything else, our thesis is, "If you can do it for free, you can do it for money." Vote selling is not in principle wrong. It has no inherent moral status. Vote selling cannot *transform* otherwise morally acceptable actions into wrongful actions. If it's morally permissible for you to vote a certain way for free, then it's permissible to vote that way for payment. If it's morally acceptable for someone to vote a certain way for free, then it's morally acceptable for you to pay her to vote that way.[2] There are cases where it's wrong for you to accept money to vote a certain way, but, in those cases, you shouldn't vote that way for free either.

There are many reasons why people oppose the commodification of votes. Perhaps the most important of these objections are that if votes are for sale, this will cause the wrong people to have too much power, cause people to use power badly, or cause people to vote in ways that harm others. We share these concerns. But, we will argue, these concerns do not justify the view that vote buying and selling are always wrong. At most, they justify the view that paying people to vote *badly* is wrong.

Imagine someone said, "If people are allowed to buy and sell sandwiches, a man who wants his wife dead might pay a cook for a poisoned sandwich. Therefore, sandwiches shouldn't be for sale." Or, suppose someone said, "If people are allowed to buy and sell sandwiches, a rich evil person might buy all the food in the world, put it in one big sandwich, and then laugh gleefully while everyone starves. We can't let that happen. Therefore, sandwiches shouldn't be for sale."

Both of these arguments are crazy. Sure, if sandwiches are for sale, these horrible things *could* happen, though the latter scenario is extremely improbable. But the proper response is not to conclude that sandwiches are the kind of thing that cannot be bought or sold. Rather, we conclude that it's fine to sell sandwiches, but not poisoned sandwiches. It's fine to buy a sandwich, but not to buy up all the food and then cause mass starvation.

Yet, when it comes to voting, people have the opposite reaction. They say, "If people are allowed to buy and sell votes, someone might pay someone else to vote in harmful ways. Therefore, votes shouldn't be for sale." They're right that these things might happen. But, as with the commodification of sandwiches, isn't the most obvious response that it's wrong to pay people to vote in harmful ways, but it's fine to sell *good* votes?

Our view is that the ethics of vote selling just is the ethics of voting. That is, in our view, there are rightful and wrongful ways to vote. Citizens do not have a specific moral duty to vote—there are a great many ways for them to discharge any duties they might have to serve the common good or to "do their part." However, people who do choose to vote have moral obligations to vote responsibly, to take the proper care to form their political beliefs in a rational manner on the basis of proper social scientific evidence, and to vote for what they justifiedly believe will best serve justice, in light of how they justifiedly expect others to vote and behave. In short, we endorse the following principle:

> *The Principle of Ethical Voting:* People who choose to vote must vote for candidates or policies they justifiedly expect to best promote justice; otherwise, they must abstain.

Note that this principle doesn't say it should be illegal for people to vote badly, or that people shouldn't possess the right to vote unless they vote well. It just says that it's morally wrong to vote in certain ways.

Given this background commitment, we then endorse the following view of vote selling and buying:

> *Permissible Vote Selling:* So long as a person conforms to the Principle of Ethical Voting, she may sell her vote.
> *Permissible Vote Buying:* It is permissible to buy votes from anyone who will conform to the Principle of Ethical Voting. Also, if you are justified in believing that voting for a particular candidate or position will serve the right ends of government, you may pay other people to vote for that candidate or position, even if those people are not themselves justified in believing that such votes will serve the right ends of government.

In short, we think many cases of vote selling are wrong, but in such cases the problem isn't really with the vote selling, but with the way people vote, period.[3] The problem is that vote selling induces people to do something they shouldn't do, period.

What Is Good Voting?

In this section, we briefly present Brennan's theory of ethical voting, as defended in his previous book, *The Ethics of Voting*. We'll provide a brief summary of the theory and the main argument for the theory. However, we won't explore all the nuances or answer all the objections to it—you can read the book for that.

Voting is an ethical issue. The way we vote can make government better or worse, and in turn, make people's lives go better or worse. Bad choices at the polls can destroy economic opportunities, produce crises that lower everyone's standards of living, lead to unjust and unnecessary wars (and thus to millions of deaths), lead to sexist, racist, and homophobic legislation, help reinforce poverty, produce overly punitive criminal legislation, and worse.

Voting is not like choosing what to eat off a restaurant's menu. If a person makes bad choices at a restaurant, at least only she bears the consequences of her actions. Yet when voters make bad choices at the polls, everyone suffers. Irresponsible voting can harm innocent people.

With that in mind, we'll first articulate a theory of what it means for a person to vote well, and then articulate an argument for that theory.

Brennan's Principle of Ethical Voting holds that a voter votes well if and only if she votes for a person or policy that she *justifiedly* believes will promote the right ends of government. Notice the term "*justifiedly*." The theory does not merely say that voters must believe that they are voting for candidates or policies that will promote the right ends of government. It is not sufficient for them to vote in a public-spirited way. Rather, they should be *epistemically justified* in believing they are voting for the right ends of government.

A belief is epistemically justified when a person has sufficiently strong evidence to warrant the belief. So, for instance, suppose Bob and Charlie both believe that the US president, as of 2014, is named Obama. Their beliefs are true. However, imagine they have different grounds for this belief. Bob believes Obama is president because he read it in numerous news reports. In contrast, Charles has been living as an isolated hermit in a mountain retreat for the past five years. He has not read or seen the news, or talked to another person since the last election. Charles believes the president is named Obama because he consulted his Ouija board, and by amazing coincidence, it spelled "Obama." Bob's belief is justified—he has good grounds for his belief. Charlie's belief is unjustified—he has bad grounds for his belief. Bob rationally believes Obama is president, but Charlie irrationally believes Obama is president.

The Principle of Ethical Voting holds that voters must have good grounds for thinking that they are voting for policies or candidates that will promote the right ends of government. In general, there are three ways that voters will violate this principle. Bad voters might vote out of 1) ignorance, 2) irrational beliefs, or 3) immoral beliefs. In contrast, good voters not only have justified beliefs about what policies candidates will try to implement, but also have justified beliefs about whether those policies would tend to promote or impede the right ends of government.

In a sense, Brennan's theory of ethical voting is an ethics of care. Consider, by analogy, a medical doctor who intends to treat a patient. We'd hold that the doctor needs to serve the patient's interests, not her own. And we'd hold that the doctor must evaluate the symptoms and form a diagnosis and treatment plan in an unbiased, rational, scientific way. The doctor should consider all the evidence and process the evidence scientifically. If the doctor does so, then the doctor has discharged her duties of care toward the patient. If she fails to do so, then she has acted negligently, and is liable for any harm she does. Brennan's view of voting ethics is much like this.

A jury is also bound by a similar ethics of care. Imagine a jury is about to decide a murder case. The jury's decision will be imposed involuntarily (through violence or threats of violence) upon a potentially innocent person. The decision is high stakes. The jury has a clear obligation to try the case competently. They should not decide the case selfishly, capriciously, irrationally, or from ignorance. They should take proper care, weigh the evidence carefully, overcome their biases, and decide the case from a concern for justice.

What's true of juries is also true of the electorate. An electorate's decision is imposed involuntarily upon the innocent. The decision is high stakes. The electorate should also take proper care. The electorate should not expose people to undue risk in the selection of policy or of rulers who will make policy. The governed have a right not to be exposed to undue risk. When elections are decided on the basis of unreliable epistemic procedures or on the basis of unreasonable moral attitudes, this exposes the governed to undue risk of serious harm. Since the governed are *forced* to comply with the decisions of the electorate, negligent decision-making is intolerable.

The reasoning above explains why it is morally important that the electorate as a whole makes decisions in a competent and reasonable way. However, there's a problem. It might be clear why it's important that the electorate as a whole vote well. But it's not clear why any individual should vote well. After all, how *we* vote has serious consequences. But how *you* vote does not.

In a large-scale election, such as a congressional election in the United States, the probability that an individual vote will decide the outcome of the election is vanishingly small. If you are a typical voter in the United States, you are much more likely to win Powerball multiple times than to cast a vote that changes the outcome of a presidential or congressional election. The expected marginal impact of an individual vote is vanishingly small. So, why think it makes sense to think individual votes are subject to moral scrutiny, if a single vote can never be expected to make a difference? If the majority of other voters are voting badly, why think there is any reason for me not to vote badly as well? In light of how little individual votes matter, one might be tempted to conclude that one may vote however one pleases.

This conclusion is not warranted. There are moral norms governing what we may or may not do when participating in collective activities, even when our individual actions make no difference.

Consider an analogy. Suppose a 100-member firing squad is about to shoot an innocent child. They will fire all at once. Each bullet will hit the child at the same time, and each shot would, on its own, be sufficient to kill her. You can't stop them, so the child will die regardless of what you do. Now, suppose they offer you the opportunity to join in and fire with them. You can make the 101st shot. Again, the child will die regardless of what you do. Is it permissible for you to join the firing squad?

Most people have a strong intuition that it is wrong to join the squad and shoot the child. Here's one plausible explanation of why it's wrong: there is general moral prohibition against participating in these kinds of activities, even if one's individual inputs do not make a decisive difference. In these kinds of cases, you should try to keep your hands clean, at least if there is no significant cost to your doing so. Suppose the firing squad threatens to kill you, too, if you do not shoot the child. In that case, it might be excusable for you to shoot. But if you suffer no significant loss by not participating, then you should not participate. Only a bad person would be willing to do so.

When the firing squad kills the child, this is a collectively harmful activity. A collectively harmful activity is an activity where a group causes harm, but individual inputs into the group's activity make no difference. In cases where we have the opportunity to engage in such collectively harmful activities, we should abide by the "Clean Hands Principle":

> One should not participate in collectively harmful activities when the cost of refraining from such activities is low.

The Clean Hands Principle is a moral principle governing whether participating in certain collective activities is permissible. It turns out that this principle can be derived from a number of prominent moral theories, such as Kantianism, rule consequentialism, and eudaimonism. (We won't go through the derivations here, though.)

This firing squad example is analogous to voting in an election. Adding or subtracting a shooter to or from the firing squad makes no difference—the girl will die anyway. Similarly, with elections, individual votes do not make a difference. In both cases, the outcome is *causally overdetermined*. The irresponsible voter is much like a person who volunteers to shoot in the firing squad. Her individual bad vote is of no consequence—just as an individual shot is of no consequence—but she is participating in a collectively harmful activity when she could easily keep her hands clean.

Again, this is just a summary of Brennan's theory of ethical voting. It doesn't go through all the complexities or arguments. For the rest of the chapter, we will just assume that the Brennanian theory of voting ethics is correct. On the basis of that theory, we say, sure, it's wrong for someone to pay someone to vote badly, but that's because that person shouldn't vote that way period. (In the same way, it's wrong to pay someone to make a poisoned sandwich for your wife.) But, we then ask, is there any reason to think it's wrong to pay someone to *vote well*, to vote in *accordance* with the Principle of Ethical Voting.

Good Voting, Commodified

We have a very restrictive, stringent view of the ethics of voting, combined with a more permissive view of the ethics of buying and selling votes. In contrast, most people have a very permissive view of the ethics of voting combined with a restrictive, stringent view of the ethics of buying and selling votes.

Most people in the US and Canada subscribe to what Brennan has previously called the "Folk Theory of Voting Ethics."[4] According to this view, people have a moral duty to vote, but few if any duties attach to the act of voting itself. People have no duty to be informed, to process political information in a rational way, or to vote for just outcomes. Instead, it's morally permissible (if not admirable) to be utterly reckless with their vote. However, the Folk Theory of Voting Ethics also holds that it's wrong to buy and sell votes, period. So, the Folk theory allows you to vote however you'd like, so long as you do it for free.

We find the Folk Theory puzzling. Consider three situations:

1 *Ignorant Ignacio:* Ignacio knows almost nothing about politics. He has never studied economics or political science. Come Election Day, he watches 30-second advertisements from two major candidates. He feels in his gut that one of the candidates has better ideas than the others, and votes for those candidates, and votes accordingly.

2 *Careless Carla*: Carla knows almost nothing about politics. She has never studied economics or political science. Come Election Day, she shows up at the polls, and sees a list of names she doesn't recognize for an office (the "comptroller") whose function she can't begin to guess. She picks the name she thinks sounds the most regal.

3 *Lackadaisical Loren*: Loren is a prominent political philosopher and political economist who has written some of the world's most important books and articles on voting. Loren has a thorough understanding of the social sciences, and has as much a claim to having sound political ideas as any person alive. Still, Loren doesn't vote, in large part because he recognizes his individual vote has almost no chance of making a difference. On

Election Day, his friend and colleague Jason pays Loren $200 to vote his conscience.

According to the Folk Theory of Voting Ethics, Ignacio and Carla did nothing wrong. Their actions might not be particularly admirable, but they aren't blameworthy either. Loren and his friend Jason, however, acted badly, and they should feel bad. Perhaps they should even go to jail.

But this seems puzzling. After all, Ignacio and Carla had no clue what they're doing, while Loren voted for what he justifiedly believed would serve the right ends of government. For all Ignacio and Carla know, they're voting for terrible candidates who will produce bad outcomes for all. In contrast, Loren has every reason to expect that the candidates he supports will produce good and just outcomes. According to Brennan's Principle of Ethical Voting, Ignacio and Carla shouldn't vote at all, for free or for money. But according to that principle, Loren is a *good voter*. If Jason pays Loren to vote, what Jason has done is paid to get Loren to vote the way people ought to vote.

People might worry that if votes were commodified, malevolent rich people—you can insert here George Soros or the Koch brothers, depending on your political predilection—would then buy up votes for their own nefarious ends. For instance, suppose there are two presidential candidates, Al and Bob. Suppose Al and Bob are identical in all respects, except for how they intend to deal with climate change. Suppose that the evidence overwhelmingly favors Al's position; in fact, the evidence is so strong that no person could be justified in advocating Bob's position. But now suppose that either George Soros or the Koch brothers—again, pick your favorite villain here—pays the majority of voters to vote for Bob. We agree that it is wrong for Soros or the Koch brothers to buy these votes, and that it is wrong for people to sell them. But we also think it would be wrong for people to vote for Bob *for free*, because doing so violates the Principle of Ethical Voting. We don't see this as being a case where commodification introduced wrongness where there wasn't any.

On the other hand, suppose you know that many careless, ignorant voters are going to vote for a harmful candidate. They will not be convinced by evidence and argument. However, suppose you could pay them to vote for what you justifiedly believe, on the basis of sound reasoning with good evidence, is the best candidate. If you do so, you make it much more likely that we'll all enjoy a good outcome. The Folk Theory of Voting Ethics holds that you did something wrong. But we think your behavior is admirable. You did a major public service—you paid for justice out of your own pocket.

The Inalienability Objection

One common argument against vote selling holds that the right to vote is inalienable, just like a right to basic liberty in the person or to free speech are inalienable. The right to vote is not like a property right to a car. You may sell a car, but you may not sell yourself into slavery. You may not sell away your right to free speech. Some kinds of rights can't be sold. The right to vote is one of those rights.

The problem with this argument is that it misunderstands what's being debated. The question we've been discussing so far is not whether a person should literally be allowed to purchase additional rights to vote. If Jaworski were to pay Brennan to vote a certain way, it's not as though Jaworski would literally come to have two votes while Brennan would then have zero. He wouldn't pay Brennan to literally transfer his right to vote the way he might buy a deed to a house. Rather, what happens in traditional vote buying and selling is that one person pays a second person to perform a certain action. Paying someone to vote is not like buying a house, and so doesn't mean that the seller loses the right to vote.

In the same way, suppose the University of Toronto pays Brennan or the College of New Jersey pays Jaworski to give a guest lecture on commodification. When we agree to give such lectures, we thereby accept certain constraints about what we'll talk about. For instance, we thereby agree not to surprise our audiences with lectures on how to distinguish speed, thrash, power, hair, black, nu, and death metal. But we don't thereby alienate our rights of free speech or transfer them to these universities. So, the worry about the inalienability of voting rights is irrelevant to the question of whether it's permissible to pay someone to vote a certain way.

Now, we could of course imagine a legal system in which the right to vote could literally be bought and sold like a car. Rather than simply paying others to vote a certain way, a citizen might buy extra rights to vote. Under that system, perhaps George Soros might come to have 1,000,000 votes all to himself, while 999,999 citizens end up with no votes at all. If the claim that the right to vote is inalienable is correct, it follows that this legal system is unjust, and that people should not buy and sell their rights to vote. However, notice that even here, the problem is not about commodification per se. If voting rights are inalienable, one may not sell these rights *because* one may not give them away, period.

"People Should Do It For Free"

One common objection to vote selling, which we have heard from many laypeople, if not philosophers and political theorists, is that people ought to be willing to vote for free, and so, for that reason, they should not be paid to vote. Voting ought to be done out of public or community spirit, or a sense of duty, not for a desire for material gain.

It's clear many people think this, but *why* they think is not so clear. One argument might go as follows:

1 Citizens have a duty to vote.
2 If you have the duty to do something, then you ought not to be paid for it.
3 Therefore, citizens ought not be paid to vote.

This doesn't seem like a sound argument to us.

First, we dispute premise 1—the claim that citizens have a duty to vote. We won't spend much time here explaining why we dispute premise 1, since Brennan has already written extensively on premise 1 in previous work.[5] (However, elements of his response can be found in Chapter 15, on the civics objection. Brennan's main counterargument to the idea that there is a duty to vote is to claim that citizens can discharge any duties they might have to serve the common good, pay debts to society, avoid free-riding, or exercise civic virtue in any number of ways besides voting.)

We also dispute premise 2. It's not clear that just because you have a duty to do something, that means you can't be paid for it. Many people believe that, under certain rare circumstances, it is permissible for governments to impose a military draft. They think that citizens who are drafted have a duty to join the military rather than flee. But they still think that drafted soldiers ought to be paid. Or, more plausibly, many people think that under certain circumstances, citizens ought not to be drafted, but they still have a duty to join the military. (For example, this was a common sentiment in the United States in World War II.) But, even if citizens have a duty to join the military, they still hold that these volunteer soldiers should be paid, rather than having to work for free. Many people also believe that it is permissible for governments to require citizens to serve on juries. They hold that citizens who are called for jury duty have, well, a duty to serve on a jury. But they still think that jurors ought to be paid. Some people even hold that citizens have a moral duty to engage in productive jobs, but, of course, citizens should be paid to work.[6] Finally, some democratic theorists believe that citizens have a duty to vote, but, because discharging this duty imposes a burden on the poor, that citizens should be paid to vote.[7] Now, perhaps all of these positions are mistaken. But some of them are at least plausible, and this shows that premise 2 is not so obviously true. It doesn't appear to be built into the concept of a duty that you can't be paid to discharge your duties.

It's not obvious why voters should be unpaid volunteers, when the other actors in government are not. Many important activities, including policing, food production, and clothing production—which are all more important than voting—are paid. Little of such work is done voluntarily. Many stereotypical exercises of civic virtue, such as holding political office, serving in the military, performing jury duty, are paid. (Jury duty doesn't pay well, but is enforced through penalties. So jurists aren't volunteers either.) Physicians and teachers are paid for their work. Why is it important that voters volunteer, when these other people do not?[8]

Semiotic Objections to Vote Selling

In Part II, we explored semiotic objections to markets in everything. One version of the semiotic objection held that introducing money into certain relationships devalues or corrupts the relationship. Money violates the shared meaning of the relationship and changes the kind of significance and value it holds for those within the relationship. For example, we sometimes exchange favors with our romantic partners, but many people believe that if we were to exchange money, this would somehow debase our relationships. As you saw in Part II, we're skeptical that this claim holds true even of romantic relationships. We're even more skeptical about whether the objection applies to voting.

Even if monetary exchanges were wrong or unhealthy in marriages or romantic relationships, the relationship of a citizen to her liberal democratic government or to her fellow citizens is not like her relationship with her spouse. (If it is, the citizen has a bad marriage.) For most of us, being a citizen of a given country just means we were born (not by choice) into a diverse society of strangers. We have basic human compassion and respect for others in our society, but most other citizens remain strangers, many of whom we have little in common with. What makes us a citizen of one place rather than another is determined by political boundaries. These boundaries are mostly the contingent results of morally arbitrary demarcations, wars, and conquest. For the most part, all we distinctively share with our fellow citizens are common tax burdens, access to some common public goods, and participation in certain mandatory social insurance schemes. Citizenship is (generally) involuntary, impersonal, and instrumental. Citizenship in contemporary liberal democracies is not much like friendship, romantic love, or family. Even if money might corrupt such relationships or violate the meaning of them—a point we've previously disputed—citizenship is almost nothing like these other relationships.

Further, in our view, it is only permissible to pay someone to vote well, or, more precisely, to pay them to vote in ways that you are justified in believing will serve the right ends of government (even if the vote seller himself doesn't know that). So, a world in which the kind of vote buying and selling we favor were widespread is likely to be a world in which voters are more likely to vote in ways that promote good and just outcomes. Now, to summarize the kinds of moves we made in Part II, we recognize that buying and selling these smart votes might signal disrespect in light of American or Canadian semiotic codes and culture. But, if so, we again take that just to mean that American or Canadian semiotic codes and culture are to that extent morally defective. Americans and Canadians ought to change the semiotics of vote buying and selling, and if they're unwilling or unable to do so, the rest of us are justified in conscientiously ignoring these codes.

Erosion and Corruption

Still, there is a closely related corruption objection that deserves further attention. It goes something like this:

The Erosion Argument

1 If people are allowed to take money to vote (even if people abide by principle 1), then this will (significantly) erode civic virtue and altruism.
2 Thus, it's wrong to buy and sell votes, even if people abide by principle 1.

The erosion argument asserts that introducing money into voting will corrupt people's moral attitudes. As a result, they will come to have less civic virtue. They will be less concerned with promoting the common good and doing their part.

Premise 1 above is an empirical claim. As we discussed in Chapter 9, anyone advancing a corruption objection needs to supply proper empirical evidence, using careful, peer-reviewed studies, that such corruption indeed occurs. In the absence of actual empirical support for the objection, we should regard as a potential problem, but not yet a real problem.

Also, it's not clear just how vote selling is supposed to erode civic virtue. What is the mechanism? Here is a plausible variation of the Erosion Argument, which makes this clearer:

The Modified Erosion Argument

1 People need to believe that voting is sacred (or has some other privileged moral status) and that money and voting must never mix. Otherwise, they will lose civic virtue and vote badly.
2 If people buy and sell votes (even if they abide by Principle 1), this will cause them or others to lose the belief that voting is sacred.
3 It is wrong to do something that causes others to lose civic virtue and vote badly.
4 Therefore, it's wrong to buy and sell votes.

This argument claims citizens will not behave well at the voting booth unless they believe that voting is a civic sacrament or has some other privileged moral status. If they see others taking money to vote—even if they are being paid to vote well—they will either stop voting or will vote badly.

Even if this were so, it wouldn't mean that vote selling is in fact wrong. It would at best show that it's useful for people to believe it's wrong. Suppose, in parallel, it turned out to be a bizarre psychological fact about people that unless most people believe God exists, they would become immoral and start killing each other. Even if this turned out to be the case, it wouldn't prove that theism is true. It would just show that people need to believe in God, to be theists, or they'll start killing each other. Atheism might still be correct.

Or, suppose that, for some bizarre reason, unless people believe in Kantian moral theory, they'll start killing each other. Again, this wouldn't imply that Kantianism is true. It might be that, say, utilitarianism is the correct moral theory, but people are too stupid, vile, and bad to handle the truth. In that case, we might want to lie and tell them Kantianism is true, even though it's not.

In general, "People will act badly unless they believe X" isn't evidence of X. So, suppose that if people believe it's permissible to buy and sell votes, they'll act badly. This doesn't mean that it's in fact wrong to buy and sell votes. Perhaps, for people to have adequate civic virtue, we need them to believe that money and voting must never mix. But that doesn't mean that in fact money and voting must never mix.

It is sometimes permissible for a person to do something, even if her doing X induces others to lose virtue or to perform wrong actions. For instance, suppose we buy food from a local grocery store. Many bystanders, upon seeing us buy food, come to believe that all human relationships are purely instrumental. As a result, they lose all moral motivation and become thieves. Now, it's regrettable this has happened, but it doesn't make our food buying wrong, nor am I responsible for their bad behavior. Instead, the thieves made a mistake—they are the ones who acted wrongly. They should not have concluded that all human relationships are instrumental, nor should they have lost their moral motivations and become thieves. I am not responsible for their depraved reaction to my innocent actions.

Similarly, suppose Bob pays Alan to vote well. Gordon witnesses this transaction, loses his sense of civic virtue, and starts voting badly. This doesn't automatically make Bob or Alan's actions wrong. Here, Gordon is the wrongdoer. He should not have lost his sense of civic virtue, nor should he have started voting badly. That was a depraved response to seeing Bob paying Alan to vote, and it's Gordon's fault (not Bob or Alan's) he had such a response.

Some might disagree and object that if you know others will have a bad response to your actions, this can transform what otherwise would have been permissible actions into wrongful actions. But this is a dangerous objection, because it licenses a kind of moral extortion. It means that people can modify your moral obligations by issuing threats, or, more broadly, by reacting badly to you. To those who still find this objection plausible, we say, "Fine. According to you, the fact that others might react badly to vote selling means that vote selling is wrong. If so, then we, Brennan and Jaworski, hereby threaten to initiate terrorist attacks on your alma mater if people vote for free. We will start murdering people unless people only vote for money." The person making the present objection is committed to the view that the only reason it remains permissible to vote for free is that our threat is insincere.

Notes

1 Satz 2012, 102; Sandel 2012a, 104–5.
2 This chapter incorporates material and ideas from Brennan 2011, 135–60. The thesis of this book ("If you can do it for free, you can do it for money") is a generalization of the view of vote commodification that Brennan defended in this earlier work.
3 For an even more radical defense of vote buying and selling than we offer here, see Freiman 2014a.
4 Brennan 2011, 3.
5 Brennan 2011, 15–67.
6 Becker 1980.
7 E.g., Ackerman and Fiskin 2005.
8 One possibility is that these other activities take significant time, whereas voting does not. However, people probably won't be paid a doctor's salary to vote. Also, voting well does take a lot of time, because it requires investments in knowledge and rationality, though voting badly does not.

PART V

Debunking intuitions

20

ANTI-MARKET ATTITUDES
ARE RESILIENT

Certain Markets Just Feel Wrong

It is difficult to shake the feeling, deep down in our stomachs, that there is just something plain wrong with buying and selling certain things. And it does seem to be a feeling in our stomachs. Notice the language that anti-commodification theorists use. Satz calls certain markets "noxious" and says they have "great distaste."[1] Sandel describes certain markets as "repugnant," "morbid," "distasteful," or as having "moral ugliness" or "moral tawdriness."[2] He agrees with certain editorialists that auctioning access to national parks is a kind of "sacrilege" because such things are "sacred" and worthy of "awe."[3] He cites Senator Barbara Boxer calling information markets on terrorism "sick."[4] Barber describes anti-consumerist asceticism as "cleansing."[5] And so on. Certain markets offend our non-rational feelings about purity and impurity.

Moral psychologist Jonathan Haidt claims that there are six "moral foundations" by which people evaluate actions as right and wrong: 1) care vs. harm, 2) fairness vs. cheating, 3) liberty vs. oppression, 4) loyalty vs. betrayal, 5) authority vs. subversion, and 6) sanctity vs. degradation.[6] Haidt contends that concern with the sanctity vs. degradation foundation is a hallmark of a conservative moral style. This concern is grounded in the psychology of disgust.

Conservatives tend to moralize their disgust reactions. (Many economic leftists who have a conservative moral style tend to do so as well.) But these disgust reactions are unreliable guides to right and wrong.

In this final chapter, we contend that opposition to markets in certain goods, or markets in general, is often based fundamentally on unreliable psychology. Many of the arguments against markets are just rationalizations of disgust reactions.

We note—and we are not the first to do so—that we were not evolved to live in large-scale impersonal societies, but to live in small-scale family clans with frequent personal interaction. Our innate moral psychology was designed for these small-scale societies. We contend that we should be deeply suspicious about anti-market intuitions, as our moral psychology has not caught up with our new environment. We have a stone-age moral psychology that is unfit for the modern world. In short, our moral intuitions are out of line with our moral demands. It could be dangerous—literally, fatal—to give too much weight to some of these intuitions. It might well be that the software of modern civilization runs badly on the hardware of our moral psychology, and the problem in this case is with the hardware rather than the software.

List of Symptoms Covered

Let us summarize the general case against the anti-commodification theorist. Throughout the book, we have found fault with the arguments the anti-commodification theorists have put forth about particular markets they dislike. Often they've relied upon questionable empirical assumptions or normative premises.

But we've also noticed some general patterns in their complaints about markets. We have offered many different arguments for why markets are not the cause of, or do not contribute as much to a whole range of problems that are often placed at the feet of market enthusiasts by anti-commodification theorists.

1. *Noxious transactions*: Sometimes, it's a matter of mere equivocation. When Debra Satz discusses noxious markets, some of her complaints are not really about markets, but about a broader category of exchanges. Slavery is noxious whether or not barter or money or some kind of economic transaction is taking place. She objects to voluntary slavery arrangements, as we do, and would object to slavery as a gift. We could describe these as "noxious gifts" if we wanted to. But if we were to defend the thesis that there are moral limits to gift giving, defenders of gift exchanges would rightly object if we were to include slavery as a reason to cast doubt on the moral standing of the gift exchange. They would say that the wrong of slavery is in no way explained by gift exchanges, that the fact that something is part of a gift exchange adds nothing to our understanding of the wrong of slavery. And we agree. Slavery is wrong independently of any kind of exchange, gift or market.

2. *Semiotics*: Sometimes, we fail to see that social conventions and social meaning are contingent, and are themselves open to criticism.

Debra Satz insists that civic respect consists, in part, in recognizing and respecting rules of etiquette. That's an important point. Sometimes, obeying etiquette is a way of demonstrating that we respect someone. Once a convention gets going, it may be a matter of morality to obey that convention, despite its contingency and, sometimes, its arbitrariness. Driving on the right-hand side of the road is not a rule we discovered in the fabric of the universe, but we do discover it in the social fabric we've overlaid on this part of the world. To ignore the social fabric on the grounds that it is arbitrary and contingent would be not only to violate mere etiquette, but to put others in danger, others who reasonably rely on adherence to the convention, and so is a matter of morality.

This example overstates the reasons for going along with contingent cultural codes. At least with driving on the right versus the left, you have good reason to comply with what others do, if you can't get them to change or if changing is too costly. After all, if one person unilaterally starts driving on the opposite side, she's likely to kill people. But suppose we determine that the social convention that attaches disrespect to kidney sales *kills* people. Here, it seems perfectly legitimate for people to say, "This is a bad convention, and I will actively flout it, even if I can't change it."

3. *Ignoring the dimensions*: At other times, anti-commodification theorists do not recognize the significant diversity of market types or modes. Market exchanges, as we have argued, involve at least nine variables, or "dimensions." We have argued that markets consist in variable times, places, and different manners. Our hypothesis is that changing these variables could change the outcome of those markets, including how repugnant we perceive a particular market to be. We recognize that this thesis requires empirical evidence, but we believe we have done enough to demonstrate a prima facie case for the claims. What's more is that recognizing the variety of market modes allows us to identify the source of repugnance not in the market as such, but in, for example, a particular mode of payment, or means of payment. It isn't the market that is repugnant, but this non-essential feature or outcome, which, in principle, can be designed out of the market.

Of course, the claim is not that markets will, of necessity, spontaneously move towards non-repugnant forms. The claim is, instead, that arguments based on the repugnance of this or that particular market are not in principle arguments against markets as such. If there is a kind of market that would not be repugnant, then that is sufficient to establish that the problem, if there is one, is not with markets as such, but rather with certain kinds of markets.

4. *Black markets*: Sometimes, anti-commodification theorists who want to push for public policy overlook the fact that we live in a non-ideal world. Making something illegal, or blocking a particular market, is not a magic wand that snaps us all in line.

In this actual non-ideal world, blocking markets using legal mechanisms often pushes those markets underground. Sometimes opponents of certain kinds of markets confuse what they see on the black market for what we can expect in an above-ground market. Sometimes, this is a matter of confusing a selection effect for a treatment effect. When markets go underground, a different group of people are attracted to buy and sell those things, and law-abiding people are disinclined to participate. But the kind of people who obey the law share other characteristics as well, characteristics that make them more likely to fight for better treatment, better service, better norms.

At other times, this is to fail to recognize that black markets rely on different enforcement mechanisms, and so incentivize different kinds of behavior. When you cannot call the police, you call on thugs. A reputation for thuggery would almost always be harmful in above-ground markets, but would help you avoid getting ripped off in black markets. This has nothing to do with the inherent features of a market in this or that good, but, rather, with the inherent features of a black market, any black market. If we prohibited coffee, we would see the same violence, the same unsavory sellers, and the same distasteful practices. We prohibited alcohol, and acted surprised when the murder rate shot up and gangs took over many streets. We should have known better. When it comes to illicit drugs, we now have no excuse.

The above lists some of our general responses to the arguments offered by anti-commodification theorists. You've seen many of our specific responses to their more specific complaints over the course of the last three parts. The more particular arguments against markets can be regarded as symptoms of a broader outlook or attitude. In the next chapter, we will try to diagnose the general problem. What makes so many people see markets in such a bad light? What makes so many of us liable to attribute evils to markets? Why do so many of us feel deep down that some, many, or even all markets are "repugnant"?

Notes

1 Satz 2012, 3–5, 9–11, 91–98, 106.
2 Sandel 2012a, 83, 133, 141, 144, 153, 166.
3 Sandel 2012a, 37, 81, 136, 142.
4 Sandel 2012a, 151.
5 Barber 2008, 39.
6 Haidt 2012.

21

WHERE DO ANTI-MARKET ATTITUDES COME FROM?

Antipathy to the market is resilient and resists disconfirmation. This antipathy is also widespread—most people tend to be naturally suspicious of the market. Here, we examine a few hypotheses about where this antipathy comes from.

Nozick's Hypothesis: Academics Hate Markets Because Markets Don't Love Them

The anti-commodification writers whom we criticize are for the most part academics. Academics are a distinctive and strange breed, and belong to a distinctive and strange culture. Perhaps that explains their aversion to markets.

The philosopher Robert Nozick suggested that academics dislike markets because they succeed in contexts that differ significantly from the market economy.[1] The problem, perhaps, is that academics are people who succeeded and excelled in the peculiar environment of the classroom, in which a central authority first set rules and then rewarded students both for how smart they are and how well they followed these rules.

In contrast, in the market, smarter people do not always receive higher incomes. The market does not always reward the very same skills and talents that teachers do in a classroom. In addition, the criteria that marked someone as "successful" and "deserving" are determined by a teacher and formed on the basis of certain education-relevant values. A detailed syllabus, and a conversation with the teacher, helps in getting clearer on exactly what is expected.

In the market, the criteria are not obvious. "Satisfying consumer demand" is the general criterion, but this gives us no substantive content. It has no predictive power unless we assume what consumers want. Furthermore, there is no obvious correlation between intelligence and attainment in an educational setting, and success on the market. Sometimes, pet rocks become trendy and popular, generating windfall profits for some who get lucky. Sometimes, a stock we buy on a whim doubles or triples in value overnight, making the whimsical wealthy. Who could have predicted the popularity of pet rocks? Or VHS over Betamax? Or that a certain stock would jump in value? Sometimes, buying decisions sweep over the market like a contagion, leaving intelligent, sophisticated, university-educated elites powerless to predict and profit from them.

Nozick thinks this explains the general antipathy that academics have towards markets. Academics succeed in the educational domain. This domain makes a great deal of sense to them. If that's so, they may wish that that domain were expanded to cover more of our lives. They want the economy to be more like a classroom, with a benevolent meritocratic and technocratic central administrator who rewards participants for rule-following and virtue.

But the domain of markets is not run by educators and the educated in accordance with rules and regulations that dominate in an academic setting. Markets are without that structure. That makes markets deeply frustrating for some. It means markets reward irrationally or, at least, non-rationally. There is no obvious standard apart from consumer demand, which is oftentimes whimsical. If he's right, that might motivate academics to look for problems with markets, and make them more susceptible to and less critical of various anti-market theories.

But there's reason to be careful with this explanation. Stephen Leider and Alvin Roth, for example, have studied the attitudes of various people towards particular markets, and towards markets in general. It turns out that generalized anti-market bias does not explain antipathy to particular markets. Those who approve and endorse markets in general sometimes have a deep aversion to markets in specific things like kidneys or sex.[2]

On the other hand, psychologist Philip Tetlock has done studies to determine which trades people of different ideologies tend to think are inherently wrong.[3] As the philosopher Gerald Gaus summarizes Tetlock's findings: "While not surprisingly, libertarians believe few transactions should be blocked, Tetlock finds that 'Marxist respondents were prototypical "censorious busybodies." Even routine market transactions … provoke [in them] a measure of moral condemnation.'" Gaus concludes, "So we should be wary of saying that a certain trade offends 'our' moral sensibilities, for 'we' have very different attitudes toward the morality of specific trades."[4] According to Tetlock, but not Roth, people's attitudes about the moral permissibility of different trades correlate with their ideologies.

Many conservatives have, in general, a positive attitude towards markets. They also have a strong antipathy towards markets in sex, pornography, in drugs, in various goods and services associated with family and religion. They are allergic to placing anything they perceive as "sacred" on the market. So while they do not have a general anti-market bias, they appear to agree with more left-liberal academics who worry about the corrosive and corrupting effects of markets.

This should not be surprising. Both left-liberals and conservatives agree on the structure of the argument. They both agree that markets have corrosive and corrupting tendencies. They just disagree about what counts as sacred or pure or divine. They disagree about what particular things are sufficiently important to protect against corruption. Left-liberals tend to worry about inequality and exploitation. Conservatives are concerned about family and the sacred. So, for left-liberals, we need to rein in the market if we want greater equality or to avoid taking advantage of the worst-off, while, for conservatives, we need to keep the market away from sex, family, and religion.

There's a separate reason to worry about Nozick's explanation, though. Once upon a time, the consensus view of academics was very different, even though the structure of the academy was more or less the same. A.O. Hirschman, writing in the *Journal of Economic Literature*, explained that during the 18th and 19th century, the prevailing opinion of academics toward the market was that it was a civilizing and positive influence.[5] Markets made us nicer, more polite, more cordial, more trusting (and trustworthy), and reduced our propensity to violence. This was called the *doux commerce* thesis, from the French for "gentle commerce." It reigned amongst the academy until the late 19th century, and the rise of Marxism. If the explanation for why academics distrust and dislike the market really were about the kind of structures and institutions that academics are more comfortable in, then we would have a difficult time explaining the prevalence of the doux commerce thesis in the academy at any point in history. And yet, that was the view. So we cannot rely on Nozick's thesis for our answer.

Confusing Economic Theory for Markets

A different possibility is the confusion of the behavioral and attitudinal assumptions of economics for purposes of explaining and predicting economic behavior, and the actual behavior and attitudes of people who go to real-world markets. One way to understand Anderson's objections to markets in women's reproductive labor, for example, is to describe it as the worry that markets cause or contribute to the attitudes, dispositions, and behaviors expected of homo economicus. In the context of her work on surrogacy, she appears to be concerned about the effect and meaning of market exchanges. She believes that it is inherent in what a market exchange is that the participants take the practical stance of thinking of the objects of sale as of merely instrumental value, there to satisfy our non-moral desires. Similarly, she also at times appears to worry that actual market exchanges can influence us to think of people and babies in this way, even if we didn't think that way prior to entering the market. Perhaps, outside of markets, we don't meet homo economicus. Indeed, she is explicitly critical of many of the assumptions of the discipline of economics as not really describing real-world, flesh-and-blood human beings. But she appears to believe that markets turn us into self-interested, crassly-calculating, instrumentally-rational creatures, who regard the objects of sale on a market as of merely instrumental value. While she regards many of the assumptions about human beings for purposes of economic modeling, explanation, and prediction as false outside of markets, she sometimes appears to believe that markets turn us into that.

But what is the basis for this widespread belief? What empirical facts can be ushered in support of the theory that markets make us selfish, or turn us into the caricature called homo economicus? There is introspection. But, as we saw in Chapter 11, the evidence for this thesis is not merely weak, but tends to falsify their predictions. Moreover, the anti-commodification theorists we have met and spoken with have told us repeatedly that, were they to run companies, they would not behave like homo economicus. In our business ethics classes, we ask our students to devise corporate social responsibility campaigns for mock companies. Our students invariably incorporate all sorts of non-profit-relevant social commitments in their corporate social responsibility statements, even though they know we, the professors who will grade them, do not think corporations must take on these commitments. (We think corporations have a large set of negative moral obligations, but that high-minded positive obligations are strictly speaking morally optional. We let them know they aren't being graded on crafting the most high-minded company.) When we ask them why they include these commitments, they tell us that some things matter more than profit. We believe them (and happen to agree with them as well).

So, invariably, they are talking about *other* people,[6] the great unwashed masses who are susceptible to being moved by the demands of the market, who are helpless in the face of institutional incentives that push us away from homo sapiens and pull us towards homo economicus. But despite years of trying to find empirical evidence of greater selfishness in more economically free countries, the anti-commodification theorists have come up empty. It's worse than that, actually, because we have discovered the precise opposite.

As we discussed in Chapter 11, people in more economically free countries are more generous. They give to more causes and contribute more of their free time. Despite widespread stories of malaise amongst capitalist countries, residents of more economically free countries report that they are happier than residents of less free economies. Despite worries of the alienating and dehumanizing effects of markets, people in economically freer countries report that they are more satisfied with their interpersonal relationships. Even though the sociological theories of left-liberal theorists predict that markets undermine trust and fairness, empirical evidence suggests the opposite. Joseph Henrich and his colleagues went to 15 small-scale societies in Africa "in search of homo economicus."[7] There, they played ultimatum, public goods, and other games with the villagers. Though they searched and searched for homo economicus, they couldn't find the crafty, calculating, and conniving creature anywhere. What they found instead was that the more market integrated a people were, the more trustworthy and fair they were, even after controlling for religiosity, culture, education, and other possible explanations.

There is strong evidence that market exchanges make us even less like homo economicus, exerting a force that pulls us closer and closer to homo reciprocans, the generous reciprocator who deals fairly with others, is cooperative, and not only trusts others, but is trustworthy in turn.

In short, there is little evidence that would vindicate the anti-commodification thesis. There is evidence that this or that particular market makes us more selfish and callous. There is evidence that presenting the mere image of money on a screen saver before students play an economic game on a computer makes those students behave more like homo economicus. But that's a response to specific features and elements that can be designed out of real-world markets.

Instead, the truth is that while *studying* economics might tend to turn us into homo economicus,[8] participating in actual markets does not. There is evidence that when students study economics, they start playing more selfishly and are more likely to cheat or defect in experimental prisoner's dilemma or trust games. But that doesn't tell us much about what happens in markets. To buy and sell something is not always to adopt the commodification attitude. We can use money and markets in contexts where we revere, respect, and preserve the dignity of the objects of sale. Studying economics can make us treat other people as instruments for our own satisfaction, but participating in markets makes us treat other people better. Markets train us to put ourselves in the shoes of others, to try and satisfy other people's preferences, to think of others as independent, autonomous creatures worthy of care and respect.

For anti-commodification theorists, all markets frame the buying and the selling of some good or service as a business decision, and so always operate within a business frame. For anti-commodification theorists, considerations of profit are controlling in a market context, and so the overjustification or crowding effect is likely to take over.

But while markets can be framed as business decisions in laboratories, and while a profit-orientation is the central conceit of analyzing and predicting markets using the tools of economics, real-world people who go to market rarely think of their decisions like that, and rarely pursue their own good and the good of the people they care about as economic models suggest that they should. Partly, this is the effect of market architecture. At auction, rare and unique items are displayed in ways that highlight their uniqueness. The manner in which the auctioneers and others write about the objects serves to decommodify them. The rituals surrounding auctions further emphasize the unique status of the goods up for bid. Despite the exchange of money, participants at auctions rarely think of themselves as engaging in a crass battle over fungible investment opportunities. They just don't think that way.

Mostly, the architecture of our market institutions is the result of spontaneous order, rather than any conscious planning or designing on the part of market participants. But even those special cases where we see homo economicus, we can introduce a non-business frame, or overcome the crowding effect, by applying the insights of market design. The time, place, and manner of markets, in combination with other social meaning conventions, can change the framing, and can preserve intrinsic motivation.

Of course, that's only true if we're dealing with ordinary people confronted with incentives that motivate them to change their decent nature. As with the black market, so with markets in general—we need to distinguish selection from treatment effects. If we begin with homo economicus and have them play economic games or participate in markets, we'll get less-than-desirable outcomes in the short term. But that's not because of markets. Put these people in positions of political power and we get less-than-desirable outcomes, but that, alone, is no reason to impugn politics. Make homo economicus teach undergraduates and the students won't be happy, but that, alone, is not sufficient to impugn the education system. So why should it impugn markets?

Generalized anti-market bias doesn't explain our anti-commodification intuitions. People who are generally pro-market share these intuitions. Perhaps there is a great deal of confusing selection for treatment effects. Maybe people really do confuse the assumptions of economics for empirical outcomes of real-world markets. But even if we have so far been successful at persuading you that all of these mistakes really are that—mistakes—we suspect you still feel uncomfortable about markets in kidneys or reading or cadavers or cultural artefacts or religious idols. That discomfort is probably best described as disgust or repugnance or nausea.

If so, then maybe a great deal of our anti-commodification intuitions are a result not of our reasoned and thoughtful engagement with the descriptive and normative facts, but a result of the fact that we are stupid monkeys in a deeply complex world. Our moral intuitions evolved in a very different context, and we should expect very many of them to misfire. Anti-commodification intuitions often misfire.

Moral Dumbfounding and Disgust

People find certain markets, such as markets in kidneys, disgusting. But just what is it that disgusts us about a market in kidneys? If we can identify it, we can eliminate it, is a thesis we suggested and defended in the last chapter. Let's try that strategy with kidneys, to see if we can identify an explanation for your disgust reaction, and to see if we can eliminate it.

Here is a list of possible worries about a market in kidneys, along with responses:

1 Exploitation: What makes a market in kidneys repugnant is the worry that the poor will become or be perceived as an "organ farm" for the wealthy. Poor people will sell organs due to economic hardship, and those organs will go to the rich. To overcome this worry, we can limit the selling of organs to all and only those who earn a certain income per year, and restrict the buying of

organs to all and only those making less than a certain amount per year. So only the rich would be permitted to sell their organs, and only the poor would be permitted to buy them. In principle, this should obviate this concern.

2　Coercion: Closely related to exploitation, we might worry that the poor will be coerced by their background economic hardship to do something that they would not choose to do if they had the economic wherewithal to say "no." There are several ways to overcome this worry. One is to again limit the selling of organs to all and only those who make a certain amount of money per year, so that economic hardship fades as a concern. Alternatively, we can institute a Universal Basic Income.

3　Commodity: We may worry that people will stop regarding their own bodies as "sacred" or "special." Instead, people may come to regard their bodies as potential profit-possibilities, as instruments for financial gain. In a previous chapter, we discussed this worry and rejected it. There, we rejected this objection because social meaning is contingent, and there is no necessary connection between markets, money, and some particular social meaning convention. Despite this response, we can add certain rituals to the buying and selling of organs that might reduce its commodity dimension, and increase its sacredness, or help decommodify it. Teachers receive a salary on the market, but we do not look at teachers as mere commodities. Cats and dogs are bought and sold, but we do not regard them as mere commodities. This worry can be overcome with good market design.

4　Access: We might worry that poor people will not be able to afford an organ. We may believe that people ought to receive kidney transplants not on the basis of ability to pay, but based on some other criteria. Worries about access are not worries about markets as such. We may believe that a free market in kidneys will result in this outcome, but then we need only offer certain constraints on the market to avoid this objection. So, for example, we can pay for kidneys using the market, but allocate on the basis of need through medicare, or through charities. We can subsidize kidney purchases. We could institute a voucher program for kidneys. Whatever mechanism we pick, we can, in principle, overcome this worry.

5　Price: One concern is that the price will be too high. If it is too high, then we might again worry about access. Interestingly, however, we might also worry that the price will be too low. If the price is too low, we might conclude that the object, a kidney, is not valued enough. We might compare the price of a kidney to other objects, and insist that a kidney, surely, is more important and significant than, say, a used Honda Civic. If so, we may worry that the price is too low. But prices are obviously variable, so price-related objections can, in principle, be easily overcome.

We could continue like this for any worry you might raise. But we suspect that the result of our strategy will, for very many readers, result in continued moral disagreement. Philosophers and psychologists have a name for this. They call it moral dumbfounding.[9] Moral dumbfounding is what happens when each of our specific moral objections are met with a good response, but we continue to insist that there must be something immoral about it. We suspect that many readers will still insist that there's something wrong with a market in kidneys, even if we overcome each particular and specific objection.

If we're right about this, then objections to markets in kidneys will have the very same structure and result as questions about the wrongness of gay marriage or incest. The intuition that it is wrong is sometimes "sticky" and appears not to be moved by rational appeals, by redescriptions of relevant context, by introducing mitigating circumstances, and so on. If that is your response to markets in certain kinds of things, then it may just be the case that you find something about the combination of the good or service in question and markets (mediated by your interpretation of what is going on in that market) *disgusting*.

In the next chapter, we ask: why should we trust our stomachs? Our answer: we shouldn't.

Notes

1 See Nozick 1998.
2 Leider and Roth 2010.
3 Tetlock 2000.
4 Gaus 2003, p. 89. Cf. to Walzer 1984, 23, 110, 116. Walzer says that there's a boundary between the spheres of the market and of politics that must not be crossed, lest it violate our understanding of these goods. Since Walzer is more or less a relativist, the fact that there are reasonable people who disagree is troublesome for him. He says that what makes it so that goods of one kind can't be traded for another is that members of a community believe this to be so. But what if not all members agree? What if some members think that majority is just confused about this?
5 Hirschman 1982.
6 Perhaps not. Brennan has a pet theory of why many academics have antipathy for the market: most professional academics have no experience of life outside academia. But they quickly discover, along their careers, that academia is full of moral corruption, from administrators gleefully violating Title VII in hiring decisions to their colleagues gleefully free-riding on others' service efforts. They think to themselves, "Well, academia is not-for-profit, so presumably business is even worse than this." In contrast, Brennan thinks his former employer, the automobile insurance firm GEICO, is saintly compared to even the best of his academic employers.
7 See Henrich et al. 2001.
8 For example, see Frank et al. 1993 (showing that exposure to "the self-interest model" encourages self-interested behavior), Wang et al. 2011 (finding that economics majors and students who took economics classes were more likely to behave in greedy ways and to rate "greed" more positively), and Gandal et al. 2005 (showing that college students planning to study economics rated values like honesty, loyalty, and helpfulness just as highly as other students, but then ranked them as much less important compared with non-economics majors by their third year).
9 See, for example, Haidt et al. 2000.

22

THE PSEUDO-MORALITY OF DISGUST

How Disgust Works

Disgust, as a moral emotion, differs importantly from other moral emotions, like anger. Anger is the typical moral emotion felt for perceived violations within the harm and fairness domain. Worries about inequality typically arouse feelings of anger, rather than disgust. We make angry rather than disgusted faces more often when it comes to lying, to cheating, to violent assaults, to concerns about exploitation, and so on. We may still describe markets that we believe will violate what some refer to as the "ethics of autonomy" as "noxious" or "repugnant." But this is not because disgust is the typical felt response. Perhaps calling these markets noxious or repugnant is based on an aesthetic decision. Some might use it not because each of the markets generates a disgust reaction, but because "noxious markets" or "repugnant markets" makes for a good category.

If you care very much about equality and exploitation, for example, thinking about a market and believing that it empirically leads to inequality and exploitation may make you angry. Your perception that something or other violates an important moral norm may in general make you angry. But anger is not subject to moral dumbfounding. You have an explanation for your anger, namely, the empirical belief that markets in this or that lead to inequality, or that markets as such have this tendency, coupled with the conviction that inequality is morally bad. If we were to convince you that this is not the empirical outcome, if you were to sincerely believe that markets do not promote inequality, or you came to believe that other considerations weigh in favor of markets despite the tendency toward inequality, then you would come to no longer be angry at markets.

Much less so with disgust. Russell and Giner-Sorolla demonstrated that an anger-response was easier to overcome when subjects were asked to re-evaluate an apparent moral violation in the presence of various mitigating circumstances. As well, people who felt anger towards a perceived moral violation—like certain sexual relations—could more easily explain their angry reactions with reasons and justifications. Those who were disgusted, on the other hand, had a much more difficult time justifying their disgust. Instead, they just begged the questions. When asked why some particular homosexual couple made them feel disgusted, subjects said things like, "because they're evil," which is another way of saying that it's wrong because it's disgusting, and it's disgusting because it's wrong.[1]

The Strange History of Repugnance Intuitions

Before we offer an attempt to "debunk" the disgust intuitions that ground some anti-commodification views, it would be worthwhile to highlight some of the various kinds of goods and services that have raised the ire of anti-commodification theorists past. It turns out that a great number of different things worried past anti-commodification theorists, worries that, as it turned out, we no longer worry so much about. Chris Freiman[2] and Martha Nussbaum[3] offer a litany of examples, including being paid for singing in the opera, for manual labor, for teaching, and for playing sports. People were also concerned about the charging of interest, and various forms of insurance, including children's insurance. Even metered parking was viewed as repugnant in the US.

Adam Smith's opera singers. Adam Smith was worried about opera singers and dancers. He wrote: "There are some very agreeable and beautiful talents of which the possession commands a certain sort of admiration; but of which the exercise for the sake of gain is considered, whether from reason or prejudice, as a sort of publick prostitution."[4]

Smith's intention was to explain the higher income that these professions attracted. According to Smith, the explanation lay in part in the disapprobation that attached not to the performance of opera singing, acting, or dancing, but to the doing of that for money. "The pecuniary recompense, therefore, of those who exercise them in this manner must be sufficient, not only to pay for the time, labour and expense of acquiring the talents, but for the discredit which attends the employment of them as the means of subsistence."[5]

In other words, these employments were noble. Singing, acting, dancing were all "higher" and "more dignified" pursuits. So noble and so dignified were they, that the people of Smith's time thought they should be above the avarice of the market. Thus, Smith thought, people who bought and sold these skills faced shame for having bought and sold them, and so had to be paid extra to induce them to do so.

But times have changed. We now do not regard paying singers, actors, and dancers as a form of pollution. When we attend the opera, if we do, we appreciate the singing, and we think nothing of the performers on stage getting a cut of the ticket sales. Of course they do, and of course they should.[6]

If we reflect on their pay, our concern, if we're concerned, has nothing to do with the in principle issue of whether or not they ought to be paid anything at all. Instead, our attention would be on how and how much they are paid. Maybe we think certain actors are overpaid, but none of us think they should be paid nothing at all, and none of us are bothered by people making their living in the arts. And while some engage in the arts for the sake of financial gain, we do not think that the arts in general are polluted by those who sing and dance for the sake of money, and not for the love of the art. If we were to poll people today, they would probably answer that the discredit was all prejudice, no reason.

Manual labor. Prior to Smith, discredit was attached to the nonleisured life of the ordinary wage laborer. Nussbaum explains that there was a general antipathy towards those who did manual work for an income in ancient Greece. Even Aristotle thought so: " ... in his view, the unleisured character of their daily activities and their inevitable preoccupation with gain would pervert their political judgment, making them grasping and small-minded."[7]

Was this anything other than rank prejudice? Aristotle and the "ancient Greek gentleman" may have their preferences about what counts as a "higher" and "more noble" form of life, and maybe they're right about the hierarchy, but it is certainly not reason that grounded their worries and objections to the use of money and payment for labor.

Teaching. While the manual laborer went in for abuse, so, too, did the teachers and educators of Aristotle's day and amongst those in the medieval church. Sophists exchanged money for philosophical instruction, and the payment was a significant part of why they were so distrusted and disliked. That same aversion to exchanging money for the teaching of spiritual and philosophical things riled some medieval church leaders.[8] By the 11th century, and in most of Europe, ecclesiastical positions within the church were often bartered for or bought with money. So, for example, the archbishopric of Norbonne was bought for one hundred thousand solidi. Pope Leo IX included condemning and banning such purchases, or "simony,"[9] as part of his reform movement at the Council of Rheims. Some had a capacious definition of simony. As Klerman explains, Bernard of Clairvaux thought that the selling of knowledge itself was a "base occupation." A proverb attributed to him reads: "A man learns for five reasons: to know, to be known to know, to sell, to instruct, to be instructed. To know is curiosity, to be known to know is vanity, to sell is simony, to instruct is charity, and to be instructed is humility."[10] Teaching, as Nussbaum explains, was regarded as an intimate and spiritual endeavor and, as such, it should be given away for free, a "pure spiritual gift."[11]

Nowadays the fact that philosophers and theologians at colleges and universities get paid is hardly worth commenting upon. Everyone we've been debating with in this book—Sandel, Satz, Radin, Anderson, and so on—gets a six-figure salary for teaching. Michael Sandel does not think that his getting paid to teach is worth mentioning in his book, and we think that's because it no longer has the power to worry anyone.

Sports. The Olympics were once a competition purely between unpaid amateurs. Then they allowed professionals in, and now the Olympics are hopelessly corrupt and disgusting. Whereas prior to permitting those who were paid for their athletic prowess the Olympics were noble and singularly exempt from any kind of graft, greed, and corruption, the Olympics are now just the playground of the rich and monocled.

Actually, none of that is true. Or, at least, if we do think the Olympics are more than a little corrupt, the explanation has little to do with permitting paid athletes to compete on the world stage. Despite the fears of the anti-commodification theorists, professional athletes appear to care as much about representing their country and doing a good job of it as the amateurs do. In fact, it is impossible to distinguish the amateurs from the professionals in terms of their behavior and character if we didn't know that one group did it as a full-time profession, while the other did it without the incentive of filthy lucre. The corruption has more to do with politics and nationalism than with markets, with the desire of governments to showcase their country's virtues through multibillion dollar expenditures on athletic venues that will crumble and go unused in the years that follow, and with the willingness of certain judges to judge not based on the actual ice dancing and figure skating abilities of the athletes, but based on some behind-the-scenes vote-trading schemes. (These judges fail to follow the ethics of proper vote selling.)

Again people worried, as they did for singing, fishing, perfuming, teaching and dancing, that "the mere presence of money would act as a corrupting influence such that the pure pursuit of the intrinsic goals of sport would be necessarily perverted."[12] But of course there is no necessary connection, as we have argued, between paying someone, and that payment somehow obliterating all other possible sources of motivation for performing the activity. Many opera singers are moved by the intrinsic values of opera, including the joys of expression, and the beauty of the art itself. The fact that they are paid is neither here nor there. The same is true of sport, many pursue sports as a livelihood because they are moved by the intrinsic pleasures and value of competition, expression, and excellence. Guidance counselors in high schools across Canada and the US give the following kind of advice: find what you love to do, then try to figure out how to make a living doing it. That's the order, not the other way around. To think otherwise is a form of prejudice.

Charging interest. Banks charge interest. Loans come with interest payments. You can pay for things with a credit card, but if you don't pay your balance completely, whatever is left over will be charged interest. The governments of several countries offer student loans, but the catch is that you'll have to pay interest.

Sometimes, the interest rates are obscene. But the mere fact of charging interest is no longer as widely regarded as an obscenity. This wasn't always so. In the not-too-distant past, the mere fact of charging interest was regarded with distaste. Holy books intoned against it, and were interpreted as prohibiting the charging of interest.

But now there are Christian bankers and Christian customers of banks. Most accept the interest that they have to pay without thinking they're going against God's will.

We can add others to this list, like paying for lawyers, children's insurance and metered parking:

Lawyer's fees. When we go to court, we pay a lawyer to represent us. Many are concerned that the rich can command better representation, and so are more likely to get a verdict that benefits them. But hardly anyone thinks that a lawyer should work for free, that providing a defense or working for the prosecution should be a profession without a salary.

That was not always so. During the 12th century, the question of whether or not a lawyer selling his services counted as simony was widely commented upon. Thomas of Chobham and others included justice as belonging to the category of the spiritual, but felt the need to explain why paying a lawyer did not count as simony: "the lawyer does not sell just advocacy, but the labor of advocating, because he labors greatly in studying and in other ways."[13] But the intuition that lawyers should not be paid remained strong. So, for example, in France during the middle ages the exchange of money for legal services was done in a round-about way: lawyers were not paid for advocating on a client's behalf, instead a client may be moved to give a "spontaneous gift" in the form of an "honora-rium."[14] This appears to have done the trick, although we're not sure why we don't perform this same trick for any number of things anti-commodification theorists find distasteful. Perhaps advertisers won't pay to advertise in sports stadiums, they merely provide an image and some text, and the stadium owners are moved to offer a spontaneous gift of placing the images in clear public view for the wonderful images. People won't pay to have sex with a prostitute, they are, instead, moved to give a spontaneous gift for the services in the form of an honorarium.

For what it's worth, when we or the anti-commodification theorists sell guest lectures for $1,000 or more per hour, the payments are called "honoraria."

Children's Insurance. From the late 19th century to the early 20th century, a battle raged between anti-commodification theorists and insurance companies. A new and strange form of insurance—children's insurance—was proposed and instituted. Insurance companies thought children should be insured against death, while anti-commodification theorists argued that such insurance places a financial value on children, and thereby substitutes the nonmonetary and noneconomic value of a child to a crude economic value.[15] "No manly man and no womanly woman," intoned the *Boston Evening Transcript* on March 14, 1895, "should be ready to say that their infants have pecuniary value."

Nowadays, we hardly even consider this an issue. Indeed, Michael Sandel doesn't even mention it despite a book full of examples of commodification intended to turn our stomachs. And maybe that's the problem—children's insurance, now no longer a bizarre and novel way of attaching a financial value to something that is beyond price, no longer has the power to turn anyone's stomach. We don't think it's disgusting; we think it responsible. We do not believe that parents are moved by the hope that their children die so they can collect on the insurance. Isn't it strange that we ever thought this? Worries about children's insurance also turned out to be a sort of prejudice.

Even in the absence of an explicit arrangement where a certain sum of money is exchanged for an untimely death, some deaths, if wrongful, can result in a court ruling of financial compensation. In a wrongful death suit, a plaintiff can attempt to recover for damages including the medical and funeral expenses, the loss of expected earnings, loss of benefits like a pension, the loss of expected goods and services the deceased would have provided, and so on. But also on this list is the possibility of recovering a financial sum for mental anguish, pain, suffering, loss of nurturing and care, the loss of love and companionship, and even loss of "consortium" (which includes sex).

At one point, the common law did not include any kind of right to sue for a wrongful death. You could sue for damages if someone was injured, but not if they died. It was by way of statutes that wrongful death suits entered onto legal avenues. While we still worry about what it means to be driving along this road, we worry a lot less. Many of us think that successful wrongful death suits at least do something in the face of a horrible tragedy. And many of us think that doing something is better than doing nothing.

Metered Parking. In the early 20th century, the United States witnessed the dawn of the parking meter. In 1932, Carl Magee invented the Park-o-meter to help ease the traffic situation in downtown Oklahoma City. In July of 1935, they were installed, and were quickly met with fierce resistance. Many thought the meters were un-American.[16] Many thought them a repugnant way of generating revenues for cities at the expense of every American's right to the free use of public streets. The arguments people raised against metered parking, and the responses on behalf of the practice, were more or less the same arguments we saw for and against pricing airline queues or access to other scarce goods.

Regarding metered parking as repugnant would now strike us as a bizarre and unusual response. We don't think anything of it. Of course there is metered parking, of course there is.

Why We Distrust Disgust

In "The Wisdom of Repugnance," Leon Kass argued that our deep-seated feelings of revulsion or repugnance are a clue to facts about ethics. When we recoil in disgust at the thought of some behavior, we are at least sometimes responding to an ingrained and "deep" wisdom—disgust and repugnance are the "emotional expression" of that wisdom, which is "beyond reason's power fully to articulate it."[17] In our classes, many of our students appear to agree with Kass. Some things, they tell us, are disgusting. Whatever might cause the disgust, insisting that it is disgusting is regarded by them as sufficient to conclude that it is wrong. Or at least prima facie wrong.

Kass admits that feeling disgusted is not an argument: "Revulsion is not an argument; and some of yesterday's repugnances are today calmly accepted—though, one must add, not always for the better."[18] How are we to assess this latter claim? By what standard is our now not feeling repulsed by, say, metered parking or children's insurance better or not better? If there is such a standard, why bother with revulsion, repugnance, and disgust at all? Why not immediately reach for that independent criterion, and evaluate our disgust reaction in light of that criterion?

Contrary to what Leon Kass, and Lord Patrick Devlin before him, suggest, repugnance is not a good guide to ethics. Repugnance, a form of disgust, changes frequently. Different cultures find different things repugnant. The very same person finds one thing repugnant when younger—olives or kissing a boy—but finds those things congenial or lovely later on in life. Even within a culture, we find different things disgusting and repugnant in one historical moment, but then we are repulsed no more. But reflection on the history of repugnance intuitions will not be sufficient to denounce it as an unreliable guide. For a successful debunking strategy, we need to demonstrate that repugnance is generally unreliable as a guide to ethics, and to articulate the causes of our repugnant reactions. It is as Martha Nussbaum says, when it comes to repugnance and disgust intuitions " … we must evaluate the cognitions they embody, as we would any class of beliefs, asking how reliable they are likely to be given their specific subject matter and their typical process of formation."[19]

This is precisely what we do in the physical realm. When it comes to our non-moral feelings of disgust in response to something in the physical world, the best theory of disgust claims that disgust evolved to aid us in avoiding invisible pathogens and other contaminants. Disgust evolved to help us not get sick. In the physical realm, what elicits disgust can be evaluated independently of our disgust response. So, knowing that disgust is an evolutionary aid to avoid pathogens and becoming sick, we can test the object of disgust for the presence of any kind of actual risk to our health.[20]

Indeed, in certain contexts, people can and should overcome their disgust response. So, for example, we think it right and proper that a doctor not be dissuaded from performing a medically-necessary surgery by her feelings of disgust. Perhaps she can't help the feeling, but she can help her response to those feelings. While disgusted, we think she still should transplant the kidney, or perform mouth-to-mouth, or perform an emergency C-Section, if that's what's necessary for good medical outcomes.

When we know that a particular object has no chance of causing us actual sickness, when we know that it is not actually contaminated, the presence of the feeling of disgust should be no guide to our action. That feeling, we might say, misfires. Mealworms may disgust us, but they are perfectly healthy to eat. Candy bars do not disgust us, but they're not good for us to eat.

Moral disgust is typically reserved to the distinctly conservative moral domain. We are more likely to make disgust, rather than angry, faces when we perceive a violation of sanctity, purity, divinity, the profound and the sacred. While it is called a conservative moral domain, it is clear that political non-conservatives often accept this foundation as part of their morality. So, for example, left-liberal Elizabeth Anderson appears to do so in her arguments against commercial surrogacy. Left-communitarian Michael Sandel clearly accepts it throughout his work on the moral limits of markets. While there are formal similarities, liberals and conservatives sometimes differ over what kinds of goods or services ought to be regarded as sacred, divine, or profound. Liberals are more likely to regard health care services as belonging to this category, regarding with suspicion the sale of these services. Conservatives tend not to worry about a market in health care.[21] While there are liberals who offer non-conservative moral foundations explanations for why they object, when they do, to a market in health care, there are at least some who think that "health" is a sacred kind of thing that ought not to be profaned by money or markets.

In arguing against disgust and repugnance as a useful guide to ethics, some want to eliminate the conservative moral domain altogether. They say that this domain is not actually a moral domain at all. Instead, it is a sort of prejudice or a kind of nonsense. What matters is violations of autonomy, or the presence or absence of harm, or the impact of something on our well-being. To think of something as "sacred" or "impure" is to go in for magical thinking.

We have come a long way in this book without limiting any moral foundations. We have argued that markets are in principle consistent with your moral foundations, whatever reasonable moral foundations you accept. We have accepted your preferred moral foundations, and have tried to show you that markets do not conflict with them. The strategy has been to have a fight at levels of abstraction above the morally foundational ones. We have not tried to convince you that all that matters is consent, or that consent functions as a trump. We have not tried to convince you that restricting market activity can only be justified in the face of harm. We have not tried to get you to abandon your worries about inequality, about exploitation, about the moral significance of communicating respectfully. Instead, we have tried to show you that, in principle, and often in practice, markets need not and often do not exacerbate wrongful inequality, that they need not and often do not lead to wrongful exploitation, that they need not and often do not express disrespectful attitudes.

In arguing against disgust, we are not abandoning our strategy. While neither of us believe the conservative moral foundation has much going for it, we want to push that debate to the pages of other books, not this one. Our argument against disgust as a heuristic for ethics is not an argument against thinking that some things are sacred or profound. We can accept the thought that kidneys, sex, and so on, are sacred, while simultaneously arguing that there are ways to design and structure a market that preserves the sacredness, the sanctity, and the purity of the objects of sale.

Fiske's Structures and Freiman's Debunking Strategy

There is a good explanation for the feeling of disgust and repugnance to market transactions. A number of psychologists have argued and presented evidence for the view that our moral reactions are dependent on our sorting of certain social relationships into certain moral categories. Alan Page Fiske distinguishes between four distinct types of psychological models: communal sharing (where "people treat all members of a category as equivalent"), authority ranking (where "people attend to their positions in a linear ordering"), equality matching (where "people keep track of the imbalances among them"), and market pricing (where "people orient to ratio values").[22] Fiske insists that these four categories or "structures" operate when we transfer things, including exchange, contribution and distribution, and that they "are the terms defining the primary standards of social justice."[23]

This view explains why we are pleased when certain kinds of goods or services are sorted into certain categories, and angry and sometimes repulsed when we sort goods or services that we think belong in one category in a different one. So, for example, sex and kidneys belong in the communal sharing category. Some, as we have seen, used to place teaching of philosophy in this category, insisting that it should be a spiritual gift. Most people think it's perfectly appropriate for us to make a gift of a kidney to a significant other, or to family members or close friends. We also think that it is perfectly appropriate to make a gift of sex to our husband or wife. We are repulsed, however, when the category of market pricing is used for these "goods" and "services." An item that intrinsically belongs to one category is instead sorted into a different (and therefore wrong) category.

When we think of real-world market exchanges, we probably automatically sort all of them into the market pricing category. When we are asked whether or not there ought to be a market in kidneys or sex or children's insurance, we are likely to translate that question into the different question of whether or not market pricing is the appropriate category for these "goods" or "services." Since market pricing is the wrong category for these, we respond with anger and disgust. It is a mis-categorization, or what Freiman calls "mismatching."[24] Sex is the kind of thing that ought to be part of a communal sharing relationship. So, too, with kidneys. We are to rely on the support and comfort of our friends and family, and not in the money we receive through an insurance payout, should one of our children die. So it is all right to exchange sex and kidneys based on communal sharing, for free, but it is not all right to do so for money, on a market.

Freiman suggests that we can also use this psychological model to help explain why we are sometimes morally dumbfounded when asked about the rightness or wrongness of a market in organs or a market in adoptions of babies. We may try to justify our objections to these markets by appealing to worries about exploitation, inequality, and so on, but should a researcher carefully eliminate even the possibility of these worries being realized, at least some subjects should still cling to a firm conviction that it is morally wrong. That is what Philip Tetlock found in one of his studies. He asked subjects if a market in organs or a market in adopting certain children would be all right with them. Almost 90% responded with moral outrage to these proposed markets. Tetlock explains their outrage like this: "[t]hese policy proposals elicit such a powerful negative response because they breach taboos; they allow people to affix dollar values to something— human bodies and babies—that well-socialized beings are supposed to regard as sacred."[25] A taboo is an absolute prohibition, without need for an explanation. Tetlock explains that describing it as a "taboo" was appropriate for about 60% of those who objected to these markets. They offered no reason, and did not feel compelled to offer an explanation "even when held accountable and pressed for one."[26]

The other 40%, the ones who offered reasons, expressed worries about the poor being compelled by their economic situation to sell their organs, and so be exploited by the rich, in the one case, and expressed worries about only healthy and attractive babies being "bought" in an adoption auction. They also worried about increases in price, such that only wealthy people could afford organs or babies. Would people change their minds if these objections were addressed? To test this, Tetlock added a series of questions, including these ones for the market in organs:

> Would you still object to markets for body organs: (a) if you lived in a society that had generous social welfare policies and never allowed the income for a family of four to fall below $32,000 per year (explaining the concept of inflation-adjusted 1996 dollars)?; (b) if society provided the less well-off with generous "organ-purchase vouchers" that increased in value as recipient income decreased (the poorer the recipient, the larger the voucher)?; (c) if it could be shown that all other methods of encouraging organ donation had failed to produce enough organs and that the only way to save large numbers of lives was to implement a market for body organs?[27]

For the pool of original subjects, 90% of which were initially opposed, about 60% remained opposed. Tetlock concluded that a market in organs is "taboo" for over half of the undergraduates who participated in this experiment. To call it a taboo is just to say that there is no general principle that justifies the opposition—it is to say that we have no reason to oppose something, except maybe for its failing to comport with a pattern or category that we use to make sense of our social lives. As Freiman has argued, Fiske's structures can here function as an explanation: subjects in Tetlock's experiment who regarded a market in organs as taboo sorted organs into the communal sharing category, and were made angry and felt disgusted at the proposal to sort them into the market pricing category instead. While we can offer explanations for taboos, these explanations are merely that. They do not rise to the level of justification. Taboos are unjustified.

A great deal of literature in social psychology appears to show that sometimes we recruit justifications for certain moral views—like opposition to a market in organs—after we have already decided to go to war. That is, we rationalize our disgust reactions, our pattern-matching, our sorting certain exchanges into one or another category, when these rationalizations play no role in explaining or justifying our objections. It is, to partially borrow Haidt's language, the disgusted dog wagging the rational tail.[28]

This, then, is the explanation of the paradox—having no moral objection to giving something away for free, while objecting to the same exchange on a market—at the heart of Freiman's "The Paradox of Commodification": we apply certain moral categories to certain kinds of transactions, and when one kind of transaction is mismatched with a category, we are repulsed and, sometimes, disgusted. But since we cannot construct a justification for our moral disgust, and since the history of our repugnance intuitions generates so many "false positives," we should ignore or discard the disgust intuitions. They are debunked.

We should note that we are not here claiming that disgust is unchangeable or always the wrong reaction. We are not claiming that disgust operates in a domain wholly separate from reason. After all, our disgust reactions have changed over time, and many of us might feel disgust in the presence of mealworms or poo-shaped chocolates but still eat them, demonstrating an ability to overcome disgust by reason. What we are claiming is that many anti-commodification intuitions are likely grounded in a disgust reaction, a reaction with a high probability of being subject to moral dumbfounding and stickiness.

Categorically Confused

Anti-commodification theorists are often just rationalizing their disgust response. What's worse is that disgusted people engage in cleansing and avoidance behavior. Rather than think hard about the issue, we turn away from it. In turning away from it, we fail to even countenance the possibility of avoiding much horror and tragedy, like the death and suffering of people on waiting lists for kidneys that could easily be assuaged with a market in kidneys.

We started by saying that we will not reject the conservative moral foundation, but have now ended with offering an argument for why we should reject disgust-based intuitions. Isn't there a conflict here?

To demonstrate why there is no conflict, let us pause for a moment to rehearse some of the conclusions of arguments we have made in prior chapters, in particular, the arguments that attempted to show how categorically confused too many anti-commodification theorists are.

Real-world market exchanges are not all performed with participants using a "business frame." It is a confusion to think that real-world market transactions operate exclusively within this frame. Depending on the design of the market, participants may operate with an ethical frame while engaging in a market exchange. The distinction between a business and an ethical frame cuts within the domain of possible market exchanges. It does not track the difference between market and non-market exchanges. The very same categorical confusion is present when it comes to relevant features of gift exchanges. Archetypal gift exchanges differ sharply from archetypal market exchanges, but not all real-world market exchanges are archetypal. The morally relevant features of a gift exchange can be, and often are, present in real-world market exchanges.

The very same categorical confusion might creep in here. We suspect that anti-commodification theorists will think that the structure of market pricing is a domain that covers every possible market exchange, while the structure of communal sharing is fundamentally at odds with market exchanges as such. By now it should be clear that that is not so. There are real-world market exchanges that would be mistakenly sorted into the market pricing category, despite the fact that a price is used. Professors at universities are paid a salary, but Michael Sandel is likely to place "being a professor of philosophy" in the communal sharing category. He would not be obviously confused, because it takes more than a price on a market for the category of market pricing to apply.

To ask whether or not there should be a market in kidneys or sex is not of a piece with asking whether or not the category of market pricing is appropriate to kidneys or sex. Those are questions about different kinds of things. In principle, the thoughts "we should have a market in kidneys" and "kidneys do not belong to the category of market pricing" are not together incoherent. And so it is that we can preserve the conservative moral foundation while simultaneously endorsing a market in sacred things. What is sacred can be sold, and the sale of it does not conflict with its sacredness, it just requires the careful design of a market.

Conclusion

John Harris is right when he writes that "there is no necessary connection between phenomena, attitudes, or actions that make us uneasy, or even those that disgust us, and those phenomena, attitudes, and actions that there are good reasons for judging unethical. Nor does it follow that those things we are confident are unethical must be prohibited by legislation or regulation."[29]

While indignation is a kind of moral emotion that can, in principle, be publicly shared, Nussbaum insists that our society "will do well to cast disgust onto the garbage heap."[30] And we agree.

If it isn't too cheeky, we'd like to paraphrase Martha Nussbaum:

> For a long time, our society, like many others, has confronted markets and market exchanges with a politics of repugnance, as many people react to the uncomfortable presence of entrepreneurs, investors, and middlemen with a deep aversion akin to that inspired by bodily wastes, slimy insects, and spoiled food——and then cite that very reaction to justify a range of

legal restrictions, from usury laws to bans on the sale of kidneys or sex. Partisans of the politics of repugnance can barely stand to think about what that capitalist did with consenting others; they say, "that stuff makes me want to throw up," and turn away from the reality of the market as from a loathsome contaminant to the body politic.[31]

If markets in kidneys and sex disgust you, you should just get over it, the way we get over our feeling of disgust when we attend a live birth. It may be disgusting, but so what? A little reflection on what is happening, on the fact that a little baby is about to enter the world, should fully trump how gross the whole thing is.

Instead of counting on a rough-and-ready heuristic grounded in our more primordial past to tell us what's right and what's wrong, we should instead rely on our considered judgments. If there's anything to be disgusted by, it is the fact that many life-saving and life-improving markets get legally blocked for want of a little reason and a little reflection.

By way of a final note, let us report our own feelings of disgust. It is not that the two of us feel no disgust, or are very low on the disgust scale. We share the very same, or at least similar, visceral feelings of disgust and repugnance as most others. The difference is in the object of our disgust.

We are not disgusted by markets in kidneys, nor by markets in sex, drugs, pornography, reading, or any of a thousand other markets. We are, instead, disgusted by the fact that people are disgusted by these markets, and fail to overcome that disgust when presented with sufficient evidence that the good outweighs the bad, that a market would save or improve our lives, that we can preserve gift relationships within a market, that sacred things can be sold without undermining or challenging their sacred status. We already know, to the extent that such things can be known, that a market in kidneys would save lives. Real living, breathing, flesh-and-blood human beings. With parents, children, with valuable and significant lives to lead. With faces and names. But third parties, the loud and obnoxious people standing on the sidelines, are screaming at the dying that saving their lives would come at the too high price of an uncomfortable turn in their stomachs. They stand in the bleacher seats, uninterested in getting involved in a market themselves, but are urging the referees to draw their weapon at the first sign of a market they think is yucky. They disgust us.

Unlike markets in organs, opposition to such markets is, truly, disgusting.

Notes

1 Russell and Giner-Sorolla 2013. See Haidt 2001.
2 See Freiman 2014b.
3 See Nussbaum 1998.
4 Smith 1776, at I.10.28.
5 Here's the full quote: "The pecuniary recompense, therefore, of those who exercise them in this manner, must be sufficient, not only to pay for the time, labour and

expense of acquiring the talents, but for the discredit which attends the employment of them as the means of subsistence. The exorbitant rewards of players, opera-singers, opera-dancers, &c. are founded upon those two principles; the rarity and beauty of the talents, and the discredit of employing them in this manner. It seems absurd at first sight that we should despise their persons, and yet reward their talents with the most profuse liberality. While we do the one, however, we must of necessity do the other. Should the public opinion or prejudice ever alter with regard to such occupations, their pecuniary recompense would quickly diminish. More people would apply to them, and the competition would quickly reduce the price of their labour. Such talents, though far from being common, are by no means so rare as is imagined. Many people possess them in great perfection, who disdain to make this use of them; and many more are capable of acquiring them, if any thing could be made honourably by them." Smith 1776, I.10.28.

6 Nussbaum 1998, 694–95, writes: "We think it entirely right and reasonable that high art should receive a high salary. If a producer of opera should take the position that singers should not be paid, on the grounds that receiving money for the use of their talents involves an illegitimate form of commodification and even market alienation of those talents, we would think that this producer was a slick exploiter, out to make a profit from the ill treatment of vulnerable and impressionable artists. On the whole, we think that, far from cheapening or ruining talents, the presence of a contract guarantees conditions within which the artist can develop her art with sufficient leisure and confidence to reach the highest level of artistic production."

7 Nussbaum 1998, 697.

8 This history is indebted to Klerman 1990.

9 At the time, "simony" was understood as the sin of trying to purchase the holy spirit. Klerman 1990 explains that Thomas of Chobham defined simony as "the making of a contract exchanging temporalia [temporal things, like money] for spiritualia [spiritual things, like the priesthood]."

10 Nussbaum 1998, 697.

11 Klerman 1990.

12 Schneider and Butcher 1993, 468.

13 Quoted in Klerman 1990.

14 For example, see http://www.barreau-saintnazaire.fr/professionhistoire.php: "The lawyer solicits no compensation from the person to whom he brings his knowledge. Quite the contrary, the latter expresses his gratitude with an 'honorarium.'" Or see http://www.avocats-picovschi.com/le-metier-d-avocat_article-1.html: "The profession then clothes itself in a definite humanism, since lawyers, often independently wealthy, exercise without any obligation towards the client, free from and independent of the power of judges and policies and claim no compensation (the honorarium being a spontaneous gift of the client's acknowledgement)." (Both of these examples were translated for us by Adam Allouba.)

15 For an analysis of this fight, see Zelizer 1981.

16 Crossen 2007.

17 Kass 1997.

18 Kass 1997.

19 Nussbaum 2009, 74.

20 Prominent theories about the nature of disgust include identifying disgust as disease avoidance. See, for example, Oaten, Stevenson, and Case 2009 or Curtis, de Barra, and Aunger 2011.

21 Tetlock 2000, 251.

22 Fiske 1992, 689.

23 Fiske 1992, 690.

24 Freiman 2014b, 15.

25 Tetlock 2000, 252.
26 Tetlock 2000, 252.
27 Tetlock 2000, 253.
28 See Haidt 2001. Freiman 2014b, writes, " … these psychological models [Fiske's four structures] explain why we cannot find acceptable supporting general principles for our anti-commodification intuitions. The reason is because these intuitions are not, in fact, supported by general principles. Instead, these intuitions are what we might call 'brute' or 'basic.' Intuitively, we can donate kidneys but not sell them *simply because* kidneys belong to the CS category rather than the MS category. There is no further underlying reason." See Freiman 2014b, 12.
29 Harris 1997, 358.
30 Nussbaum 2009, 75.
31 Nussbaum's (2010, xiii) words were: "For a long time, our society, like many others, has confronted same-sex orientations and acts with a politics of disgust, as many people react to the uncomfortable presence of gays and lesbians with a deep aversion akin to that inspired by bodily wastes, slimy insects, and spoiled food—and then cite that very reaction to justify a range of legal restrictions, from sodomy laws to bans on same-sex marriage. Partisans of the politics of disgust can barely stand to think about what that gay teenager did with his friends; they say, 'that stuff makes me want to throw up,' and turn away from the reality of gay life as from a loathsome contaminant to the body politic."

23

POSTSCRIPT

How to Prove Us Wrong

What can't money buy? There are things people shouldn't do, period, and money shouldn't buy those things for that reason. There are things people shouldn't have, period, and money shouldn't buy those things. But the money is incidental here.

Our thesis is that there are no inherent limits to markets. That doesn't mean that every market transaction is good or permissible. There are things people shouldn't have, such as slaves or child porn, in which case they also shouldn't buy and sell these things. But here the problem isn't the *market* in those things; it's those things, themselves. There are things people shouldn't do, such as kill innocent people, in which people shouldn't buy and sell services in doing those things. But, again, the problem isn't the *market* in those services; it's those services, period. There are ways of producing and selling goods that are immoral, and that sometimes gives us reason to avoid doing business with certain vendors or buying certain goods. But here it's not because the goods or services in question are the kinds of things that must not be bought or sold, but because the particular way they are being produced or sold violates basic business ethics. So, to use one of our previous examples, if all for-profit colleges are of immorally low quality and exploit their customers, then they are immoral businesses. But it doesn't mean that buying and selling education is inherently wrong; it just means that all the current sellers have bad business ethics.

The commodification debate concerns what things can be for sale. More precisely, it concerns whether there are some things that can be traded, given away, and exchanged for free, but which are wrongful to buy and sell.

Over the past 22 chapters, we've examined dozens of supposedly noxious or repugnant markets, and dozens of arguments purporting to show that these markets are immoral. In each case, we found serious flaws with those arguments. After explaining specifically why we are skeptical of particular anti-commodification arguments, we laid out general grounds for skepticism. We argued that many times when anti-commodification theorists complain about a market in some good, they are merely complaining about the particular form of that market. However, we pointed out, it seems like there is always a different way of buying and selling that good or service that eliminates the anti-commodification theorist's complaint. We also expressed a worry about the basic intuitions anti-commodification theorists rely upon. Our argument does not rest upon this worry, but, nevertheless, we worry that many anti-commodification theorists are reifying disgust reactions, or that they are skeptical of markets in general because we human beings were not designed to live in market societies.

What we want to do now is lay out what it would take to make a successful anti-commodification argument. Here's a roadmap for how to prove us wrong. Let's say you think that some good or service G must not be for sale. Now ask these questions:

1 *Asymmetry:* Is it permissible for people to have G, period? Is it permissible for people to give G away or take G for free? You need to show us "yes." You need to find an asymmetry where it's okay to have and exchange something, but not on the market. Otherwise, your complaint isn't really about the market.
2 *Design-insensitivity:* Whatever your objection is to buying and selling G, is there some alternative form of the market that would remove that objection? In principle, could someone sell it in a different way, at a different time, in a different place, and would your objection go away? You need to show us "no." You need to demonstrate that there is no way of designing a market that would overcome the objection.

This is a tall order, but that's what it takes. Otherwise, the objections will miss their mark. We will either be complaining about something other than the market, or we will be complaining about contingent features of markets, about the *how*, not the *what*.

Having a Conversation

Michael Sandel says he can't promise "definitive answers" to the questions about what should and should not be for sale. But he says he wants to "at least prompt discussion of these questions … "[1] Elsewhere he says that we need to have a conversation about these questions, about what it means to put a price tag on pregnancy and procreation, or about just how we should express the way we value education and learning.[2]

This book and our other articles on the topic are our contribution to that conversation. We welcome having that conversation. (Indeed, we can put a price on it. Brennan reasonably estimates that partaking in this conversation will pay him at least an additional $45,000 in 2016 and $300,000 over the next 30 years of his career.[3])

Part of having a good conversation is responding to the other people in the conversation. A few years ago, Sandel wrote the lead essay in a *Boston Review* debate about commodification. He said that markets crowd out morals and make us more selfish and corrupt.[4] Herbert Gintis (see Chapter 11 for a summary of his research on this issue) pointed out that Sandel not only lacked evidence for this claim, but, contrary to Sandel, the available evidence (some of which Gintis himself had produced) strongly indicates Sandel is wrong. In fact, as far as we know, markets tend to ennoble us rather than corrupt us.[5] But in subsequent talks over a year later, such as a talk delivered at Brown University on October 24, 2013, Sandel continues to advance the same criticisms. We'd like to see him take his critics seriously rather than brushing them off. We'd like to know why he finds Gintis's work unpersuasive.[6]

One final point: having a conversation means leaving our guns at home. When Sandel asks us to talk about what should and shouldn't be for sale, we hope he intends for this to be a conversation in good faith, where if we can't reach consensus, we won't try to force the other side to comply with our point of view. We hope that if Sandel can't convince everyone to see the light as he sees it, he won't resort to forcing them to comply with his vision of right and wrong. So, we assume that Sandel doesn't intend that this conversation carry over into the voting booth. After all, when we vote on what can and can't be for sale, we're not having a conversation anymore. We're instead just pushing around the people with the minority opinion. We're using the coercive power of government to force them to submit to our point of view.

However, if we're wrong about that, if Sandel really does want it to come to a vote, we'll accept that on one condition: let there be a market in those votes.

P.S.: We Commodified This Book

Most books are commodified, but this book is extra-commodified.

Take a look at our Acknowledgments section. You might notice something strange. In addition to the normal sort of thanks you'd expect to see, we have three tiers of Acknowledgments. Each person or group listed there paid for his or her acknowledgment. The highest tier, the Silvermint Tier, cost $25. In exchange, sponsors receive their name in print in that tier, a few chapters of this book sent to them early, and the right to publish a short message in the acknowledgments. (Some of the sponsors declined to publish a message.) The Silvermint Tier is named after UConn philosophy and women's studies professor Daniel Silvermint, who paid an undisclosed amount to have the highest tier named after him. The next tier, the Platinum Tier, cost $10. In exchange, sponsors get their name in print, plus the introductory chapters (Part I) sent to them early. The lowest tier, the

Gold Tier, cost $1. In exchange, sponsors get their name in print. You might notice some sponsors are listed five times. These sponsors gave us $5 and asked to be listed five times. In total, we raised over $600 in sponsorships. We made it clear to sponsors that while we both give money to charity, we intend to use this money selfishly, to promote our own narrow self-interest.

We wish to thank Chris Nelson for suggesting we commodify the acknowledgment sections. (He didn't pay us for this acknowledgment.)

Is it permissible for us to commodify our book this way? We think the answer is yes. But rather than justify that, we leave that as an exercise—a "final exam"— for the reader, whom we now thank for reading, regardless of whether the book was purchased, borrowed, or stolen.

Notes

1 Sandel 2012a, 11.
2 http://www.theguardian.com/books/2012/may/27/michael-sandel-reason-values-bodies. He also stated this at a lecture at Brown University on Thursday, October 24, 2013.
3 Georgetown's McDonough School of Business pays faculty who publish in top venues (such as the journal *Ethics* or the academic press Routledge) a large summer research bonus. In addition, since publications help raises, and raises build upon past raises, a good article or book now can easily be worth $300,000 over the course of a career.
4 Sandel 2012b, https://www.bostonreview.net/forum-sandel-markets-morals
5 Gintis 2012, https://www.bostonreview.net/gintis-giving-economists-their-due
6 In the *Boston Review* debate, Sandel wrote a one-paragraph response to Gintis, but he seemed to just ignore Gintis's main criticisms. So, while Sandel has technically written a response to Gintis, he hasn't really responded.

BIBLIOGRAPHY

Ackerman, Bruce, and James Fiskin. 2005. *Deliberation Day*. New Haven: Yale University Press.

Allan, Bradley M., and Roland G. Fryer, Jr. 2011. "The Powers and Pitfalls of Education Incentives," *The Hamilton Project*, Washington, D.C.: Brookings Institution.

Al-Ubayli, Omar, Houser, Daniel, Nye, John, Paganelli, Maria Pia, and Xiaofei Sophia Pan. 2013. "The Causal Effect of Market Priming on Trust: An Experimental Investigation Using Randomized Control," *PLoS One* 8(3): e55968. doi: 10.1371/journal.pone.0055968

Anderson, Elizabeth. 1990. "Is Women's Labor a Commodity?," *Philosophy and Public Affairs* 19: 71–92.

——1995. *Value in Ethics and Economics*. Cambridge, MA: Harvard University Press.

——2000a. "Why Commercial Surrogate Motherhood Unethically Commodifies Women and Children: Reply to McLachlan and Swales," *Health Care Analysis* 8: 19–26.

——2000b. "Beyond Homo Economicus: New Developments in Theories of Social Norms," *Philosophy and Public Affairs* 29: 170–200.

Appadurai, Arjun. 2005. "Commodities and the Politics of Value," in *Rethinking Commodification: Cases and Readings in Law and Culture*, ed. Martha M. Ertman and Joan C. Williams. New York University Press, 2005.

Archard, David. 2002. "Selling Yourself: Titmuss's Argument against a Market in Blood," *Journal of Ethics* 6: 87–103.

Ariely, Dan. 2013. *The Honest Truth about Dishonesty: How We Lie to Everyone, Especially Ourselves*. New York: Harper.

Austen-Smith, D., and R. Fryer. 2005. "An Economic Analysis of 'Acting White'," *Quarterly Journal of Economics* 120: 551–83.

Barber, Benjamin. 2008. *Consumed*. New York: W. W. Norton and Company.

Becker, Gary. 1957. *The Economics of Discrimination*. Chicago: University of Chicago Press.

Becker, Lawrence. 1980. "The Obligation to Work," *Ethics* 91: 35–49.

Berggren, Niclas, and Therese Nilsson. 2013. "Does Economic Freedom Foster Tolerance?" *Kyklos* 66: 107–207.

Bertrand, M., Goldin, C., and Lawrence Katz. 2010. "Dynamics of the Gender Gap for Young Professionals in the Financial and Corporate Sectors," *American Economic Journal: Applied Economics* 2: 228–55.

Birch, Sarah. 2009. *Full Participation*. Manchester: University of Manchester Press.

Bloch, Maurice, and Jonathan Parry. 1989. "Introduction: Money and the Morality of Exchange," in *Money and the Morality of Exchange*, ed. Maurice Bloch and Jonathan Parry, pp. 1–33. New York: Cambridge University Press.

Bowles, S. 1998. "Endogenous Preferences: The Cultural Consequences of Markets and Other Institutions," *Journal of Economic Literature* 36: 75–111.

Brennan, Andrew. 1992. "Moral Pluralism and the Environment," *Environmental Values* 1: 15–33.

Brennan, Jason. 2011. *The Ethics of Voting*. Princeton: Princeton University Press.

——2012a. *Libertarianism: What Everyone Needs to Know*. New York: Oxford University Press.

——2012b. "For-Profit Business as Civic Virtue," *Journal of Business Ethics* 106: 313–24.

Brennan, Geoffrey, and Alan Hamlin. 1995. "Economizing on Virtue," *Constitutional Political Economy* 6: 35–60.

Buchanan, James. 2003. "Politics without Romance," *Policy* 19: 13–18.

Burtt, Shelley. 1990. "The Good Citizen's Psyche: On the Psychology of Civic Virtue." *Polity* 23: 23–38.

Camera, Gabriele, Casari, Marco, and Maria Bigoni. 2013. "Money and Trust among Strangers," *Proceedings of the National Academy of Science of the United States of America*, early online edition, 2013. Available at http://www.pnas.org/content/early/2013/08/21/1301888110.

Cameron, Judy, and W. David Pierce. 1994. "Reinforcement, Reward, and Intrinsic Motivation: A Meta-Analysis," *Review of Educational Research* 64: 363–423.

Campbell, David E. 2001. "Making Democratic Education Work," in *Charters, Vouchers, and Public Education*, ed. Paul E. Peterson and David E. Campbell, pp. 254–55. Washington, DC: Brookings Institution.

Carlisle-Frank, Pamela, and Joshua M. Frank. 2005. "Owners, Guardians, and Owner-Guardians: Differing Relationships with Pets," *Anthrozoos* 19: 225–42.

Carruthers, Bruce G., and Laura Ariovich. 2010. *Money and Credit: A Sociological Approach*. London: Polity Press.

Carruthers, B.G., and W. N. Espeland. 1998. "Money, Meaning, and Morality," *American Behavioral Scientist* 41: 1384–1408.

Charity Aids Foundation. 2012. *World Giving Index* 2012. Available at https://www.cafonline.org/publications/2011-publications/world-giving-index-2011.aspx/.

Christiano, Thomas. 2008. *The Constitution of Equality*. New York: Oxford University Press.

Cohen, G. A. 2009. *Why Not Socialism?* Princeton: Princeton University Press.

Conly, Sarah. 2013. *Against Autonomy*. New York: Cambridge University Press, 2013.

Cowen, Tyler. 1998. *In Praise of Commercial Culture*. Cambridge, MA: Harvard University Press.

Credeur, Mary Jane, and Mary Schlangenstein. 2013. "Airlines Fight for First- and Business-Class Passengers," *Bloomberg*, May 30, 2013. Available at http://www.businessweek.com/articles/2013-05-30/airlines-fight-for-first-and-business-class-passengers.

Crittenden, Jack. 2007. "Civic Education," in *Stanford Encyclopedia of Philosophy*, ed. Edward Zalta. Available at http://plato.stanford.edu/entries/civic-education/.

Crossen, Cynthia. 2007. "When Parallel Parking Was New and Meters Seemed Un-American," *Wall Street Journal*, July 30, 2007. Available at http://online.wsj.com/news/articles/SB118574808780081653?mod=hps_us_editors_picks&mg=reno64-wsj&url=http%3A%2F%2Fonline.wsj.com%2Farticle%2FSB118574808780081653.html%3Fmod%3Dhps_us_editors_picks.

Curtis, Valerie, de Barra, Micheal, and Robert Aunger. 2011. "Disgust as an Adaptive System for Disease Avoidance Behavior," *Philosophical Transactions of the Royal Society B* 366: 389–401.

Dagger, Richard. 1997. *Civic Virtues: Rights, Citizenship, and Republican Liberalism*. New York: Oxford University Press.

Deci, E. L., Koestner, R., and Ryan, R. M. 1999. "A Meta-Analytic Review of Experiments Examining the Effects of Extrinsic Rewards on Intrinsic Motivation," *Psychological Bulletin* 125: 627–68.

Delong, Brad. 2002. *Macroeconomics*. New York: McGraw Hill.

Easley, David, and Jon Kleinberg. 2010. *Networks, Crowds, and Markets: Reasoning about a Highly Connected World*. Cambridge: Cambridge University Press.

Eisenberger, Robert, and Judy Cameron. 1996 "Detrimental Effects of Reward: Reality or Myth?," *American Psychologist* 51: 1154–66.

Ekelund, Robert, Ressler, Rand, and Robert Tollison. 2006. *Microeconomics: Private and Public Choice*. New York: Prentice Hall.

Fabre, Cécile. 2006. *Whose Body is it Anyway?* New York: Oxford University Press.

Finnis, John. 1997. "Law, Morality, and 'Sexual Orientation'," in *Same Sex: Debating the Ethics, Science, and Culture of Homosexuality*, ed. John Corvino. New York: Rowman and Littlefield.

Fiske, Alan Page. 1992. "The Four Elementary Forms of Sociality: Framework for a Unified Theory of Social Relations," *Psychological Review* 99: 689–723.

Frank, Robert H., Gilovich, Thomas, and Dennis T. Regan. 1993. "Does Studying Economics Inhibit Cooperation?" *The Journal of Economic Perspectives* 7: 159–71.

Franklin, Mark N. 2001. "Electoral Participation," in *Controversies in Voting Behavior*, 4th edition, ed. Richard Niemi and Herbert Wiesberg, pp. 83–100. New York: CQ Press.

Freeman, Samuel. 2007. *Rawls*. New York: Routledge Press.

Freiman, Christopher. 2014a. "Vote Markets," *Australasian Journal of Philosophy* 92: 759–774.

——2014b. "The Paradox of Commodification," unpublished manuscript. Williamsburg, VA: College of William and Mary.

Frey, Bruno S. 2002. *Inspiring Economics: Human Motivation in Political Economy*. Northampton: Edward Elgar Publishing.

Fry-Revere, Sigrid, and Bahar Basanti. 2014. "Desperate Times Demand Innovative Solutions: Compensated Kidney Donations." Best Thinking. Available at https://www.bestthinking.com/articles/medicine/internal_medicine/nephrology/desperate-times-demand-innova tive-solutions-compensated-kidney-donation?tab=versions.

Galston, William. 2007. "Pluralism and Civic Virtue." *Social Theory and Practice* 33: 625–35.

Gandal, Neil, Roccas, Sonia, Sagiv, Lilach, and Amy Wrzesniewski. 2005. "Personal Value Priorities of Economists," *Human Relations* 58: 1227–52.

Gaus, Gerald F. 2003. "Backwards into the Future: Neo-Republicanism as a Post-Socialist Critique of Market Society," *Social Philosophy and Policy* 20: 59–91.

——2008. *On Politics, Philosophy, and Economics*. Belmont, CA: Thomson-Wadsworth.

Gauthier, David. 1987. *Morals by Agreement*. New York: Oxford University Press.

Gell, Alfred. 1992. "Inter-tribal Commodity Barter and Reproductive Gift-Exchange in Old Melanesia," in *Barter, Exchange and Value: An Anthropological Approach*, ed. Caroline Humphrey and Stephen Hugh-Jones, pp. 1–20. Cambridge: Cambridge University Press.

Gilbert, Pablo. 2012. "Is There a Human Right to Democracy? A Response to Cohen," *Revista Latinoamericana de Filosofía Política* 1: 1–37.

Gintis, Herbert. 2012. "Giving Economists Their Due," *Boston Review*, June 25, 2012. Available at http://www.bostonreview.net/gintis-giving-economists-their-due.

Goldin, C., and Lawrence Katz. 2008. "Transitions: Career and Family Life Cycles of the Educational Elite," *American Economic Review* 98: 363–69.

Gorman, Linda. 2013. "Discrimination," *The Concise Encyclopedia of Economics* 2013 online edition. Available at http://www.econlib.org/library/Enc1/Discrimination.html.

Gregory, Christopher A. 1982. *Gifts and Commodities*. London: Academic Press.

Grier, Katherine. 2006. *Pets in America: A History*. Chapel Hill: UNC Press.

Gwartney, James, Lawson, Robert, and Joshua Hall. 2012. *Economic Freedom of the World: 2012 Annual Report.* Toronto, ON: Fraser Institute. Available at http://www.freetheworld.com/2012/EFW2012-complete.pdf.

Haidt, Jonathan. 2001. "The Emotional Dog and its Rational Tail: A Social Intuitionist Approach to Moral Judgment," *Psychological Review* 108: 814–34.

——2012. *The Righteous Mind: Why Good People are Divided by Politics and Religion.* New York: Pantheon Press.

Haidt, Jonathan, Bjorklund, Fredrick, and Scott Murphy. 2000. "Moral Dumbfounding: When Intuition Finds No Reason." Unpublished manuscript.

Hanson, Robin. 2013. "Should We Vote on Values but Bet on Beliefs?" *Journal of Political Philosophy* 21: 151–78.

Harris, John. 1997. "'Goodbye Dolly?' The Ethics of Human Cloning," *Journal of Medical Ethics* 23: 353–60.

Hayek, F. A. 1960. *The Constitution of Liberty.* Chicago: University of Chicago Press.

Hazlitt, Henry. 1988. *Economics in One Lesson.* New York: Three Rivers Press.

——1998. *Economics in One Lesson,* 50th Anniversary Reprint Edition. New York: Laissez-Faire Books.

Healey, Kieran. 2006. *Last Best Gifts: Altruism and the Market for Human Blood and Organs.* Chicago: University of Chicago Press.

Henrich, Joseph, Boyd, Robert, Bowles, Samuel, Camerer, Colin, Fehr, Ernst, Gintis, Herbert, and Richard McElreath. 2001. "In Search of Homo Economicus: Behavioral Experiments in 15 Small-Scale Societies," *American Economic Review* 91: 73–78.

Hirschman, Albert. 1970. *Exit, Voice, and Loyalty.* Cambridge, MA: Harvard University Press.

——1982. "Rival Interpretations of Market Society: Civilizing, Destructive, or Feeble?" *Journal of Economic Literature* 20: 1463–84.

Hoffman, Mitchell, and John Morgan, "Who's Naughty? Who's Nice? Experiments on whether Pro-Social Workers are Selected Out of Cutthroat Business Environments," October 25, 2013. Available at http://ssrn.com/abstract=2345102 or http://dx.doi.org/10.2139/ssrn.2345102.

Hoxby, Caroline. 2003a. "School Choice and School Productivity: Could School Choice be a Tide that Lifts All Boats?" in *The Economics of School Choice,* ed. Caroline Hoxby, pp. 287–342. Chicago: University of Chicago Press.

——2003b. "School Choice and School Competition: Evidence from the United States," *Swedish Economic Policy Review* 10: 9–65.

Hussain, Waheed. 2012. "Is Ethical Consumerism an Impermissible Form of Vigilantism?" *Philosophy and Public Affairs* 4: 111–43.

Jamieson, Alistair. 2009. "Brain-Eating Tribe Could Help Find Treatment for Mad Cow Disease," *The Telegraph,* November 19, 2009. Available at http://www.telegraph.co.uk/news/worldnews/australiaandthepacific/papuanewguinea/6603676/Brain-eating-tribe-could-help-find-treatment-for-mad-cow-disease.html.

Jha, Saumitra. 2013. "Trade, Institutions, and Ethnic Tolerance: Evidence from South Asia," *American Political Science Review* 107: 806–32.

Kaman, Vicki S., and Charmine E. J. Hartel. 1994. "Gender Differences in Anticipated Pay Negotiation Strategies and Outcomes," *Journal of Business and Psychology* 9: 183–97.

Kass, Leon R. 1997. "The Wisdom of Repugnance." *New Republic* 216: 17–26.

Kelman, Steven. 1981. "Cost-Benefit Analysis: An Ethical Critique," *AEI Journal of Government and Society Regulation,* January/February 1981: 33–60.

Klerman, Dan. 1990. "Slavery, Simony, and Sex," unpublished manuscript. Chicago: University of Chicago Law School.

Krawiec, Kimberly D. 2010. "Price and Pretense in the Baby Market," in *Baby Markets: Money and the New Politics of Creating Families,* ed. Michele Bratcher Goodwin, pp. 41–56. New York: Cambridge University Press.

Krugman, Paul. "The CPI and the Rat Race," *Slate,* Sunday, Dec. 22, 1996. Available at http://www.slate.com/articles/business/the_dismal_science/1996/12/the_cpi_and_the_ rat_race.html.

Krugman, Paul, and Robin Wells. 2009. *Economics,* Second Edition. New York: Worth Publishers.

Lacetera, N., Macis, M., and R. Slonim. 2013. "Economic Rewards to Motivate Blood Donation," *Science* 40: 927–28.

Landes, Elisabeth M., and Richard Posner. 1978. "The Economics of the Baby Shortage," *The Journal of Legal Studies* 7: 323–48.

Leider, Stephen, and Roth, Alvin E. 2010. "Kidneys for Sale: Who Disapproves, and Why?" *American Journal of Transplantation* 10: 1221–27.

Levitt, Steven, and Stephen Dubner. 2008. *Freakonomics.* New York: William Morrow.

——2009. *Superfreakonomics.* New York: Harper Collins.

Luckner, Stefan, Schroder, Jan, and Christian Slamka 2012. *Prediction Markets: Fundamentals, Designs, and Applications.* Berlin: Gabler Verlag.

Lue, Todd W., Pantenburg, Debbie P., and Phillip M. Crawford. 2008. "Impact of the Owner-Pet and Client-Veterinarian Bond on the Care that Pets Receive," *JAVMA* 232: 531–40.

Maddison, Angus. 2003. *Contours of the World Economy: 1–2030 AD: Essays in Macroeconomic History.* New York: Oxford University Press.

Mankiw, Gregory. 2008. *Principles of Economics,* 5th Edition. New York: Southwestern College Publishers.

Mauss, Marcel. 1954. *The Gift: Forms and Functions of Exchange in Archaic Societies.* London: Cohen and West.

Mazar, Nina, Amir, On, and Dan Ariely. 2008. "The Dishonesty of Honest People: A Theory of Self-Concept Maintenance," *Journal of Marketing Research* 45: 633–44.

McCloskey, Deirdre. 1991. *If You're So Smart: The Narrative of Economic Expertise.* Chicago: University of Chicago Press.

——2008. *The Bourgeois Virtues.* Chicago: University of Chicago Press.

——2011. *Bourgeois Dignity.* Chicago: University of Chicago Press.

McConnell, Campbell, Brue, Stanley, and Sean Flynn. 2014. *Economics,* 20th Edition. New York: McGraw-Hill.

Mellstrom, Carl, and Magnus Johannesson. 2008. "Crowding Out in Blood Donation: Was Titmuss Right?" *Journal of the European Economic Association* 6: 845–63.

Mickel, Amy E., and Lisa A. Barron. 2008. "Getting 'More Bang for the Buck': Symbolic Value of Monetary Rewards in Organizations," *Journal of Management Inquiry* 14: 329–38.

Milanovic, Branko. 2007. *The Haves and the Have Nots.* New York: Basic Books.

Mitchell, Terence R., and Amy E. Mickel. 1999. "The Meaning of Money: An Individual-Difference Perspective," *Academy of Management Review* 24: 568–78.

Molotch, Harvey. 2012. *Against Security: How We Go Wrong at Airports, Subways, and Other Sites of Ambiguous Danger.* Princeton: Princeton University Press.

Mueller, Dennis. 2003. *Public Choice III.* New York: Cambridge University Press.

Mueller, John, and Mark G. Stewart. 2011. *Terror, Security, and Money: Balancing the Risks, Benefits, and Costs of Homeland Security.* New York: Oxford University Press.

Murray, Charles. 2012. *Coming Apart: The State of White America, 1960–2010.* New York: Crown Forum.

Nordhaus, William. 1996. "Do Real-Output and Real-Wage Measures Capture Reality? The History of Lighting Suggests Not," in *The Economics of New Goods,* ed. Timothy F. Bresnahan and Robert J. Gordon, pp. 29–70. Chicago: University of Chicago Press.

Norris, Pippa. 2000. *A Virtuous Circle: Political Communications in Postindustrial Societies.* New York: Cambridge University Press.

North, Douglas. 1990. *Institutions, Institutional Change, and Economic Performance.* New York: Cambridge University Press.

Nozick, Robert. 1998. "Why Do Intellectuals Oppose Capitalism?" Cato Policy Report, January/February.

Nussbaum, Martha. 1998. "'Whether from Reason or Prejudice': Taking Money for Bodily Services," *The Journal of Legal Studies* 27: 693–724.

——2009. *Hiding from Humanity: Disgust, Shame, and the Law.* Princeton: Princeton University Press.

——2010. *From Disgust to Humanity: Sexual Orientation & Constitutional Law.* Oxford: Oxford University Press.

Oaten, M., Stevenson, R., and T. Case. 2009. "Disgust as a Disease Avoidance Mechanism: A Review and Model," *Psychological Bulletin* 135, 303–321.

Ostrom, Elinor, ed. 2003. *Trust and Reciprocity: Interdisciplinary Lessons from Experimental Research.* New York: Russell Sage.

Pateman, Carol. 1998. *The Sexual Contract.* Stanford: Stanford University Press.

Paulhus, D. L. 1991. "Measurement and Control of Response Biases," in *Measures of Personality and Social Psychology Attitudes*, ed. J. P. Robinson, pp. 17–60. San Diego: Academic Press.

Pillutla, M., and X. P. Chen. 1999. "Social Norms and Cooperation in Social Dilemmas," *Organizational Behavior and Human Decision Process* 78: 81–103.

Posner, Richard. 1987. "The Regulation of the Market in Adoptions," *Boston University Law Review* 67: 59–72.

Radin, Margaret Jane. 1997. "Market-Inalienability," *Harvard Law Review* 100: 1849–1937.

——2000. *Contested Commodities.* Cambridge, MA: Harvard University Press.

Ramcharan, Thigarajan, and Arthur J. Matas. 2002. "Long-Term (20–37 years) Follow-Up of Living Kidney Donors," *American Journal of Transplantation* 2: 959–64.

Rasmussen, Dennis. 2008. *The Problems and Promise of Commercial Society: Adam Smith's Response to Rousseau.* University Park, PA: Pennsylvania State University Press.

Rawls, John. 1971. *A Theory of Justice.* Cambridge, MA: Harvard University Press.

——1993. *Political Liberalism.* New York: Columbia University Press.

——2001. *Justice as Fairness: a Restatement.* Cambridge, MA: Harvard University Press.

Richerson, Peter J., and Robert Boyd. 2008. "The Evolution of Free Enterprise Values," in *Moral Markets*, ed. Paul Zak, pp. 107–41. Princeton: Princeton University Press.

Roback, Jennifer. 1986. "The Political Economy of Segregation: The Case of Segregated Streetcars," *Journal of Economic History* 56: 893–917.

Rosenfield, David, Folger, Robert, and Harold F. Adelman. 1980. "When Rewards Reflect Competence: A Qualification of the Overjustification Effect," *Journal of Personality and Social Psychology* 39: 368–76.

Rus, Andrej. 2008 "'Gift vs. Commodity' Debate Revisited," *Anthropological Notebooks* 14: 81–102.

Russell, P.S., and R. Giner-Sorolla. 2013. "Bodily-moral Disgust: What it is, How it is Different from Anger and Why it is an Unreasoned Emotion," *Psychological Bulletin* 139: 328–351.

Sandel, Michael. 1998. What Money Can't Buy: The Moral Limits of Markets: The Tanner Lectures on Human Values Delivered at Brasenose College, Oxford, May 11 and 12. Available at http://tannerlectures.utah.edu/_documents/a-to-z/s/sandel00.pdf.

——2012a. *What Money Can't Buy.* New York: Farrar, Straus, and Giroux.

——2012b. "How Markets Crowd Out Morals: Opening the Debate," *Boston Review*, May 1, 2012. Available at https://www.bostonreview.net/forum-sandel-markets-morals.

Satz, Debra. 2012. *Why Some Things Should Not Be for Sale.* New York: Oxford University Press.

Schmidtz, David. 2006. *Elements of Justice.* New York: Cambridge University Press.

——2013. "Property," in *The Oxford Handbook of the History of Political Philosophy*, ed. George Klosko, pp. 599–610. New York: Oxford University Press.

Schmidtz, David, and Jason Brennan. 2010. *A Brief History of Liberty.* Oxford: Wiley-Blackwell.

Schneider, Angela J., and Robert B. Butcher. 1993. "For the Love of the Game: A Philosophical Defense of Amateurism," *Quest* 45: 460–69.

Shariff, Azim F., and Ara Norenzayan. 2007. "God is Watching You: Priming God Concepts Increases Prosocial Behavior in an Anonymous Economic Game." *Psychological Science*, 18: 803–9.

Slater, Margaret, di Nardo, Antonio, Pedocini, Ombretto, dalla Villa, Paulo, Candeloro, Luco, Alessandrini, Barbara, and Stefania del Papa. 2008. "Cat and Dog Ownership and Management Patterns in Central Italy," *Preventative Veterinary Medicine* 85: 267–94.

Smith, Adam. 1776 (1904). *An Inquiry into the Nature and Causes of the Wealth of Nations.* Edwin Cannan, ed., Methuen & Co., Ltd.

——1981. *An Inquiry into the Nature and Causes of the Wealth of Nations*, Vol 1. Indianapolis: Liberty Fund.

Smith, Charles W. 1990. *Auctions: The Social Construction of Value.* Berkeley: University of California Press.

Somin, Ilya. 2013. *Democracy and Political Ignorance.* Stanford: Stanford University Press.

De Soto, Hernando. 2000. *The Mystery of Capital.* New York: Basic Books.

Stevens, Cynthia K., Bavetta, Anna G., and Marilyn E. Gist. 1993. "Gender Differences in the Acquisition of Salary Negotiation Skills: The Role of Goals, Self-efficacy, and Perceived Control," *Journal of Applied Psychology* 78: 723–35.

Stevenson, Betsy, and Justin Wolfers. 2008. "Economic Growth and Subjective Well-Being: Reassessing the Easterlin Paradox," *Brookings Papers on Economic Activity* 39: 1–102.

Stoebenau, Kirsten. 2010. "'Côtier' Sexual Identity as Constructed by the Urban Merina of Antananarivo, Madagascar," *Études Océan Indian* 45: 93–115.

Taylor, James Stacy. 2005. *Stakes and Kidneys: Why Markets in Human Body Parts are Morally Imperative.* Surrey: Ashgate.

Tenbrunsel, Ann E., and Max Bazerman. June 1, 2011. "Launching into Unethical Behavior: Lessons from the *Challenger* Disaster," *Freakonomics.com*. Available at http://www.freakonomics.com/2011/06/01/launching-into-unethical-behavior-lessons-from-thechallenger-disaster/.

Tetlock, Philip E. 2000. "Coping with Trade-Offs: Psychological Constraints and Political Implications," in *Elements of Reason: Cognition, Choice, and the Bounds of Rationality*, ed. Arthur Lupia, Matthew D. McCubbins, and Samuel L. Popkin, pp. 239–263. New York: Cambridge University Press.

——2005. *Expert Political Judgment.* Princeton: Princeton University Press.

Titmuss, Richard. 1971. *The Gift Relationship.* New York: Pantheon Press.

Tomasi, John. 2012. "Response: Markets as Fairness," *Boston Review*, May/June 2012. Available at http://new.bostonreview.net/BR37.3/ndf_john_tomasi_markets_morals.php.

Transparency International. 2012. *Corruption Perceptions Index 2012.* Available at http://cpi.trans parency.org/cpi2012/results.

Vansteenkiste, Maarten, Lens, Willy, and Edward L. Deci. 2006. "Intrinsic versus Extrinsic Goal Contents in Self-Determination Theory: Another Look at the Quality of Academic Motivation," *Educational Psychologist* 41: 19–31.

Von Neumann, John, and Oskar Morgenstern. 1944. *Theory of Games and Economic Behavior.* Princeton: Princeton University Press.

Walzer, Michael. 1984. *Spheres of Justice.* New York: Basic Books.

Wang, Long, Malhotra, Deepak, and J. Keith Murnighan. 2011. "Economics Education and Greed," *Academy of Management Learning & Education* 10: 643–60.

Weil, David. 2009. *Economic Growth*, Second Edition. New York: Prentice Hall.

Zak, Paul, ed. 2008. *Moral Markets.* Princeton: Princeton University Press.

Zak, Paul, and Stephen Knack. 2001. "Trust and Growth," *Economic Journal* 111: 295–321.

Zelizer, Viviana. 1981. "The Price and Value of Children: The Case of Children's Insurance," *American Journal of Sociology* 86: 1036–56.

——1989. "The Social Meaning of Money: 'Special Moneys'," *American Journal of Sociology* 95: 342–77.

——1994. *Pricing the Priceless Child: The Changing Social Value of Children*. New York: Princeton University Press.

——1995. *The Social Meaning of Money*. New York: Basic Books.

——1997. *The Social Meaning of Money*. Princeton: Princeton University Press.

——2007. *The Purchase of Intimacy*. Princeton: Princeton University Press.

——2013. *Economic Lives: How Culture Shapes the Economy*. Princeton: Princeton University Press.

Zwolinski, Matt. 2008. "The Ethics of Price-Gouging," *Business Ethics Quarterly* 18: 347–78.

INDEX

Page numbers in *italics* refer to figures. Page numbers in **bold** refer to tables.

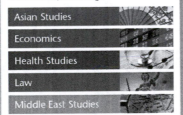